Burst of Flavor

Burst of Flavor

Kusuma Cooray

The Fine Art of Cooking with Spices

A LATITUDE 20 BOOK

University of Hawai'i Press   Honolulu

06 05 04 03 02 01   5 4 3 2 1

Library of Congress Cataloging-in-Publication Data

Cooray, Kusuma.
    Burst of flavor : the fine art of cooking with spices / Kusuma Cooray.
        p.   cm.
    "A Latitude 20 book."
    Includes index.
    ISBN 0-8248-2372-9 (cloth : alk. paper)   ISBN 0-8248-2416-4
    (pbk. : alk. paper)
    1. Cookery (Spices)   2. Spices.
    TX819.A1 C66 2001
    641.6'383-dc21   00-062948

Designed by Bonnie Campbell, Running Feet Books
Printed by Everbest Printing Co., Ltd., China

Lovingly dedicated to

Ranjit George Cooray

Contents

Fish & Shellfish

Starters

Poultry, Meat

Soups

Vegetables

Legumes

Chutneys, Relishes

Grains

Desserts

Salads

Foreword

HAWAI'I IS A SPECIAL PLACE THAT BLENDS THE best of Asia and America with a strong local tradition. Hawai'i's regional cuisine has a unique taste that incorporates the same blend of East and West into creative dishes. Building on these Hawai'i traditions and on strong links with the resort and visitor industries, the Culinary Institute of the Pacific at Kapi'olani Community College offers the opportunity to become a skilled culinarian, knowledgeable in both Asian and Western cuisine.

Our unique location in the Pacific and our diverse ethnic society bring an interesting mix of talent and expertise to our campus. The Culinary Institute of the Pacific at Kapi'olani Community College thrives on this diversity. Our goal is to be a premier culinary institute for Asia and the Pacific by building on the talents and reputations of our outstanding chefs. Associate Professor and Chef Instructor Kusuma Cooray is such an individual.

Chef Cooray hails from the lovely island of Sri Lanka. She has trained at Le Cordon Bleu in London, the National Bakery School in London, and La Varenne Ecole de Cuisine in Paris. She was personal chef to heiress Doris Duke and later executive chef of the renowned restaurant The Willows and the Banyan Gardens in Honolulu. During her tenure The Willows won, in consecutive years, the prestigious Travel/Holiday Award. Kusuma is a certified executive chef and certified culinary educator of the American Culinary Federation and a fellow and master craftsman of the Cookery and Food Association. She is also a Maitre Rotisseur and Counseiller Culinaire for the Hawaii-Pacific Region of the Chaine des Rotisseurs. Kusuma has cooked for many VIPs, including Jacqueline Kennedy Onassis, her excellency Chandrika Bandaranaike Kumaratunge, president of Sri Lanka, and his royal highness Prince Charles of Britain. She was also featured in promotions for the *Cooking Across America* series produced by the Food Network.

This book is a visual and culinary delight that allows Chef Cooray to share her special talent and creativity with you as she does with her students. Enjoy!

John Morton
Provost, Kapi'olani Community College

Acknowledgments

BURST OF FLAVOR WAS PUT TOGETHER WITH THE help of many. First, my thanks and admiration to some of the pillars of the food world: Julia Child, Anne Willan, Diana Kennedy, André Soltner, Jacques Pépin, and the late James Beard and Louis Szathmary. Knowing them and their work is an inspiration to me.

I lovingly remember Peggy Pavel, who first worked with me on the framework for this book. Thanks also to Victor Pavel for his kind input.

My gratitude to the vice president of the University of Hawai'i and Chancellor for Community Colleges Joyce Tsunoda, Provost John Morton, and Dean of Instruction, Leon Richards, the University of Hawai'i, and Kapi'olani Community College and Culinary Institute of the Pacific for the enthusiastic support they extended to me. I would also like to thank Bert Kimura, Dean Carol Hoshiko, Robin Fujikawa, Dennis Kawaharada, and librarian Mary Marko for their help.

Thanks to Charles H. Lamoureux, Ray Baker, and Karen Shigematsu of Lyon Arboretum for providing plant materials.

A heartfelt thank you to graphic artist Helen Hamada, who was always there for me and worked tirelessly for many months on typesetting this project. To Errol de Silva of Camera Hawai'i, who lent his expert artistic style to capture my cuisine in sixty tantalizing pictures—a thank you from the bottom of my heart. Sincere thanks to wine expert Richard Field of R. Field Wine Company for his notes to readers on wines to match my food.

A loving thank you to Tish Kuruppu for typing part of the manuscript and assisting me with food styling, as well as sharing the fun that came with it. Thanks to the crew at Camera Hawai'i for their hard work. Thanks to Louise Pagotto, my superb editor, who worked with so much energy and enthusiasm. I appreciate her guidance and support.

Thanks to my dear friend Winnie Myers for cheering me from the sidelines, and I greatly appreciate the well-wishes from friends and family from many parts of the world. I am thankful to all my students, past and present, who make me feel special. Thank you to the many thousands of guests who spent their evenings dining at the Ka'Ikena La'uae Restaurant.

I express gratitude to my publisher, William Hamilton, director of the University of Hawai'i Press, for valuable suggestions and guidance, and for making my dream come true.

Finally, a loving thank you to my husband, Ranjit George Cooray, for sharing in my vision and contributing to the success of this book.

Introduction

CERTAINLY, WHILE WE ARE CONCERNED ABOUT our dietary needs and nutrition, we should enjoy the pleasures of eating. The continuing interest in nutrition and the dynamic influence of ethnic and international cuisines have sparked a keen interest in spices for cooking.

Fragrant spices of India are often admired but not fully understood. Many ask questions about their haunting fragrance and the intriguing flavors they impart to food. True, some people are experts at using spices, and books on Indian cuisines abound, but many say it is tedious to use spices as suggested in Indian recipes. There are unlimited queries on how to use spices and in what combinations in foods other than Indian. Spices are a mystery to many who love cooking, and a great many others have yet to be exposed to the joys of cooking with spices.

The search for these exotic flavors and flavor combinations is on. In response to this search, I have written this book.

Me and My Kitchen

My mental kitchen is a highly moveable feast. I was born in Sri Lanka and grew up on spicy curries, fresh fruit, seafood, vegetables, curd, and treacle. I went to England and France for my culinary education and apprenticeship. There I gained a taste for ripe cheeses, wine and crusty breads, Dover sole, Scottish salmon, crème fraîche, and raspberries. But my love for spices and herbs never diminished.

Since 1988, I've been at the University of Hawai'i's Kapi'olani Community College, now the Culinary Institute of the Pacific. Here I teach Continental and International Cuisine to students who cook for the Ka'Ikena La'uae Restaurant, also referred to as Ka'Ikena Restaurant. It is one of Hawai'i's most popular restaurants.

Hawai'i is a melting pot of high-energy, East-West influences. Almost fifteen years ago, I began to entice numerous diners with the fragrances of Asian spices in foods ranging from soup to nuts, from entrées to desserts. Many kitchens in four countries have helped me develop the guiding principles that I now bring to you and your kitchen in this book.

The most basic of these principles is that there is no unbridgeable gap between East and West, or between Asia and other Pacific countries. I see no conflicts among the food cultures of the world. Each has much to give the others; with appreciative handling, even the most foreign ingredients and flavors live together harmoniously and bring out the best in each other.

You and Your Kitchen

Fresh ingredients are vital to nutritious and pleasurable eating. Buy your fruits and vegetables as fresh as possible and during their particular harvest seasons, when they are bursting with flavor. Let your demand for freshness extend to seafood, meat, and poultry, too.

For the sake of good health, cook with the least amount of fat and use the best-quality oil. I use mainly olive oil and butter in moderation.

Elaborate special equipment is unnecessary. A coffee grinder can be used for any amount from ¼ cup to 3 cups of spices. For smaller quantities, e.g., 1–2 tablespoons, use a pharmacy-type marble mortar. A handy chopper works well for small quantities of moist spices, ginger, garlic, shallots, onions, or raw herb pastes. Use the food processor for a large quantity, for chopping onions, grinding nuts, or mixing dough and batters.

Today's market supplies are so abundantly varied and today's cooks are so well traveled that some readers will find spices and herbs such as saffron, fennel, fenugreek, and tamarind familiar. Other spices will be strangers to you; however, by using them in the recipes in this book, you will become familiar with them, too. My hope is that this book will unfold to you a burst of flavors, fragrant and delicious, global in scope and exotic in overtones.

About Spices

Spices are derived from aromatic plants or parts of plants like roots, barks, buds, flower parts, fruits, stems, leaves, and even gum resins, and are all usually available in dry form.

A Brief History

Sanskrit writings from three thousand years ago describe the importance of spices. History documents that King Solomon's men sailed the Arabian Sea and traded spices with India. Later, spices enticed many Greeks and Romans from the West and Chinese from the East to sail the seas in search of these aromatic plants. In the thirteenth century, Marco Polo returned to Venice with news of spices on the Malabar Coast in India. Navigators like Vasco da Gama, Christopher Columbus, and Magellan were all lured by these fragrant spices and explored new routes to capture this lucrative trade for their own countries. Soon spices became as priceless as gold. International commerce flourished as the search for spices became competitive. By the 1500s Portugal took over the spice trade from the Arabs and controlled India's Malabar Coast, Java, Sumatra, and Ceylon. By 1612 Ceylonese had to pay their taxes in spices and currency. Around 1636 the Dutch ousted the Portuguese from the Spice Islands

and took over Ceylon. The Dutch had a monopoly over the fragrant spices—nutmeg, mace, cloves, and true cinnamon—that were native to Ceylon. The Dutch were as cruel as the Portuguese and tortured the natives, demanding enormous amounts of cinnamon bark. When quotas were not met, men were punished by death and women were whipped.

In 1796 the British ousted the Dutch from the Indian subcontinent. Queen Victoria is known to have loved curries and spicy food, but the British traded more in tea, sugar, and other commodities than in spices. It was in the eighteenth century that the United States started bartering in spices. As the nineteenth century approached, spices were being grown in South America and many other countries.

Medicinal Properties

Three-thousand-year-old Ayurvedic scripts list the medicinal properties and curative value of spices. Fragrant spices are said to be able to calm the nerves and soothe the senses, not just please the palate. Cloves are said to act as an antiseptic. Fennel, cardamom, and cloves are used as a mouth freshener. They also aid digestion and prevent heartburn. Turmeric is a noted antiseptic and is used to treat skin diseases. Legumes are cooked with the addition of asafoetida or ginger to counteract flatulence. Fenugreek tea is said to help stomach disorders such as gastritis. Coriander with ginger made into a tea acts as a decongestant. As a general rule, spices stimulate the appetite, enhance liver function, and increase blood circulation.

Ayurvedic medical scripts also document the effect of spices on the body. Spices are categorized (not scientifically) into "warm" and "cool." Cardamom, cinnamon, nutmeg, mace, and dried ginger are said to be warm. Black mustard seeds, fenugreek, and coriander are said to be cool spices. Generally, warm spices are used in cold weather, cool spices are used in warm weather. For example, a meat dish with hot garam masala (a blend of roasted, ground warm spices) is

Introduction

perfect when the weather is cold. "Warm" spices are said to generate internal body heat. "Cool" spices are believed to take heat away from the body and cool the system.

Many spices are said to fall in between the spectrum of warm and cold. These are also categorized as neutral and are generally used in any weather or climate.

All spices and herbs have assigned medicinal properties according to the ayurvedic medical system. Many westerners are confused with this system, but to many Asians, traditions handed down by generations of ancestors have instilled a deep understanding of the complexity of spices and herbs.

Culinary Properties

Most spices add fragrance and create special flavors in food. Many, such as oil-fried black mustard seeds, add color and enhance the appearance of a dish. Turmeric gives a delicate blush if not overused. Saffron, the most expensive spice in the world, adds a golden hue and a haunting aroma. Saffron, the stigmas of the crocus flower, is said to color 700,000 times its own weight in water. Fenugreek, when cooked in oil or simmered in coconut milk, gives an unexplainable mystical aroma. Coriander has a lemony aroma when coarsely crushed and gives food a crusty texture. Spices are fragrant and aromatic, seductive and tantalizing. Not all are as hot as people mistakenly believe. In fact, the only two spices commonly used to impart hotness are pepper and chilies.

Blending

Spices can be used singly or in combination. A well-known blend of spices is garam masala. The spices are roasted and ground to create this aromatic blend. Some other spice blends, such as cumin and coriander, are ground or crushed raw (unroasted), releasing their fragrance. Once crushed or ground, they lose their volatile oils quickly and thus lose some of their fragrance. Some spices are ground fine; others are ground coarse. Still others are fried whole in oil, or ground to a paste with the addition of a liquid like water or vinegar. Those blends that are ground with liquids are known as wet spice mixes or pastes. To roast spices, use a heavy skillet; add the spices, and roast on low heat until the spices are crisp to the bite. Stir often to avoid scorching. Spices may also be roasted in a baking pan in a moderately hot oven. Spices used in these numerous ways give subtle aromas and appealing nuances to foods cooked with them.

Buying Spices

When buying whole or fresh spices, look for the crispest, most fragrant spices. Avoid limp and mildewed or discolored spices. Readymade ground spice blends should be in airtight, sealed containers or packets.

Storing Spices

Ground spices remain fresh up to three or four months. Whole spices, if stored right, will keep for two to three years. Spices should be stored in airtight containers in a cool dry place, away from heat or sunlight. Heat robs them of their flavor, and dampness causes the product to absorb moisture and to cake. Wet spice mixes or pastes will stay fresh for four to five months when stored in the refrigerator in airtight, nonreactive containers. All spice containers must be tightly sealed to retain the spices' volatile oils.

Flavor, the Heart of Cuisine

Good food gratifies the senses—sight, smell, and taste. Spice cookery sounds glamorous, extravagant, and complicated. Complicated it is not. It is just basics—essential to good food, and to good health. I cook simply, with fresh, natural ingredients, spices, and herbs so that the food is nutritious yet pleasing to all the senses.

The key to good spicing is to use spices in the right portions. Food should not be overdone with spices. As particular spices have medicinal or antiseptic value, they will add to the health value of your food.

The art of spicing is in the delicacy of spicing. Into slowly simmering soups, I drop selected spices to draw out the layers of fragrances. I add whole fried spices to give fragrance to sometimes monotonous legumes. I roll a fillet of beef in crushed spices and roast it for a fragrant crust. I rely on ground spices to give flavor to vegetables, seafood, and meat.

Single spices and herbs have individual tastes to be enjoyed. To some foods I give a breath of a single crushed spice; other foods, I barely brush with a single pungent herb—what an enticing, elusive aroma! Fragrances of spices and herbs are the ethereal bonding between texture and flavor.

How to Use This Book

The aim of this book is to share recipes written in a simple style and to provide explicit instructions that are easy to follow and allow you to visualize the dish you are about to cook. Because the appearance of the dish is an important element in cuisine, I included pictures of the prepared dishes. Your guests can enjoy food displayed with aesthetic care.

To get the most out of the recipes, first read the introductory directions to each recipe: they are enlivened with anecdotes and reminiscences or food history and serving suggestions. Then read the recipe thoroughly. All weights and measures are given in American measures, and an easy conversion table can be found at the back of the book (page 245). It is important to use one set of measures or the other without mixing the two.

Use measurements, temperatures, and timing as a guide, but use your judgment. My recipes include many ingredients, but the dishes are not necessarily difficult to prepare. The ingredients used are readily available in large city supermarkets and ethnic markets. Simple preparation techniques are used most often. Make sure you read the glossary, too. It is well worth delving into. It explains unfamiliar spices and herbs, ingredients, and cooking techniques and terms—all of which appear in bold text in the recipes. Reference recipes are in bold with the relevant page number. For example, the recipe for Tomato-Orange Soup (see page 30) calls for 2 cups of **Defatted Chicken Stock**. The recipe directs the reader to the Defatted Chicken Stock recipe (see page 45) to prepare the stock as instructed. The recipes are in categories to assist you in formulating a menu. A dining experience is not complete without a carefully selected wine. The relationship between wine and food is vital to the taste of both, and Richard Field provides valuable notes on wine in his essay beginning on page xvii. He offers suggestions to help you pick the wines to match the food you prepare.

On a final note, cooking is more than following a recipe—make it an adventure. Improvise and be artistic. Experiment and innovate. Enjoy and delight your family and guests.

Notes on Wine

Richard Field

AS CHEF COORAY OBSERVES, "GOOD FOOD gratifies the senses—sight, smell, and taste." Good wine must do this, too, and much more. Wine that heightens our enjoyment of the dish before us is more important than serving a wine that may be great in its own right. To a certain degree, I subscribe to the casual approach of simply matching wines you like with foods you like.

It is important, however, to distinguish between casual food and uniquely spiced, compelling food like the food presented in this book. Chef Cooray offers exotic fragrances, unusual textures, and complex flavors that present wonderful opportunities to pair wines to match the intensity of fragrance, flavor, and varied textures of her recipes.

It really comes down to this—wine must provide pleasure for our sight, smell, taste, and our imaginations. It is with food that wine can create new contexts and that the very same dish served with a thought-provoking wine becomes a new sensory experience. It is in our minds that the experiences, the myriad nuances, combinations, and impact on the senses created by unique personal pleasures, occur. And with some care and forethought, that wonderful experience lives on in the mind forever.

Starters

A large variety of wines are available that will pair well with many of the starters. White wines that are crisp, light bodied, and slightly earthy with a citrus edge are my rec-

ommendation. Examples would be German Riesling, Fumé Blanc, Sancerre, or Pouilly-Fuissé. Other excellent choices would include Pinot Gris from Oregon or Germany, French Chablis, or a delightful Malvasia white wine. Rosé wines that are either dry or slightly sweet without a bitterness in the finish would enhance the starter dishes. I prefer a Vin Gris. Red wines should be fresh, fruit driven, and low in tannins. Meeting all of these requirements are Lambrusco, Beaujolais, Pinot Noir, Zinfandel, and Grenache. If you prefer Champagne, I recommend you serve an extra-dry Brut, or a Rosé. The Goat Cheese–Stuffed Peppers, an appetizing starter in this section, is exotic and delicious, and I suggest serving it with a light Mediterranean-styled red wine like Mivervois, Fitou, and Côte du Roussillon.

Soups

Wines are a wonderful accompaniment to both the tasty hot soups and the chilled soups Chef Cooray presents. Serve a heavier wine, like a dry Rosé or unoaked Chardonnay, with the hot soups. Serve a delicate lighter wine, like a German Riesling, with the chilled soups.

Fish and Shellfish

Bright, off-dry German Riesling Kabinett pairs well with seafood. With Lobster with Honey Butter Sauce, Grapefruit, and Avocado, another of Chef Cooray's specialties, I suggest Vouvray Sec or ripe Pinot Gris. With Seared Scallops with Pear Salad, bright

German Riesling Kabinett is a great match. For hearty Baked Fish in Tomato Sauce with Fried Eggplant, my suggestion is a fruit-forward Pinot Noir or a Zinfandel. Champagne or dry sparkling wine enhances seafood dishes. Aligoté, Sancerre, and Chablis are other excellent choices.

Poultry and Meat

The hearty dishes in this section pair well with a variety of wines. A dry Rosé like Bandol Rosé is my choice for Skillet-Roasted Spicy Chicken with Pomegranate Sauce. Cru Beaujolais like Moulin-a-Vent, Morgon, and Chateauneuf-du-Pape, or a red Rioja are all excellent choices for duck dishes, especially Duck with Sweet Potatoes and Red Cabbage Salad. Red wines that are crisp and full bodied are my recommendation for meats. Examples are Beaujolais, Chinon, young Côtes-du-Rhône, and fruity Merlot. Serve Roast Carved Rack of Lamb with Pickled Cherries with a rich, full-bodied Pinot Noir or with a fine Bordeaux.

Legumes

With tomato-based legume dishes, try light, fruity Pinot Noir or a Gamay. Avoid very dry wines. With pasta, Italian Pinot Grigio or a dry Riesling is my recommendation.

Salads

With the variety of salads in this section of the book, Champagne or Cava are good choices. Muscadet and Sancerre are great partners as well. Other choices are Alsace Pinot Gris, Italian Pinot Grigio, or a dry Riesling.

Dessert

With chocolatey desserts, Sauternes or Eiswein is my recommendation—but chocolate is difficult to match unless you are very familiar with both the dessert and the wines. With Black Plum Soup with Lemon Ice Cream and Lemon Curd, Chef Cooray's house specialty in her restaurant, a rich new-world Moscato d'Oro is a delightful partner, but you may try a slightly sparkling Moscato d'Asti.

These rules for serving wines with dishes are really only guides. The best guide should be your palate. However, I am often asked, What if I want to serve just a single wine for all the courses? A bright, off-dry German Riesling Kabinett would be my recommendation. It is low in alcohol and has no oak taste to it. This Riesling works well with most dishes.

Knowledge of wine is a lifetime lesson. The only way to master it is to start with enjoying, pairing, and comparing them.

Burst of Flavor

Starters . . .

Tantalizing Beginnings

The wafting aromas of appetizers add an aura of suspense to a meal; a lovely connection is made with special party guests or family gathered around the table to dine.

I am inspired by aromas and tastes from around the world. I remember the crispy **poppadom** my mother often made for us to remind us of our dinner to come. Sometimes placed beside the poppadom was a tiny bowl of deep-fried red chilies, seasoned with lemon juice and a sprinkling of salt—she soaked them in curd before frying them. I loved to munch on the crispy poppadom. It was just enough to whet my appetite—like a discreet door opening to the enjoyment of the rest of the dinner.

Poppadom was just right for my palate then. Today I am enchanted by many more aromas and tastes from around the world. Scottish salmon, every bite of it rich and velvety; juicy oysters; caviar heaped on blinis, with sips of champagne, the epitome of taste sophistication—all leave my mouth tingling in expectation of what is to come.

Another favorite of mine is the sweet, peeled plum tomato, cleverly trimmed and positioned to hold swirls of anchovy, wisps of red onion, and the tiniest of tiny **Niçoise olives,** as if they were tumbling out of it. It is garnished with a tuft of crispy watercress. All glistening with green **virgin olive oil,** it comes to life with the addition of crusty garlic bread.

Hot brioche, crowned with almost-melting ripe brie; grilled shrimp on sweet sugarcane skewers; silken purée of fruit with slivers of more fruit—these can tantalize even the most sophisticated of palates.

The recipes in this chapter range from cold to hot, mild to pungent, simple to fancy. They are all so right for this day and age, tasty and fragrant and in small portions for the many guests today who dine on a selection of appetizers only. For others, I hope these appetizers will open a door for you to the rest of the menu—as they do for me.

The Rose (Sliced Smoked Salmon)

Smoked salmon is used for this stylish appetizer that has both dramatic color and form. Once the ingredients are prepared, putting the dish together is fun. Salmon roe and **tobiko** (flying fish roe) are used to enhance the overall color of the dish. Both salmon roe and tobiko have a crisp texture and pop in the mouth to give a pleasantly salty flavor.

The tart, marinated cucumber and the hot flavor of the freshly ground black peppercorns help to balance the richness of the dish. Buttered toast or lavosh may be served as an accompaniment. Both offer a crunchy texture in contrast to the silken smoothness of the salmon.

4 ounces smoked salmon, thinly sliced

Seasonings for Chopped Salmon
2 tablespoons cream cheese, whipped
½ teaspoon snipped dill
½ teaspoon snipped chives
*½ teaspoon **capers***
Freshly ground black pepper to taste
Salt to taste

Marinated Cucumber
1 small seedless cucumber
Fresh lemon juice to taste
*2 teaspoons **extra virgin olive oil***
Freshly ground black pepper to taste
Salt to taste

Garnish
1 tablespoon salmon roe
2 tablespoons extra virgin olive oil
1 tablespoon tobiko
12 chives

Directions
Roll up a slice of salmon to resemble the center of a rose. Wrap 3 more slices, one after another, loosely around the rolled up center, to resemble a rose. Make 4 salmon roses.

Chop the remaining salmon and place it in a small bowl. Add cream cheese, dill, chives, capers, and black pepper and salt to taste. Mix to combine.

For marinated cucumber, trim ends of the unpeeled cucumber and slice lengthwise into extremely thin ribbons. Place in a small bowl; add lemon juice, olive oil, and black pepper and salt to taste. Mix and set aside to marinate for 15 minutes.

Presentation
Place a spoon of the seasoned chopped salmon in the center of a plate. Place a salmon rose on top, and arrange marinated cucumber by the side of the rose.

To garnish, combine the salmon roe with the olive oil and drizzle on the plate. Sprinkle tobiko on the plate, and place chives beside the rose.

4 servings

Seared Scallops with Haricots Verts and Shiitake Mushrooms

This appetizer is very glamorous. The crunchy **haricots verts** and the seared scallops are enlivened by the nutty flavor of the black **mustard seeds** in the tart sauce. It is important to cook the mustard seeds in hot oil so their flavor is released. Together with the garlic, they add elegance to an otherwise simple sauce.

The scallops need to be seared in an extremely hot skillet; this process will keep them crusty outside and juicy inside.

Crème fraîche should be made ahead of time. Sour cream is a good substitute for crème fraîche.

12 large scallops
2 teaspoons olive oil
¼ pound haricots verts
2 ounces shiitake mushrooms

Seasoned Crème Fraîche
*½ cup **Crème Fraîche** (see recipe, page 243)*
1 teaspoon chopped yellow onion
*1 teaspoon **capers***
1 tablespoon snipped chives
1 teaspoon cracked black peppercorns
1 tablespoon fresh lemon juice

For Haricots
2 tablespoons chopped sun-dried tomatoes
½ cup orange juice
1 tablespoon olive oil
1 teaspoon black mustard seeds
2 cloves garlic, sliced
*1 cup tomato **concassée***
Salt and freshly ground black pepper to taste

For Mushrooms
1 tablespoon olive oil
1 tablespoon chopped shallots
1 teaspoon minced garlic
Salt and freshly ground black pepper to taste

Garnish
8 chives

Directions
Trim and wipe scallops, toss in olive oil, and refrigerate. Trim and **blanch** haricots. Slice shiitake mushrooms. In a bowl, whisk together all the ingredients for seasoned crème fraîche. Soak sundried tomatoes in orange juice for 5 minutes. Pour olive oil into a sauté pan and place on high heat; add black mustard seeds and stir until the seeds splutter. Add garlic and cook for 2 minutes. When garlic turns a light gold color, add soaked sun-dried tomatoes and cook for 3 minutes. The sun-dried tomatoes will have absorbed almost all the orange juice. Add haricots verts, tomato concassée, and salt and pepper to taste. Stir around to coat the haricots verts with the seasonings and keep warm until ready to serve. To another sauté pan, add 1 tablespoon olive oil and sauté shallots, garlic, and shiitake mushrooms on high heat, adding salt and pepper to taste. Takes 3 to 4 minutes.

Place a skillet on high heat for a few minutes to get it to searing temperature; drop in the scallops, and sear for about 3 minutes on each side. Skillet must be extremely hot to sear the scallops. Season with salt and ground black pepper to taste.

Presentation
Place 3 scallops on each plate, arrange haricots beside the scallops, and spoon the bits of tomato on the scallops. Spoon the mushrooms around the scallops. Decoratively spread a little crème fraîche on the plates. Garnish with chives.

4 servings

Chicken Satay

Satay is a Southeast Asian favorite. Small pieces of marinated meat are threaded on skewers and broiled or grilled over charcoal. The taste of the satay with the aromatic blend of spices and herbs is divine.

Lemongrass gives the marinade in this recipe a wonderful aroma. If lemongrass is unavailable, a tablespoon of lemon zest will do. The **curry leaves** give the dish a unique fragrance, but you can make this marinade without them. Curry leaves are now available in most oriental stores in larger cities. The textures and flavors of the spice and herb combination used for the marinade meld together quite nicely in this Southeast Asian delicacy. Many Ka'Ikena La'uae Restaurant guests request the recipe.

24 bamboo skewers
2 cups water
1 pound boneless, skinless chicken breast or thigh

Marinade
1 bulb lemongrass, chopped
1 teaspoon chopped ginger
1 teaspoon chopped garlic
1 shallot, peeled and sliced
2 seeded, chopped fresh red chilies
1 sprig curry leaves
*⅛ teaspoon **turmeric***
*1 teaspoon roasted ground **coriander***
1 tablespoon light soy sauce
1 tablespoon dark brown sugar
¼ cup hot water
2 tablespoons coconut milk
2 tablespoons peanut butter
2 tablespoons fresh lime juice
Salt to taste

For Grilling
3 tablespoons peanut oil

Garnish
1 small cucumber, peeled
*3 tablespoons **rice wine vinegar***

2 teaspoons sugar
Lime juice to taste
Salt to taste
*2 tablespoons ginger **julienne***
12 sprigs of Chinese parsley
2 tablespoons crushed roasted peanuts

Directions
Soak bamboo skewers in water for at least half an hour to prevent the skewers from burning before the chicken is cooked.

Cut chicken into 2-inch strips. Place lemongrass, ginger, garlic, shallot, red chilies, curry leaves, turmeric, coriander, soy sauce, and brown sugar in the blender and purée, gradually adding hot water, coconut milk, and peanut butter. Season with lime juice and salt to taste, and blend to combine.

In a small pan, reserve 4 tablespoons of this marinade mix for the satay sauce. Pour the rest over the chicken, and leave to marinate for 2 hours. When done marinating, thread chicken on skewers and brush with peanut oil; broil or grill the chicken, turning the skewers and brushing again with peanut oil. Cook 4 to 5 minutes per side.

For the satay sauce, place the reserved marinade mix in a small pan on low heat. Sprinkle ¼ cup water on the mix and cook for 3 to 4 minutes.

For the garnish, slice the cucumber into long thin ribbons using a peeler. Once the cucumber is sliced with a peeler, the seeds and core remain intact and can be discarded. Add rice wine vinegar, sugar, lime juice, and salt to taste, and mix.

Presentation
Drizzle satay sauce on appetizer plates, place cucumber ribbons and 4 satay sticks on each plate. Strew ginger, Chinese parsley, and peanuts on the plate.

6 servings

Salmon with Marinated Avocado

...ndied ginger adds a ...n taste of the salmon ...of the avocado in this ...n sugar and **balsamic vinegar** in the crust add a rich caramel taste to the cooked salmon. Dill adds a subtle perfume and brings all the taste elements together. The final touches, cracked black peppercorns and a drizzle of balsamic vinegar, are all the more dramatic. Preserved ginger is a good substitute for candied ginger.

1 pound trimmed salmon fillet
Salt to taste
2 large ripe avocados

Dressing
1 tablespoon white wine vinegar
2 tablespoons olive oil
1 tablespoon chopped candied ginger
2 teaspoons cracked black peppercorns
Salt to taste

Crust
2 tablespoons chopped candied ginger
¼ cup broken-up dill sprigs
1 tablespoon light brown sugar
1 tablespoon balsamic vinegar
2 teaspoons cracked black peppercorns
Salt to taste

To Sear Salmon
2 tablespoons olive oil

Garnish
1 tablespoon candied ginger
1 tablespoon cracked black peppercorns
1 tablespoon balsamic vinegar
6 dill sprigs

Directions
Cut salmon into 6 portions, season with salt to taste, and set aside. Peel avocados, remove pits, cut into ¼-inch-thick slices, and place in a dish. In a small bowl, whisk together ingredients for dressing with salt to taste. Pour on avocado, and chill in the refrigerator for 15 minutes. At this point, place appetizer plates in a warm oven for 10 minutes.

Mix ingredients for crust with salt to taste. Coat one side of each salmon portion with the mix. Heat olive oil in a skillet over high heat, sear the crusted sides of the salmon for 2 minutes, turn over, and sear for 4 minutes more.

Presentation
Place marinated avocado and salmon on hot appetizer plates. Strew plate with candied ginger and cracked black peppercorns, drizzle balsamic vinegar, and garnish with dill.

6 servings

Goat Cheese-Stuffed Peppers

Goat cheese, rich and creamy, is paired with crunchy spices in this elegant starter. Roasted and crushed spices release their flavor and aroma. The **fennel** seeds impart a sweet taste, while **coriander** adds a lemony taste and **cumin** a pungent bite. Together with the white sesame seeds, these spices form the crust that enhances the appearance of the stuffed peppers and offsets the creaminess of the goat cheese.

I cook the hot wax peppers briefly in sweetened, acidulated boiling water (described in the recipe). This procedure helps to remove the hotness of the peppers.

4 wax peppers, each 4 to 5 inches long
2 cups water
2 tablespoons white vinegar
1½ tablespoons sugar
2 cups ice water

Stuffing
¾ cup goat cheese
1 sliced green onion
1 tablespoon sliced basil
1 tablespoon chopped tomato
Salt to taste
Freshly ground black pepper to taste
1 small egg white, stiffly beaten

Spice Topping
¼ teaspoon roasted, crushed fennel seeds
¼ teaspoon coriander seeds
¼ teaspoon cumin seeds
½ teaspoon white sesame seeds

Garnish
*1 cup lettuce mix (**frisée** and **red oak leaf lettuce**)*
½ cup diced tomato
3 tablespoons olive oil
1 tablespoon white vinegar
Salt to taste
Freshly ground black pepper to taste
1 teaspoon black sesame seeds

Directions
Preheat oven to 475°F.

Halve peppers, slicing through stems down to tail ends. Remove core and seeds, and discard. Wash peppers.

Boil water with vinegar and sugar (sweetened, acidulated water); add peppers and cook for 30 seconds. Drain off water and leave peppers in ice water to chill.

For stuffing, place goat cheese in a medium bowl and beat with a whisk to soften. Mix in green onion, basil, and tomato. Season with salt and pepper to taste. In a separate bowl, beat egg white until it forms stiff peaks; fold into stuffing mixture. Stuff pepper halves.

For the spice topping, place the spices in a spice grinder. Pulse 3 to 4 times to crack open the seeds. Mix with the white sesame seeds and sprinkle on the peppers.

Place on a baking sheet and bake in the preheated oven for 5 minutes.

Presentation
Place 2 pepper halves on each appetizer plate, and garnish with frisée and lettuce. Mix tomato, oil, and vinegar together, and season with salt and freshly ground black pepper to taste. Drizzle on the plate. Sprinkle black sesame seeds around the peppers.

4 servings

Curry-Flavored Mussels

Always use live mussels for cooking—never ones that are frozen or "on ice." Unlike oysters, they are not eaten raw. Avoid picking unusually heavy or light mussels; heavy ones can be full of sand, and light ones have too little flesh. Pick mussels that are tightly closed.

To clean the mussels, scrub them well with a brush under cold running water. Using a knife, scrape off any barnacles and cut off the fibrous beards between shell hinges. Soak mussels for 20 minutes in brine (2 tablespoons salt to 4 pints of water), and rinse a few times in cold water to get rid of all the sand. Spices add an exotic fragrance and flavor to the broth and take away the strong fishy smell of the mussels. **Curry leaves** provide a pungent aroma to the broth, and chilies are for those who dare to bite into them.

You may do without the curry leaves and substitute the peel of a lemon for the **lemongrass.** Many greens are available today; you may pick your favorite ones to partner with this dish. I have picked strong-flavored greens that have a peppery bite to them.

20 to 24 large mussels

Spicy Court Bouillon

2-inch piece of ginger, crushed
2 sprigs curry leaves
4 bulbs lemongrass, crushed or zest of 2 lemons
*1 teaspoon **coriander** seeds, crushed*
*1½ teaspoons **cumin** seeds, crushed*
2 cups water
1 cup dry white wine
*6 whole **green chilies***
2 tablespoons lemon juice

To Finish
¼ cup full cream or coconut milk

Green Salad
*1 cup **mizuna***
1 cup watercress sprigs
*1 cup **dandelion** leaves*
2 tablespoons sliced yellow onion
2 tablespoons fresh lemon juice
*1 tablespoon **balsamic vinegar***
Salt to taste
Freshly ground black pepper to taste

Directions
Prepare mussels for cooking and set aside.

Place the ingredients for the spicy court bouillon in a pan; simmer to reduce to 1½ cups, about 10 minutes. Place mussels in the reduced liquid, cover pan, and steam for 4 to 5 minutes or until the mussels open. Pick out any unopened mussels and discard them. Place mussels in wide serving bowls. Pick out and place the cooked chilies and a few curry leaves on the mussels in each bowl.

Add cream or coconut milk to the liquid left in the pan from steaming the mussels, bring to a simmer, and strain into a bowl through a cheesecloth-lined strainer to rid the liquid of any remaining sand. Ladle over the mussels in the serving bowls.

Presentation
Place salad greens and onion in a medium-size bowl and season with lemon juice, balsamic vinegar, and salt and black pepper to taste. Toss lightly to coat greens. Arrange on salad plates.

Serve mussels and salad with hot crusty bread.

4 servings

Caviar Bites Nureyev

For the cocktail party at Shangri-La in honor of Rudolf Nureyev, I created these glamorous bites with caviar; they rested on the blinis on top of a heaping of **chenna**—not on the usual sour cream! (We provided lots of Tattinger and Stolichnaya, too!) I named these morsels after the master of ballet himself.

Prepare blinis mix 2 hours in advance, and chenna may be made a day in advance.

*1/2 cup **Chenna** (see recipe, page 242)*
Salt to taste
Freshly ground black pepper to taste
*1/2 recipe **Buckwheat Blinis** (see recipe, right column)*
1/4 cup hot, full cream
4 tablespoons beluga caviar
20 dill sprigs for garnish

Condiments
2 medium-size hard-cooked eggs
1/2 white onion, chopped fine
2 lemons, cut in wedges and seeded

Directions
Season chenna lightly with salt and black pepper to taste; soften by kneading it gently. Cook blinis (each 1-inch wide), brush with hot cream, top with chenna, and crown with a portion of caviar.

Presentation
Place the caviar bites on a serviette-lined silver platter, and place a bouquet of dill sprigs on the serviette.

For condiments, grate egg whites and yolks separately and place in 2 bowls. Spoon onions and lemon wedges into 2 other bowls.

Place condiments on a silver platter.

6 to 8 servings

Buckwheat Blinis

Buckwheat is not a grain and is not related to wheat. Its seeds are called groats, roasted and labeled **kasha**. Unroasted groats are ground to a fine flour, **buckwheat flour,** which is used for blinis. Blinis are small, Russian yeast pancakes usually served with caviar and sour cream.

Here is a light and easy-to-prepare recipe. These 1/2-inch-diameter blinis, with a whisper of spices, are dainty and elegant.

1 cup buckwheat flour
4 medium egg whites
1 cup whole milk
*Pinch of **nutmeg***
*Pinch of ground **mace***
Salt to taste
Freshly ground black pepper to taste
1/4 cup olive oil

Directions
Place flour, egg whites, and milk in a medium bowl. Using a wooden spoon, beat to a smooth batter. The batter can also be beaten in a food processor and takes only 2 to 3 minutes. Add nutmeg, mace, and salt and black pepper to taste. Beat a few seconds. Cover batter and leave in refrigerator for 2 hours.

Bring batter to room temperature and beat in 1 tablespoon olive oil.

Heat a crêpe pan. Add 1 teaspoon of olive oil, and when almost smoking, drop teaspoons of batter into the pan about 1-inch apart. When bubbles appear on the uncooked sides, turn blinis over using a spatula and brown the bottoms. Similarly, cook remaining blinis. The blinis should be crisp and a nice brown color. Serve them hot. Blinis may be placed covered in a warm oven for 1 hour.

6 to 8 servings

Grilled Shrimp with Melons in Port Wine

Use large shrimp for this hot and spicy appetizer. The accompanying sweet-and-sour melon, specked with cracked black peppercorns, is a lively contrast to the hot shrimp. Crushed **shiso** leaves add a unique flavor to the dressing; fresh shiso leaves make a fragrant garnish. A good substitute is mint, a relative of shiso.

8 bamboo skewers
1 cup water
8 large shrimp, heads and tails on

Fruit
½ ripe honeydew melon
2 pounds watermelon
1 starfruit

Dressing for Fruit
2 cups white port wine
1 tablespoon white wine vinegar
1 tablespoon fresh lime juice
3 tablespoons powdered sugar
4 crushed shiso leaves
*4 whole **cloves***
*1-inch piece of **cinnamon** stick*
*1 blade of **mace***
5 black peppercorns, cracked

Coating for Shrimp
*1 teaspoon ground **cumin***
*1 tablespoon **chili paste***
Fresh lime juice to taste
Salt to taste
2 tablespoons olive oil

Garnish
4 shiso leaves

Directions
Soak 8 bamboo or wooden skewers in 1 cup water for at least half an hour to prevent the skewers from burning while grilling. Peel, devein, and clean shrimp, leaving heads and tails on.

Slice the melons open and remove seeds. Scoop some of the fruit with a medium-size melon-ball cutter (to make 2 cups of melon balls). Slice the starfruit into 8 slices. Place all in a medium-size bowl.

For the dressing, place port wine, vinegar, lime juice, and sugar in a **nonreactive** saucepan. Bring to a slow simmer. Remove from heat and add the shiso leaves, cloves, cinnamon, mace, and cracked black peppercorns. Cover and set aside to cool. Once the dressing is cooled to room temperature, strain and discard shiso, cloves, cinnamon, mace, and black peppercorns. Pour this strained dressing on the fruits and leave to marinate for 1 to 2 hours in the refrigerator.

To the shrimp, add cumin, chili paste, and lime juice and salt to taste. Mix to coat shrimp. Skewer shrimp (1 per skewer) starting from the tail end. Shrimp are skewered so that they do not curl up after cooking. Brush with olive oil and grill about 3 minutes per side.

Presentation
Arrange fruits on serving plates, and drizzle the dressing on. Remove shrimp from the skewers. Place 2 shrimp each on fruit and garnish with shiso leaves.

4 servings

Broiled Quail

These broiled birds are spicy, sweet, and tangy. The chutney in the marinade leaves a shiny glaze on the birds when done cooking. **Endive** adds a hint of bitterness, and the tart orange juice helps combine these tastes together.

For best results, use a spicy mango chutney for the marinade.

4 quail, washed and wiped clean inside and out

Marinade
1 teaspoon minced ginger
1 teaspoon minced garlic
*1 teaspoon **chili paste***
3 tablespoons mango chutney (use any brand)
Juice of 1 lime
Salt to taste
4 tablespoons melted butter

For Deglazing
Juice of 1 orange
¼ cup sherry
Salt to taste

Orange Dressing
2 tablespoons orange juice
1 tablespoon olive oil
1 teaspoon Dijon mustard
Salt to taste

Garnish
*1 **endive** cut into a **julienne***
1 orange, peeled and segmented
Peel of 1 orange cut into a fine julienne
8 sprigs of watercress

Directions
Split each bird down the back and remove the backbone and neck. Make 2 cuts on either side of the breastbone. These cuts allow you to flatten out the bird by pressing down with a meat mallet. Cut wing tips and tuck the wings behind where the neck was. Make a cut in the skin at the rear end of the bird and tuck the leg ends through this cut.

Lay birds on a cutting board and, with fingertips, loosen skins without tearing them. In a small bowl, mix ginger, garlic, chili paste, chutney, lime juice, and salt to taste. Rub the mixed marinade all over the birds, including under skins; brush skin side with melted butter. Place in the refrigerator to marinate at least 5 hours.

Place skin side down on a rack on a broiler pan. Broil for 6 to 8 minutes, 6 inches away from the heat. Turn birds over, brush with pan drippings, and broil 2 to 3 minutes. To test for doneness, prick through thigh. If juices run clear, it is done; if not, cook 1 or 2 minutes more.

Place birds on 4 hot plates and keep warm. Leave the broiler pan on the stovetop on high heat. Deglaze pan with orange juice and sherry, scraping the brown bits. Season with salt to taste.

In a small bowl, whisk together ingredients for dressing with salt to taste; add endive and toss to coat with dressing.

Presentation
Arrange the dressed endive around the birds to resemble a nest; drizzle deglazed pan juices on the plates around the endive. Garnish with orange segments, orange julienne, and watercress sprigs.

4 servings

Lamb in Lettuce

This elegant starter combines an abundance of pleasing flavors and tastes. The spicy lamb morsels studded with raisins are enclosed in delicate lettuce, simmered, and marinated in a honey vinaigrette to complement the tart pineapple.

Use butter lettuce or green leaf lettuce to wrap these lamb rolls. Avoid using the coarse outer leaves as they could turn bitter during the cooking process.

8 large lettuce leaves

Stuffing
2 tablespoons olive oil
1 cup minced yellow onion
1 pound coarse-ground lean lamb
½ teaspoon ground **cumin**
½ teaspoon ground **coriander**
¼ teaspoon ground **cinnamon**
Pinch of ground **cloves**
¼ cup raisins
¼ cup chopped garden mint leaves
Salt to taste
Freshly ground black pepper to taste

Honey Vinaigrette
2 tablespoons honey
2 tablespoons apple cider vinegar
2 tablespoons fresh lemon juice
¼ cup olive oil
Salt to taste

Garnish
2 rings of fresh pineapple, halved
4 sprigs of garden mint

Directions
Blanch lettuce for 2 seconds; dip in ice water. Wipe dry. Heat oil and sauté onion on medium heat for 5 minutes. Add lamb and spices, and cook on high heat for about 6 minutes. Stir in raisins and mint, with salt and black pepper to taste. Cool.

Spread open lettuce leaves on a board; divide stuffing between the leaves. Fold the 2 ends of each leaf to enclose stuffing and roll up to secure; place in a sauté pan.

For vinaigrette, place honey, vinegar, lemon juice, olive oil, and salt to taste in a small bowl. Whisk until emulsified. Save 1 tablespoon. Pour balance on the lettuce rolls to cover; bring to a slow simmer for about 3 minutes. Remove from heat, place lamb rolls in a dish, and pour the juices on the rolls. Leave to marinate in the refrigerator for 2 hours.

Bring the lamb rolls to room temperature. Brush pineapple with the reserved vinaigrette and grill for 2 to 3 minutes.

Presentation
Place grilled pineapple on appetizer plates. Arrange 2 lamb rolls each on pineapple, drizzle the reserved vinaigrette over it, and garnish with mint.

4 servings

Deviled Shrimp

As the name implies, this dish is very hot and spicy. The **tamarind** gives a spark of tartness as well as a deep golden brown color. It is a favorite of many back home. Serve as an appetizer or as a main dish with rice to accompany.

1 pound shrimp
3 tablespoons vegetable oil
2 yellow onions, peeled and thinly sliced
1 bulb **lemongrass,** crushed
1 sprig **curry leaves**
1 teaspoon each minced ginger and garlic
1 teaspoon **cayenne pepper**
1 teaspoon crushed red pepper
1 teaspoon paprika
3 tablespoons **Tamarind Juice** (see recipe, page 203)
2 teaspoons light brown sugar
Salt to taste

Directions
Peel and devein shrimp. Heat oil, add onion, lemongrass, and curry leaves, and sauté on high heat until onions turn a golden brown. Add ginger, garlic, spices, tamarind juice, brown sugar, and salt to taste. Cook for 6 to 8 minutes on low heat, stirring to avoid burning the spices.

Add shrimp and fold to combine with the spicy onion mix. Cook on high heat for 3 to 4 minutes. Remove and discard lemongrass.

Presentation
Serve hot or at room temperature.

6 to 8 servings

Seared Scallop Salad

Earthy mushrooms, spinach, and tomatoes laced with a mildly spiced, tart dressing liven up these sweet seared scallops.

12 large scallops
Salt and freshly ground black pepper to taste
2 tablespoons olive oil

For Salad
2 teaspoons minced shallots
2 teaspoons minced garlic
2 medium-size **portabella mushrooms,** stems removed, sliced
Salt to taste
1 cup seeded, diced tomato
1 cup spinach leaves, sliced 1/4-inch long

For Dressing
2 tablespoons olive oil
1 tablespoon **balsamic vinegar**
1 tablespoon fresh lemon juice
1/8 teaspoon **cayenne pepper**
1/2 teaspoon ground **coriander**
Salt and freshly ground black pepper to taste

Directions
Trim scallops. Pull off the small tendon or sinew on the side of each scallop. This gets rubbery if left on and cooked. Season with salt and black pepper to taste. Heat a skillet with olive oil, and sear scallops on high heat about 3 to 4 minutes on each side. Remove scallops from skillet, add shallots and garlic, and sauté 2 to 3 minutes. Add mushrooms, season with salt, and cook 4 minutes. In a medium-size bowl, add the sautéed shallots, garlic, and mushrooms to the rest of the salad ingredients. In a small bowl, whisk ingredients for dressing, and pour on salad. Season with salt and black pepper to taste. Toss to combine.

Presentation
Arrange salad on plates and place 3 scallops each on the salads.

4 servings

Starters

Smoked Salmon Salad with Creamy Pineapple

Refreshing! The slightly salty salmon and the tart, creamy pineapple bring out the best in each other. The cucumber must be young and seedless to make the cucumber cups. You can make this dish without the cucumber cups; if you do, slice the cucumber and place them attractively on the plate.

Smoked Salmon Salad

4 ounces smoked salmon, coarsely chopped
*¼ cup tomato **brunoise***
1 tablespoon red onion brunoise
Freshly ground black pepper to taste
Fresh lemon juice to taste
*½ cup **chervil** sprigs*

Creamy Pineapple

1 cup finely diced pineapple
2 tablespoons cream cheese, whipped
1 tablespoon mayonnaise
Salt to taste

Garnish

1 cucumber
8 chives
4 chive flowers

Directions

Place the ingredients for salmon salad in a small bowl and toss lightly, adding black pepper and lemon juice to taste.

In a separate bowl, mix the ingredients for the creamy pineapple.

For the garnish, trim the ends of the cucumber, and using a mandoline, slice into long, thin ribbons. Using 2 ribbons of cucumber, circle to form a cup. Makes 4 cups total.

Presentation

Place cucumber cups on appetizer plates. Spoon salmon salad into each cup and then tie 2 chives each around each cup. Tie a knot to hold the chives in place and stick in a chive flower. Spoon the creamy pineapple around the cucumber cups.

Serve **Naan Bread** (see recipe, page 168) or toasted brown bread as an accompaniment.

4 servings

Grilled Eggplant Napoleon

A vegetarian delight! Roasted and crushed **fennel** and **cumin** give the melted goat cheese with crunchy pine nuts a surprising flavor twist.

Spice combinations such as fennel and cumin or cumin and **coriander** are used in everyday Sri Lankan cooking. To keep flavors lively, we change these combinations often.

Use a plump, pear-shaped eggplant with a purple, shining black skin.

1 eggplant
1 teaspoon salt
1 tablespoon minced garlic
2 tablespoons olive oil
½ cup goat cheese
1 teaspoon crushed, roasted fennel seeds
1 teaspoon crushed, roasted cumin seeds
Salt to taste
Freshly ground black pepper to taste
2 tablespoons pine nuts, roasted and chopped
*¼ cup **chiffonade** of basil leaves*

Vegetables
1 red onion, sliced ⅛-inch thick
Salt to taste
Freshly ground black pepper to taste
1 red bell pepper
1 cup washed and trimmed spinach leaves
2 tomatoes

For Baking
1 tablespoon olive oil

Garnish
*1 tablespoon tomato **brunoise***
2 teaspoons olive oil
2 sprigs of basil

Directions
Cut the eggplant along its length into 6 slices ¼-inch thick, sprinkle with 1 teaspoon of salt, and leave aside for 5 minutes; wash and wipe dry. Rub in the garlic and brush with olive oil. Grill 3 to 4 minutes on each side of the eggplant slices to char lightly.

Season goat cheese with spices, and salt and black pepper to taste. Fold in pine nuts and basil.

Season onion with salt and black pepper to taste, brush with the remaining olive oil, and char on the grill about 3 minutes. Oil the red bell pepper and char until the skin is black. Remove skin and seeds. When cool, cut into thin strips. In a sauté pan on high heat, wilt the spinach for 10 seconds, seasoning with a pinch of salt. Slice tomatoes very thin and season with salt and black pepper to taste.

Preheat oven to 375°F.

To assemble, place a slice of eggplant on an oiled baking sheet, spread a portion of seasoned goat cheese, and cover with a portion of onion and bell pepper. On top of that, place a slice of eggplant, add goat cheese, spinach, and tomato, ending with another slice of eggplant. Top with a little goat cheese, onion, and bell pepper. Drizzle with olive oil, place in the oven, and bake for 5 minutes or until heated through.

Presentation
Using a spatula, remove eggplant from the baking sheet and place on plates. Sprinkle tomato brunoise on the plates, drizzle with olive oil, and place sprigs of basil by the eggplant.

2 servings

Roast Beets, Ricotta and Endive with Citrus Vinaigrette

The sweetness of the beets contrasts dramatically with the slightly bitter flavor of both the beet greens and **endive**. The creamy ricotta spiked with cracked black peppercorns, along with the tart vinaigrette, harmonize all the flavors in the dish. These ricotta-sandwiched beets, with the wiry roots still on, are a visual delight.

4 medium-size beets
1 tablespoon olive oil

For Cooked Beet Greens

1 teaspoon olive oil
1 tablespoon chopped yellow onion
1 teaspoon chopped garlic
1½ cups sliced beet greens (saved from the beets)
Salt to taste
Freshly ground black pepper to taste
*2 teaspoons **balsamic vinegar***

Ricotta Stuffing

1 cup ricotta cheese
2 teaspoons snipped chives
1 teaspoon cracked black peppercorns
*Pinch of grated **nutmeg***
Salt to taste

Garnish

2 oranges, peeled and cut in segments
2 small endive, leaves separated and trimmed
*Zest of 1 orange cut into a fine **julienne***

Dressing

Juice of 1 orange
2 tablespoons olive oil
2 teaspoons Dijon mustard
1 teaspoon sugar
Salt to taste

Directions

Preheat oven to 375°F.

Brush beets with olive oil, place in a roasting pan, and roast in the preheated oven for 1 hour.

To cook the beet greens, heat oil and sauté onion and garlic for 3 to 4 minutes on medium heat. Stir in beet greens and cook 4 to 5 minutes or until greens are soft. Season with salt and black pepper to taste, and mix in the vinegar.

Trim the leaf ends of the roasted beets, peel and cut across into 2 slices each, leaving the wiry root ends on.

Mix together the ricotta stuffing with salt to taste.

Presentation

Spoon the sautéed beet greens onto the center of the plate and place a beet slice on the beet greens. Spoon a portion of ricotta stuffing on the beet, and top with a slice with the wiry root end on.

Arrange orange segments and endive around the beet greens, with the leaf tips pointing toward the edge of the plate; sprinkle orange zest julienne on beets.

Whisk the dressing ingredients in a small bowl with salt to taste and drizzle dressing on the endive and beets.

4 servings

Lobster with Marinated Leeks and Tomato and Lemon Chutney

This sophisticated dish is perfect for a special party, well worth the preparation time. Leeks have an affinity for **nutmeg** and are enlivened with just a hint of it. The specks of red pepper add not only to the appearance of the dish but to the taste as well. The sweet and spicy chutney combines pleasingly with the lobster and leeks.

½ recipe **Tomato and Lemon Chutney**
   (see recipe, page 200)
2 lobsters, 1½ pounds each

Marinated Leeks
2 leeks
2 cups water
½ cup tomato **concassée**
1 tablespoon olive oil
1 tablespoon white wine vinegar
Pinch of nutmeg
Pinch of crushed red pepper flakes
Salt to taste
Fresh lemon juice to taste

For Hot Aioli
2 small egg yolks
2 teaspoons Dijon mustard
2 tablespoons champagne vinegar
4 cloves garlic, peeled and finely chopped
⅛ teaspoon **cayenne pepper**
Salt to taste
½ cup olive oil

Garnish
1 tablespoon **tobiko**
4 sprigs of dill

Directions
Make tomato and lemon chutney and set aside.

Cook lobsters in boiling water for 8 to 10 minutes. Cool, remove heads, and save for stock. Crack the claws and remove the meat. Cut the underside of the lobster tail, remove the meat in one piece, and cut the tail meat crosswise into 6 slices per tail.

To make marinated leeks, cut root ends off leeks and discard. Cut off green parts and save to use in the stock. Slice white parts lengthwise, soak in 2 cups fresh water for 5 minutes, and wash in fresh water to get rid of sand and grit. Cut in ½-inch-thick diagonal slices (about 1½ cups). Cook in fresh simmering water for 3 minutes, strain, and while still warm, mix with tomatoes and remaining ingredients. Add salt and lemon juice to taste. Place in the refrigerator for at least 1 hour or as long as 1 day.

For hot aioli, blend egg yolks, mustard, vinegar, garlic, and cayenne with salt to taste in a blender. Add oil in a stream and blend until the consistency is like thick mayonnaise.

Presentation
Place a spoonful of leeks in the center of an appetizer plate. Place 2 slices of lobster on the leeks and a dollop of chutney on the lobster. Place another slice of lobster and a claw on the chutney. Spoon aioli on the lobster and top with tobiko.

Drizzle the plate with aioli, allowing it to blend into the dressing from the leeks. Strew the remaining tobiko around the leeks and garnish with dill.

4 servings

Seafood Mousse

This rich and elegant mousse has a melt-in-your-mouth texture. It is important to process the seafood to a very fine consistency and pass it through a sieve to achieve a smooth texture. The mousse has only a hint of spice and is partnered with a lively sauce and a tart relish. The nuances of taste in this dish are enjoyed in every mouthful.

2 tablespoons melted unsalted butter
8 four-ounce molds

Seafood Mousse

6 ounces trimmed scallops
6 ounces peeled and deveined shrimp,
  heads and tails removed
3 medium egg whites
*¼ teaspoon **cayenne pepper***
*Pinch of freshly grated **nutmeg***
Salt to taste
Freshly ground white pepper to taste
2 to 2½ cups heavy cream

Spicy Beurre Blanc

½ cup white wine
1 tablespoon chopped shallots
1 teaspoon cracked black peppercorns
*Pinch of ground **cloves***
Pinch of nutmeg
½ cup heavy cream
½ pound unsalted butter, chilled
Salt to taste
Lime juice to taste

Relish

1 tomato, seeded and cut into small dice
*1 tablespoon **capers***
1 tablespoon small-diced red onion
1 teaspoon snipped chives
1 teaspoon coarse-ground black pepper
Fresh lemon juice to taste
Salt to taste

Garnish

12 chives
*2 teaspoons **tobiko***

Directions

Butter the molds and set aside.

Wipe the seafood to remove any excess moisture and place in the work bowl of a food processor. Process to a smooth consistency.

Add the egg whites and seasonings with salt and white pepper to taste. Process for 10 seconds, scrape down the sides of the work bowl, add the cream gradually, and process for 10 seconds more. The mix should be the consistency of whipped cream. You may not need all the cream. Pass the mix through a sieve for a smooth-textured mousse.

Preheat oven to 250°F.

Spoon 2 to 2½ ounces of the seafood mousse mix into each mold. Cook in a covered **bain marie** in the preheated oven for 30 minutes.

While the mousse is cooking, make the beurre blanc. Place wine, shallots, spices, and cream in a pan, and reduce to ½ cup (about 5 to 6 minutes on moderate heat). Gradually whisk in the butter; season with salt and lime juice to taste. Strain, cover, and keep it warm.

To make the relish, place all the ingredients with lemon juice and salt to taste in a small bowl and toss to combine.

Presentation

Unmold mousse onto the center of each plate and spoon sauce around the mousse. Garnish each with relish and chive. Top each mousse with a little tobiko.

8 servings

Grilled Spicy Swordfish

These spicy swordfish skewers are accompanied by a crunchy salad with a zesty dressing. All the flavors combine for a pleasing sensation.

6 ounces trimmed swordfish, cut into 1-inch cubes

For Marinade
*½ teaspoon **cayenne pepper***
*1 teaspoon ground **cumin***
*1 tablespoon **fish sauce***
1 tablespoon tomato ketchup
1 tablespoon white vinegar

For Grilling
8 skewers, soaked in ½ cup water
1 tablespoon olive oil

For Dressing
2 tablespoons fresh lemon juice
1 teaspoon crushed red pepper flakes
1 tablespoon honey
Salt to taste

For Salad
*1 red onion cut into a fine **julienne***
1 cucumber, peeled, seeded, and cut into a fine julienne
2 tablespoons carrot julienne
½ teaspoon roasted cumin seeds
½ cup whole basil leaves

Directions
Place the fish in a **nonreactive** bowl. Add ingredients for marinade to the fish, mix, and refrigerate 4 hours. Thread fish on skewers, brush with oil, and cook on a hot grill for 5 minutes on each side. Mix the dressing and pour over salad; toss well to coat.

Presentation
Spoon salad on plates and place 2 skewers of fish.

4 servings

Pacific Fish Salad

Using fresh fish is essential to this salad. Any snapper such as **opakapaka** or **onaga** is ideal for this Pacific Island delicacy. The occasional bite into **coriander** seeds adds a dash of spiciness to this otherwise sweetish fish salad.

1 pound white fish fillet
3 limes, juiced and strained
½ red onion, cut into thin slices, and soaked in ice water
1 ripe tomato, peeled, seeded, and cut into thin slices
*1 **green chili**, halved, seeded, and chopped fine*
1 teaspoon coriander seeds, crushed
Salt to taste
½ cup freshly squeezed, thick coconut milk

Garnish
*¼ cup garden mint **chiffonade***

Directions
Skin fish fillet and slice into ⅛-inch-thick slices. Place on plate and sprinkle with lime juice. To extract juices, place another plate on fish and weigh down with an unopened can of food weighing 10 to 12 ounces. Leave in the refrigerator for at least 4 hours. Drain off all juice and wipe fish dry.

Drain water from onion, wash in fresh water, wipe dry, and place in a small bowl. Add tomatoes, green chili, coriander seeds, and salt to taste. Toss to combine.

Presentation
Arrange tossed onion and tomatoes on a platter. Place fish slices on top, pour coconut milk over them, and garnish with mint chiffonade. Serve chilled.

4 servings

Blackened Spicy Ahi with Pineapple Relish and Mint Chutney

Chef Paul Prudhomme created the classic blackened red fish years ago and put New Orleans on the map. Many flew to New Orleans just to taste this dish. The dish was so popular that soon New Orleans ran out of red fish! We have many versions of this dish in Hawai'i. Blackened spicy tuna is my version of the classic, a favorite with the Ka'Ikena La'uae Restaurant guests. This spice mix has a noticeable Sri Lankan flavor. Rather than adding flour to the spice mix, I add **yellow split peas** to help the spices adhere to and aromatize the fish, which will be served rare.

8 ounces center-cut tuna fillet, trimmed
1½ tablespoons peanut oil

Mint Chutney
1 cup garden mint leaves
½ cup plain yogurt
1 teaspoon chopped shallots
1 teaspoon chopped ginger
*1 **green chili,** seeded and chopped*
2 tablespoons lime juice
2 tablespoons water
1 teaspoon sugar
Salt to taste

Spice Mix for Ahi
1 tablespoon yellow split peas
*1 tablespoon **coriander** seeds*
*1 tablespoon **cumin** seeds*
*Seeds of 2 **cardamom** pods*
*1 teaspoon **fenugreek** seeds*
1 teaspoon black peppercorns
1 teaspoon white sesame seeds
*1 teaspoon **cayenne pepper***
2 teaspoons salt

Pineapple Relish
½ cup finely diced pineapple
¼ cup chopped basil
1 tablespoon chopped, roasted macadamia nuts
1 tablespoon roasted, grated coconut
Salt to taste
Fresh lemon juice to taste

Garnish
16 chives

Directions
Trim the tuna fillet into a log shape, approximately 2 inches by 5½ inches. Brush with half the oil.

To make mint chutney, place all the ingredients in a food processor and process till smooth. Season with salt to taste.

For the crust, heat a skillet and add the split peas, coriander, cumin, cardamom, fenugreek, black peppercorns, and white sesame seeds. Roast on medium-high heat for 4 to 5 minutes or until the seeds are crisp. Remove from heat and place the seeds in a blender. Grind to a coarse texture, spoon onto a plate, and mix in cayenne pepper and salt.

Dredge tuna in the spice mix to coat all sides. Brush an iron skillet with the remaining oil and place on high heat. When the skillet is very hot, sear the tuna for 30 seconds per side; slice thin. The tuna will still be rare inside with a crisp crust around. In a small bowl, toss together ingredients for relish and add salt and lemon juice to taste.

Presentation
Mold relish on plates and place the fish in overlapping half-circles around the relish. Spoon mint chutney on the plates and garnish with chives.

4 servings

Soups . . .

To Warm the Heart

Soup—the word originally meant "a cup of nourishment." Today, soups are valued for both their nourishment and simplicity. In small portions, they tease the palate; in large ones, they're satisfying meals in themselves.

Widely varied specialty soups from around the world come in many forms: clear soups, thick soups, and puréed soups; some are hot, and some are cold; some are based on vegetables, and some on fruits, seafood, or meats; some are hearty and some are wickedly rich. Many soups rely on flour and fat, or egg yolk and cream for thickening. While many people love these rich soups, many more yearn for lighter and healthier fare.

I have some wonderful soup memories. Chef Paul Bocuse's truffle soup with a crown of golden puff pastry was out of this world. Biting into the truffle—I felt regal! I recall Chef Yamadate's sparkling fish broth, in its pristine beauty, served in a pretty little bowl with a Japanese garden scene. Its flavor and beauty warmed my heart.

Memories of my mother's soups will live with me forever. The fragrance of her soups hinted at the herbs or spices she added. A serving of her chicken soup always contained two peeled garlic cloves, a sliver of ginger, and two or three peppercorns. Of course, these lovely garlic and ginger garnishes weren't raw —they came from mother's soup pot, the soft garlic melting into a silken purée with the first two mouthfuls. We reveled in my mother's lentil soups laden with fresh vegetables; the vegetables were crunchy and colorful. Her creamy **gotukola** soup, based on the juice of freshly ground gotukola, is thickened naturally by the disintegrating rice grains. Enriched with a spoonful of coconut milk, this soup surpasses many cream soups in flavor.

Inspired by these memories, I have selected the soups for this chapter. The foundation I use for some of these soups is a good, fat-free stock of fish, chicken, or beef, as well as vegetables. For some other soups, I use fruits, yogurt, cream, buttermilk, milk, and wine—all with the enchanting perfume of herbs and spices.

Tomato-Orange Soup

The day was sunny and breezy, and the place was Doris Duke's Tudor-style mansion on the Atlantic coast in Newport, Rhode Island. The soup was perfect for that summer day, and the special guest was Jacqueline Kennedy Onassis. The hint of ginger in the soup is refreshing against the slightly sweet and tart orange. All the flavors in the soup blend soothingly in the mouth.

4 large oranges

Soup

1 pound ripe tomatoes
*1 tablespoon **extra virgin olive oil***
1 yellow onion, peeled and chopped
*½-inch piece of **cinnamon** stick*
4 black peppercorns
1 teaspoon grated ginger
*2 cups **Defatted Chicken Stock** (see recipe, page 45)*
1 teaspoon sugar
Salt to taste
Freshly ground white pepper to taste

Garnish

1 orange
2 cups crushed ice
4 sprigs of orange leaves

Directions

Slice the oranges ½-inch below the stem ends and save tops for garnish. Scoop out the oranges, removing all the orange pulp and most of the pith. Save orange juice for the soup (about 1 cup). Wash the orange shells, wipe, wrap in plastic wrap, and put them in the freezer.

For soup, core and chop tomatoes. Heat oil in saucepan, add onion, and cook for 4 minutes to soften. Add tomatoes, cinnamon, peppercorns, ginger, and stock. Simmer until tomatoes are soft, about 8 minutes. Remove from heat and pass the soup through a sieve, pressing with a wooden spoon to help get most of the tomato pulp. Return soup to the saucepan. Season with the reserved orange juice, sugar, and salt and white pepper to taste. Chill until ready to serve.

To make the garnish, peel the orange zest extremely thin and cut into a very fine **julienne. Blanch** and rinse in cold water.

Presentation

To present the soup, fill soup plates with crushed ice and embed frozen orange shells.

Ladle chilled soup into orange shells and top with orange zest julienne. Place orange leaf sprigs and sliced stem ends beside the soup-filled orange shells.

4 servings

Burst of Flavor

Roast Butternut Squash Soup with Candied Walnuts

This is one of Ka'Ikena La'uae Restaurant's popular soups. Squash has a natural affinity for spices, especially **cinnamon** and **cloves.** Along with **cardamom,** this threesome is often used in **garam masala,** a fragrant blend of roasted ground spices. The candied walnuts add texture and help balance the richness of the soup.

For Candied Walnuts

½ cup walnuts

2 tablespoons unsalted butter

2 tablespoons sugar

1 tablespoon honey

⅛ teaspoon ground cinnamon

To the Soup

2 pounds butternut squash

1 tablespoon olive oil

¼ cup chopped yellow onion

1 leek, white part only, chopped

2 pints **Defatted Chicken Stock** (see recipe, page 45)

1 teaspoon ground dry ginger

½ teaspoon each ground cinnamon and cloves

¼ teaspoon ground cardamom seeds

Salt to taste

Freshly ground white pepper to taste

1 cup heavy cream

Garnish

3 tablespoons **Crème Fraîche** (see recipe, page 243)

Directions

Place walnuts in a pan on low heat. Allow walnuts to get slightly crisp.

Add butter, sugar, and honey; cook for 5 to 6 minutes or until nuts are coated with the sugar and honey glaze. Dust with cinnamon. Spoon walnuts onto a wax paper–lined pan. Do not use the walnuts until they are dry.

Preheat oven to 300°F. Halve butternut squash, remove seeds, place on a baking pan skin side up, and bake for 30 to 40 minutes. Scoop out the soft insides of the squash while the squash is still warm (it comes off the skin easily) and set aside. Discard the skin.

In a heavy-bottomed pan, heat 1 tablespoon of olive oil and add onions and leeks. Cook 4 to 5 minutes on low heat. Add the stock, butternut squash, spices, and season with salt and white pepper to taste. Simmer for 30 minutes. Stir in cream, remove from heat, and purée in a food blender. Heat the soup back to a simmer.

Presentation

Ladle into soup bowls, and top each portion with a dollop of crème fraîche and a candied walnut.

6 servings

Ranjit's Pot-Au-Feu

This spice-laced broth with vegetables, chicken, and beef is a nourishing meal for family and guests. The blend of three spices, **coriander, cumin,** and **cinnamon,** is commonly used in Sri Lanka to flavor meat and chicken soup. By the time it's finished cooking, the vegetables are soft and melt in the mouth, the beef is tender and moist, and the chicken almost falls off the bone (easily pulled off with tongs).

Ranjit, my husband, garnishes this delicious medley of tastes and textures with grated Parmesan cheese. Crusty garlic bread and a crisp green salad complete this homey dinner.

The leftover soup is a welcome treat the next day.

1 fryer chicken (1½ to 2 pounds)
1 pound beef chuck
1 tablespoon olive oil
*4 pints **Defatted Chicken Stock** (see recipe, page 45)*
1 teaspoon crushed coriander seeds
½ teaspoon crushed cumin seeds
1-inch piece of cinnamon stick
1 teaspoon whole black peppercorns
12 garlic cloves, peeled

Vegetables
6 small carrots, leaves trimmed, with an inch of stem left on
6 to 8 small red potatoes, unpeeled
6 leeks, white part only
6 small boiling onions, peeled
Salt to taste
12 string beans, trimmed
*2 whole sprigs of **curry leaves***

For Green Salad
2 cups broken-up romaine lettuce
1 cup broken-up butter lettuce
1 cup broken-up green leaf lettuce

For Dressing
*1 tablespoon **balsamic vinegar***
1 tablespoon fresh lime juice
1 tablespoon Dijon mustard
2 tablespoons olive oil
Salt to taste
Freshly ground black pepper to taste

Directions
Skin and wash chicken inside and out; wipe dry. Cut beef in 1½-inch cubes. Heat oil in a heavy-bottomed pan on high heat. Place chicken in pan and sear about 6 minutes or until it's a light golden color. Set aside. Add beef to pan and sear for 4 to 5 minutes.

Add stock, spices, and garlic. Return chicken to pan, cover, and simmer on low heat. Make sure chicken is immersed in the stock; if not, add more stock or water.

After 1 hour, add all the vegetables but the string beans. Cover and simmer for 30 minutes. Season with salt to taste. Turn off heat and let dish rest until serving time.

Before serving, bring soup to simmer, add string beans, and lay the curry leaves on top. Cover and simmer 10 minutes. Serve.

Place salad greens in a medium-size bowl. In a small bowl, whisk dressing ingredients together, adding salt and black pepper to taste. Pour on the salad and toss gently to coat the greens.

Presentation
Ladle soup into soup bowls. Serve with green salad and crusty garlic bread.

8 or more servings

Lentil Rasam with Spicy Garlic Custard

Tamarind is an essential ingredient in this broth from the north of Sri Lanka. It is popular in many other parts of the country, too. There are several variations, many extremely spicy. I prefer this mild version, served in small portions as a stimulating starter. Its dash of spiciness is refreshing with the rich garlic custard.

Spicy Garlic Custard
6 timbale molds
1 tablespoon vegetable oil
4 large garlic cloves, peeled
1 cup water
1 tablespoon unsalted butter
1 tablespoon sugar
2 tablespoons port wine
1 egg and 2 yolks
½ cup whole milk
*Pinch of **cayenne pepper***
Salt to taste

Broth
*½ cup **pink lentils***
6 cups cold water
2 tomatoes, sliced
2 teaspoons chopped ginger
1 small yellow onion, peeled and sliced
*1 teaspoon **coriander** seeds, crushed*
*1 teaspoon **cumin** seeds, crushed*
*2-inch piece of **cinnamon** stick*

Seasoning
*3 tablespoons **Tamarind Juice** (see recipe, page 203)*
Salt and freshly ground black pepper to taste

To Enrich Soup
1 tablespoon unsalted butter
1 shallot, peeled and thinly sliced
*⅛ teaspoon **asafoetida,** optional*

Garnish
4 to 5 whole Chinese parsley leaves

Directions
Preheat oven to 275°F.

Wipe timbale molds and apply oil generously. Place garlic in a sauté pan with 1 cup water and simmer for 8 minutes. Remove garlic from water. Heat butter in a sauté pan, add cooked garlic cloves, and sprinkle with sugar. Stir to coat garlic with the butter. Add port wine and cook about 10 minutes on low heat. Mash the garlic to a purée using the back of a spoon.

Place egg, egg yolks, and milk in a small bowl. Add a pinch of cayenne and salt to taste; whisk until smooth. Fold in the garlic purée and ladle about ¼ cup custard mix into each timbale mold; place in a baking pan. Cook in a **bain marie** in the preheated oven for 20 minutes. To check for doneness, insert a toothpick into the custard. The toothpick should come out clean if the custard is done.

Wash lentils in 4 to 5 changes of water. Place in a pot with 6 cups water and add the tomatoes, ginger, onion, and spices. Bring to a boil. Reduce heat and simmer for 40 minutes. Skim off the film that floats to the top. Season with tamarind juice, salt and black pepper to taste. Remove from heat, pass through a fine strainer, and place the broth aside. About 4½ cups are needed.

Heat butter in saucepan, add shallots, and cook 1 minute on high heat until shallots turn golden brown. Turn off heat, stir in asafoetida, and in a few seconds, pour in the broth slowly, discarding the sediment.

Presentation
Ladle soup into bowls. Remove custards from timbale molds and place one in the center of each soup serving. The custards come off the molds easily if you run a knife tip around the top edge of the custard to release it. Garnish each custard with a Chinese parsley leaf.

4 to 5 servings

Watercress Soup

Nutmeg has a sweet, fruity overtone and is wonderful with greens such as watercress and spinach. It loses its spark soon after grinding, so it is best to use a hand grater and grind it straight into the soup.

1 bunch of watercress, washed
1 tablespoon olive oil
1 tablespoon chopped yellow onion
1 cup **Defatted Chicken Stock** *(see recipe, page 45)*
3 cups whole milk
Pinch grated nutmeg
Salt to taste
Freshly ground white pepper to taste

To Bind Soup
1 egg yolk
½ cup full cream

Garnish
¼ cup watercress leaves

Directions
Trim off tough stem ends of watercress and chop into ½-inch pieces—about 3 cups. Reserve ¼ cup of watercress leaves for garnish. Heat olive oil in saucepan, add onion, and cook on low heat for 3 to 4 minutes. Add watercress and stir until wilted. Pour in stock and milk, and simmer for 5 to 6 minutes. Purée until smooth using an immersion blender or regular blender, strain into pan, and season with nutmeg, and salt and white pepper to taste. In a small bowl, whisk together egg yolk and cream, and stir into soup. Simmer 1 minute, stirring the soup to avoid curdling.

Presentation
Ladle soup into soup bowls and garnish with watercress leaves.

4 servings

Spicy Chestnut Soup

Chestnut soup is elegant, perfect for Christmas and Thanksgiving dinners. It is very rich and should be served in small portions. **Garam masala** is a fragrant blend of several roasted spices. Its fragrance mellows the rich soup perfectly.

2 tablespoons olive oil
1 teaspoon chopped garlic
2½ cups fresh chestnuts (about 1½ cups after peeling)
3 cups **Defatted Chicken Stock** *(see recipe, page 45)*
1 cup whole milk
1 teaspoon garam masala
Salt to taste
Freshly ground black pepper to taste
¼ cup full cream

Caramelized Apple Garnish
1 green apple
1 tablespoon sugar

Directions
Reserve 1 tablespoon oil and heat the rest in a saucepan on high heat. Add garlic and cook for a few seconds to a golden brown. Turn heat to medium, stir in chestnuts, and add stock and milk. Cover saucepan and cook for 30 minutes. Remove from heat and purée the soup using an immersion blender or a food blender. Pour back into the saucepan; season with garam masala and salt and black pepper to taste. Stir in cream and simmer for 1 minute.

Presentation
Peel, core, and thinly slice apple. Heat reserved olive oil in a small sauté pan. Add apples, sprinkle with sugar, and sauté until the apples are golden on the edges. Ladle soup into deep soup bowls and garnish each portion with a few caramelized apple slices.

4 servings

Mulligatawny

Mulligatawny is a spicy soup that is very popular in Sri Lanka. It literally means "pepper water" and originally was a thin broth. Down through the ages, it changed into a spice-flavored soup, loved by many from both East and West. My version is lighter, and the flavor of the apples blends well with the many spices in the rich chicken stock. The pinch of **turmeric** in the soup gives it an appetizing light yellow blush. **Cumin** and **coriander** seeds give it a piquancy. The robust flavor and aroma of the final sprinkling of crushed roasted **fennel** seeds are a wonderful contrast to the sweet-and-tart apple-studded soup.

Soup Stock

3 pints **Defatted Chicken Stock** (see recipe, page 45)

1 potato, peeled and cut into small dice

1 yellow onion, peeled and cut into small dice

1 tomato, chopped

1 bulb **lemongrass,** crushed

6 **cardamom** pods

2-inch piece of **cinnamon** stick

1 teaspoon roasted, ground cumin seeds

1 teaspoon roasted, ground coriander seeds

Pinch of turmeric

1 teaspoon black peppercorns, crushed

2 tablespoons **Tamarind Juice** (see recipe, page 203)

Fresh lime juice to taste

Salt to taste

To Enrich Soup

1 tablespoon unsalted butter

2 shallots, peeled and thinly sliced

1/4 cup thick coconut milk

1 tart green apple, cut into 1/4-inch cubes

2 teaspoons dark-roasted, crushed fennel seeds

Garnish

1 tablespoon whole Chinese parsley leaves

Directions

Place chicken stock in a saucepan, and add potatoes and onions. Bring to a boil, lower heat, and simmer for 15 minutes. Add tomato, lemongrass, and all the spices. Simmer for 20 minutes, stirring often with a wooden spoon, and crushing the vegetables as you stir. Season with tamarind juice; add lime juice and salt to taste. Remove from heat and pass through a strainer.

To enrich the soup, heat butter in a saucepan, add shallots, and sauté 1 to 2 minutes till golden brown. Pour in the strained soup and simmer for 10 minutes. Stir in coconut milk and apples. Simmer 3 to 4 minutes. Remove soup from heat, sprinkle in the roasted, crushed fennel seeds, and cover. Let stand for 5 minutes before serving.

Presentation

Stir soup and ladle into bowls. Garnish with Chinese parsley leaves and serve.

4 servings

Seafood in Tamarind Broth

This lightly spiced broth, specked with herbs, makes an appetizing backdrop to seafood. I serve freshly fried **poppadom** with this hearty soup. Poppadom is a wafer-thin Indian flatbread made with lentil flour. It may be fried or grilled. It has become very popular in the last few years and is available in many health food and specialty grocery stores. Hot crusty bread is just as good.

Hot and Spicy Rouille

*1 fresh red **chili pepper,** seeded*
3 large garlic cloves
1 slice of bread, crusts removed
1 tablespoon cold whole milk
1 large egg yolk
*¼ teaspoon ground **cumin***
⅔ cup olive oil
Salt to taste
Fresh lime juice to taste

Seafood in Tamarind Broth

1 tablespoon olive oil
2 spiny lobsters, split lengthwise and cleaned
8 ounces snapper, cut into 4 pieces
8 shrimp, peeled and deveined
4 shrimp heads (reserved from the shrimp)
8 Manila clams
*5 cups **Tamarind Broth** (see recipe, page 203)*
*1 minced red **serrano chili***
1 minced green serrano chili
2 green onions, chopped fine
1 tomato, peeled, seeded, and chopped fine
Fresh lime juice to taste
Salt to taste

Garnish

1 lime, thinly sliced
4 sprigs of Chinese parsley

Directions

To prepare rouille, chop red chili pepper and garlic cloves. Soak bread in milk; then squeeze out the milk. Place chili pepper, garlic, and bread in a food processor, and blend to a smooth paste. Add egg yolk and cumin, and process. Gradually add olive oil and process until the mixture is thick. Season with salt and lime juice to taste. Refrigerate until ready to use.

Heat oil in a heavy, wide pan. Add lobster and snapper. On high heat, sear for 4 minutes. Add shrimp, shrimp heads, clams, and tamarind broth. Cover pan and simmer for 5 minutes. Add minced chilies, green onions, and tomato; season with lime juice and salt to taste. Cover pan and remove from heat.

Presentation

Ladle broth into shallow, wide bowls and spoon in the seafood. Place the shrimp heads attractively in the soup. Spoon rouille over seafood. Garnish with lime slices and Chinese parsley.

4 servings

Cucumber-Yogurt Soup

This pale green soup specked with bits of walnuts, black **mustard seeds,** and **cumin** seeds is a summer beauty. The garnish adds elegance to an otherwise simple presentation.

Roasted and crushed mustard and cumin seeds, along with the walnuts, give the yogurt-cloaked cucumber a seductive flavor.

Using the same ingredients specified for the soup, you can make an elegant salad, too. Grate all the cucumber and place in a strainer over a bowl to remove the liquid. Add the walnuts and spices to the cucumber; season with lemon juice, salt, and black pepper to taste. Toss and garnish with chopped green onions and dill.

Whether you make a soup or salad, pick seedless cucumbers, available at most supermarkets. If seedless cucumbers are not available, remove the seeds from regular cucumbers before grating.

For the Soup

2 large cucumbers, peeled
1 pint plain yogurt
¼ cup roasted walnuts, chopped coarse

Seasonings

½ teaspoon black mustard seeds, roasted
  and crushed
¼ teaspoon cumin seeds, roasted and crushed
Fresh lemon juice to taste
Freshly ground black pepper to taste
Salt to taste

Garnish

*½ cup cucumber **julienne***
4 green onions or chives
4 sprigs of dill
1 tablespoon roasted, chopped walnuts

Directions

Grate 1 cucumber (avoiding the seeds) and place in a strainer over a bowl to allow the liquid to drain off.

For the soup, seed the other cucumber and discard the seeds. Chop and place in a food processor with yogurt, and blend until smooth. Remove to a medium-size bowl. Add the drained, grated cucumber, walnuts, and spices with lemon juice, black pepper, and salt to taste. Chill. Tie up cucumber julienne into 4 bundles using the green onions or chives.

Presentation

Spoon soup into serving bowls. Place a cucumber bundle with dill sprigs tucked between the cucumber and green onion ribbon in the center of each soup, making sure that it sits above the level of the soup. Sprinkle roasted, chopped walnuts on the soup.

4 servings

Chicken and Winter Melon Soup

Winter melon is a bland vegetable that comes to life with the tastes and textures of the cashew nuts and mushrooms in rich chicken broth. A tasty stock is essential to this soup. Reducing the stock helps to concentrate the flavor, resulting in a richer stock. When the soup is completed, it should have a naturally slightly salty taste without the addition of extra salt. Add salt to taste sparingly.

This soup has Chinese overtones, but I use cashew nuts instead of the peanuts traditionally found in some Chinese soups. Cashew nuts, a Sri Lankan favorite, are a fine substitute for peanuts. Their creamy taste and texture add a unique touch to the soup. Soak the raw cashew nuts before cooking; this softens the texture of the nuts.

½ cup unsalted cashew nuts
1½ cups hot water
6 large dried shiitake mushrooms, stems removed
6 ounces boneless chicken thigh meat
2 pounds winter melon

Soup Stock
*8 cups **Defatted Chicken Stock** (see recipe, page 45)*
*1 piece **star anise***
*1 teaspoon **five-spice powder***
2-inch piece of ginger, thinly sliced
Freshly ground black pepper to taste

Seasonings
*1 tablespoon **mushroom soy***
Salt to taste

Garnish
4 green onions, trimmed and sliced fine

Directions
Soak cashew nuts in ½ cup of hot water for 30 to 40 minutes. In a separate small bowl, soak mushrooms in 1 cup hot water for 15 minutes and cut into quarters. Cut chicken into 1-inch pieces and refrigerate. Peel, seed, and cut winter melons into 1-inch cubes.

Place the soup stock ingredients in a pot and add the cashew nuts drained from the soaking water. Add the mushrooms with their soaking water. On medium heat, reduce to about 5 cups. Reduction takes about 35 to 40 minutes. Add chicken and winter melon. Simmer for 20 minutes.

Season with mushroom soy. Taste and add more salt if needed.

Presentation
Serve in wide bowls. Garnish with green onion.

To add elegance, you might want to serve the soup in a winter melon "bowl." To make the bowl, cut a 6-inch slice off the stem end of the winter melon. Scoop the pulp from the melon. Remove and discard seeds from the pulp (use the pulp to make the soup).

Dip the scooped winter melon in a pot of boiling water and cook for 7 to 8 minutes. Remove from boiling water, wipe dry, and place on a serviette-lined platter. Ladle the hot soup into the winter melon bowl.

4 to 6 servings

Vegetable Soup with Tapioca

This vegetable soup, fragrant with **mace,** is thickened with tapioca and enriched with cream. Tapioca is a starch extracted from cassava root. It is available in pellet form, referred to as pearl tapioca.

¼ cup tapioca
½ cup water

Vegetable Soup

1 tablespoon olive oil
1 medium yellow onion, peeled and thinly sliced
1 large carrot, peeled and thinly sliced
2 cloves of crushed garlic
5 cups Vegetable Stock (see recipe, page 46)
2 cups tomato concassée
Salt to taste
Freshly ground black pepper to taste
¼ cup full cream
1 tablespoon snipped chives
¼ teaspoon ground mace

Directions

Sprinkle tapioca in ½ cup water and set aside. For the vegetable soup, heat oil in a pot, add onion, and sauté for 6 to 7 minutes or until light golden. Add carrots, garlic, and vegetable stock. Stir, cover, and simmer for 20 minutes. Add tomatoes, season with salt and black pepper to taste, and simmer for 15 minutes. Blend using an immersion blender or food blender. Avoid overblending; it will cause too much froth. A minute is fine. Strain mixture back into a clean pot. Add tapioca; simmer, stirring constantly (to avoid lumps) for 6 to 7 minutes. Stir in cream, snipped chives, and ground mace, and remove from heat.

Presentation

Ladle into bowls and serve hot.

4 servings

Avocado Soup Kamehameha

A specialty of The Willows restaurant, this soup is a winning starter for lunch or dinner.

Avocados are believed to have been introduced into the United States in Florida around 1830. Avocado is called butterfruit in some countries. In the olden days, British ships stocked it to serve lesser officers, calling it midshipman's butter.

Just a hint of **cayenne pepper** and **coriander** add spark to the rich, buttery soup.

1 large avocado peeled, pit removed
1 teaspoon chopped yellow onion
⅛ teaspoon cayenne pepper
¼ teaspoon ground coriander
1 cup Defatted Chicken Broth (see recipe, page 45)
2 tablespoons cream sherry
1 cup half-and-half cream
Salt to taste
Freshly ground white pepper to taste

Garnish
6 lemon slices

Directions

Blend all ingredients in a processor or blender with salt and white pepper to taste. Chill.

Presentation

Ladle into chilled bowls, with a lemon slice floating on each.

6 servings

Defatted Beef Stock

A good stock is the foundation of a good soup. The homemade stocks to follow provide nutrition and full-bodied flavor.

There are a few golden rules to remember when making stocks. Never cover a stock. Initially, bring it to a boil and then simmer on low heat so ingredients release their flavors. Skim throughout cooking to remove fat and grease.

The end result is a rich and flavorful stock. Roasted red onions give a deep brown color to the stock. It is unsalted and not overly spiced. Cool the stock as quickly as possible and refrigerate in sterilized, covered containers. Stock will keep three to four days if properly refrigerated. You may freeze it and bring it out for cooking when needed.

Commercial bouillon, broths, and canned base should be a last resort. They rarely measure up to homemade stocks and broths.

Beef stock can be brown or white. The difference between brown stock and white stock is that the bones and vegetables are roasted until browned for the brown stock, as in this recipe.

Veal bones may be substituted for beef if you wish.

4 pounds beef bones, cut into 2- to 3-inch pieces
4 pounds beef shank, sliced into 3-inch pieces
3 medium-size red onions, cut into medium dice
3 medium-size carrots, cut into medium dice
3 leeks, white parts only, washed and sliced ½-inch thick
3 stems celery, sliced ½-inch thick
8 quarts water
6 large tomatoes, cut into medium dice
6 cloves garlic, peeled
1 tablespoon black peppercorns
6 whole **cloves**
1 teaspoon **coriander** seeds

Directions

Preheat oven to 400°F.

Place bones and shank in a roasting pan and roast for 40 minutes to brown them well.

Move bones and meat from the roasting pan to a large stockpot (about 10-quart size). Drain off the fat collected in the roasting pan, and add onions, carrots, leeks, and celery. Place in the oven for 25 minutes to roast. Add the browned vegetables to the stockpot along with 8 quarts of water, tomatoes, garlic, and spices.

Place on high heat, bring to a fast boil, reduce heat to low, and simmer for 6 hours. Skim as often as necessary to remove the film that collects on the surface of the stock. Strain stock through a cheesecloth-lined strainer, cool, and refrigerate. Remove any fat solidified on the surface before use.

Yields 1 gallon

Burst of Flavor

Asian-Style Beef Stock

This light but flavorful spicy stock makes a tasty base for soups.

6 pounds beef rib bones
6 quarts cold water
2 red onions, unpeeled
2-inch piece of ginger, sliced
4 whole **star anise**
2-inch piece **cinnamon** stick
10 black peppercorns
6 whole **cloves**
1 cup chopped Chinese parsley roots

Directions

Wash beef bones and place in a pot (about 8-quart size) with 6 quarts cold water. Bring to a slow simmer, skim to remove the film that collects on the surface.

Preheat oven to 350°F.

Wash red onions and halve them lengthwise. Place cut side down in a roasting pan. Roast in the preheated oven for 35 minutes. Peel onions when cool enough to handle.

Reduce heat to low. Add the roasted onions, ginger, spices, and Chinese parsley roots, and simmer for 5 hours. Skim as often as necessary to remove the film.

Strain stock through a cheesecloth-lined strainer, cool, and refrigerate. Remove any fat solidified on the surface before use.

Yields 3 to 4 pints

Defatted Chicken Stock

This is a fast and easy way to make a chicken stock. Use it as a base for soups and stews. This clear, pale-gold stock is nutritious and tasty.

For a darker-colored stock, roast the chicken bones for 40 minutes in a preheated, 400°F oven and continue to cook as stated in the recipe.

6 pounds chicken back bones
6 pints cold water
2 medium yellow onions, peeled and sliced
1 carrot, sliced
2 stems celery, sliced
3 leeks, white parts only, washed and sliced
1-inch piece of **cinnamon** stick
1 teaspoon crushed **coriander** seeds
1 teaspoon crushed **cumin** seeds
8 black peppercorns
4 whole **cloves**

Directions

Wash chicken bones, place in a pan with 6 pints cold water and the rest of the ingredients, and bring to a slow boil. Skim off the froth.

Reduce heat to low and simmer for 2½ hours. Skim as often as necessary to remove the film that collects on the surface of the stock.

Add more water if needed to keep the bones covered with liquid. Pour through a cheesecloth-lined strainer, cool, and refrigerate stock. Remove any fat solidified on the surface before use.

Yields 2½ pints

Fish Stock

Simply spiced yet fragrant, this stock is light and refreshing.

Use very fresh whitefish bones cut up into 3- to 4-inch pieces. Rinse off thoroughly before use.

Fish stock is delicate. Refrigerate, but be sure to use it up within one to two days. Its lovely flavor diminishes if it's frozen.

Fennel and **cinnamon** add a touch of sweetness to the stock. Salt this according to taste.

2 pounds whitefish bones
2½ pints water
1 yellow onion, peeled and thinly sliced
3 leeks, white parts only, washed and thinly sliced
2 stems celery, sliced
4 sprigs garden mint
2 slices ginger
3 tomatoes, quartered
1 teaspoon fennel seeds
1-inch piece of cinnamon stick
1 cup white wine
Juice of 1 lemon

Directions

Place washed fish bones in a large, stainless steel pan with the rest of the ingredients. Bring to a boil, reduce heat to low, and simmer 35 to 40 minutes, skimming frequently.

Pour through a cheesecloth-lined strainer, cool, and refrigerate.

Yields 1½ pints

Vegetable Stock

Good cooks are aware of the goodness of vegetable stocks.

Roasting vegetables before they go into the stockpot ensures a deep amber-colored product; slow cooking makes the broth clear and helps to enrich it as well. Use this vegetable stock in soups, to glaze vegetables, or to cook grains and legumes.

Vegetables

2 medium-size, unpeeled yellow onions, halved
3 leeks, white part only
2 celery stems
2 whole carrots
1 cup whole mushrooms or mushroom stems (any kind)

For Stock

3 garlic cloves, unpeeled
3 medium-size whole tomatoes
*1-inch piece of **cinnamon** stick*
*4 whole **cloves***
*1 teaspoon **coriander***
*1 teaspoon **cumin** seeds*
8 black peppercorns
4 pints water

Directions

Preheat oven to 400°F.

Place vegetables on a baking sheet and place in the preheated oven. Roast until vegetables turn a golden brown, about 30 minutes. Place roasted vegetables in a pot with the rest of the ingredients and bring to a boil. Turn heat to low and simmer 1 hour. Pour stock through a cheesecloth-lined strainer, cool, and refrigerate.

Yields 2 pints

Tamarind Broth

This broth is excellent in fish and seafood preparations. Tart and slightly sweetish, **tamarind** brings out the best in seafood.

1 tablespoon vegetable oil
1 red onion, peeled and sliced
2 cloves garlic, sliced
3 slices ginger, crushed
3 bulbs crushed **lemongrass**
10 black peppercorns
1-inch piece of **cinnamon** *stick*
4 tomatoes chopped
¼ cup **Tamarind Juice** *(see recipe, page 203)*
4 cups water
Salt to taste

Directions
Heat oil in a medium-size stainless pot and sauté onion, garlic, ginger, and lemongrass for 5 minutes or until the vegetables are wilted. Add the spices, tomatoes, tamarind juice, and water, and bring to a slow boil. Turn down heat and simmer 45 minutes. Season lightly with salt to taste. Pour through a fine strainer. Cool and refrigerate. Keeps well for 3 to 4 days.

Yields 2 cups

Lemongrass Broth

Redolent of the sweet aroma of **lemongrass,** this clear broth leaves a lovely telltale fragrance behind. It is easy to make. Use it as a soup base, or to steam or poach seafood.

4 pints cold water
6 bulbs lemongrass, crushed
2 green onions, sliced
4 slices ginger
6 cloves garlic, peeled
½ teaspoon black peppercorns
1 yellow onion, peeled and sliced
2 teaspoons salt

Directions
Place all ingredients in a medium-size pot on high heat and bring to a boil. Turn heat to low and simmer for 45 minutes. Season with salt to taste. Pass broth through a cheesecloth-lined strainer. Cool and refrigerate. Keeps well for 3 to 4 days.

Yields 2½ pints

Fish & Shellfish . . .

Bounty of the Seven Seas

My childhood home in Moratuwa, Sri Lanka, was only three hundred yards away from the Indian Ocean. We often feasted on crab, prawns, and squid, all with a delicate, unforgettable sweetness. The end of the southwest monsoon rains heralded the big catch: an abundance of kingfish (**ono** in Hawaiian), tuna, trevally, and snapper, as well as such small fry as anchovies, sardines, and herring. In those days we never bought fish from the market. The fishermen brought it fresh to our back doorstep.

Kingfish was a family favorite. My mother seared a center-cut chunk of about four pounds, **braised** it in a creamy sauce made with stone-ground **mustard seeds,** and garnished it with onion rings sautéed to a rich, golden brown. Another favorite was anchovies threaded on six-inch skewers. Mother marinated them in lime juice, **turmeric,** salt, and freshly ground black pepper, then fried them until golden brown and crisp. In Paris I tasted mussels poached in wine and luscious scallops in a butter-rich cream sauce for the first time.

In Newport, Rhode Island, I attended my first clambake! Maine lobsters were the sweetest I've tasted anywhere. These sea-fresh memories intermingle with others on America's Atlantic coast: plucking periwinkles from rocks on the shore bordering Doris Duke's Rhode Island mansion "Rough Point"; or cooking a freshly caught, plump black bass from the lake in her "Duke Gardens" in New Jersey.

In multiethnic Hawai'i, Asia-Pacific cuisines evolved with seafood as a central focus. My first taste of ocean-fresh raw fish here was thinly sliced red snapper **sashimi** that lay gracefully on a haystack of shredded radish and wisps of pink pickled ginger. We ate these morsels after dipping them in soy sauce and Japanese horseradish. Chunks of glistening raw tuna amid tufts of tiny seaweed on a smooth green ti leaf, seasoned with sea salt, **chili pepper water,** and sesame oil stimulated my appetite.

Soon I was familiar with Hawai'i seafood. I started cooking it with spices, roasted or raw, and ground or popped in oil. I flavored it with **curry leaves** and **green chilies** or mint and **tamarind**—just as we did at home.

The dishes in this section are easy to prepare, tasty, and appealing to the eye. The recipes rely on fresh ingredients and simple techniques. For the tempting tastes and flavors, I borrow seasonings and spices from far-away shores across the seven seas.

Grilled Tuna

Lime juice and coconut milk combined with salt and pepper make a tasty dressing often used in Sri Lanka. The addition of pineapple to this dressing gives it a taste combination that complements fish cooked rare. This dish may be served as an entrée or in smaller portions as an appetizer.

1 pound tuna fillet, cut into 4 portions
1 tablespoon olive oil
Fresh lime juice to taste
Salt to taste

Vegetables
4 pearl onions, peeled and halved
1 small **jicama,** peeled and cut
   into **batonnet**
½ bell pepper, cut into batonnet
¼ peeled pineapple, cut into batonnet
1 tablespoon olive oil
2 teaspoons sugar
1 teaspoon fresh lime juice
Salt to taste

Salad
4 leaves of radicchio
½ cup **red oak leaf lettuce**
¼ cup **frisée**
½ cup basil leaves
8 yellow teardrop tomatoes, cut in halves
8 red teardrop tomatoes, cut in halves
Salt to taste

For Dressing
3 tablespoons fresh lime juice
3 tablespoons coconut milk
2 teaspoons cracked black peppercorns
Salt to taste
2 tablespoons olive oil

Garnish
2 teaspoons aged **balsamic vinegar**
12 candied coconut slivers

Directions
Coat fish with olive oil and season with lime juice and salt to taste. Refrigerate until ready to grill.

Brush vegetables and pineapple with olive oil and sprinkle on sugar and lime juice with salt to taste. Grill for 3 to 4 minutes.

Grill fish on high heat about 3 minutes per side for rare.

Place salad greens and tomatoes in a medium-size bowl. Season with salt to taste.

To make the dressing, whisk lime juice, coconut milk, cracked black peppercorns, and salt to taste in a small bowl. Gradually add oil and whisk thoroughly to emulsify. Pour on the salad and toss to combine.

Presentation
Arrange grilled vegetables, pineapple, and salad on plates. Place the fish on top of the salad. Drizzle balsamic vinegar on the plates and garnish with coconut slivers.

4 servings

Burst of Flavor

Sri Lankan Shrimp Curry

This curry has become one of Ka'Ikena La'uae Restaurant's specialty dishes. Serve the curry with rice or rice pilaf, and chutney.

1½ pounds of shrimp
2 tablespoons vegetable oil
1 teaspoon dill seeds
*1 teaspoon **fenugreek** seeds*
*1 teaspoon **fennel** seeds*
*1 sprig **curry leaves***
2 teaspoons minced ginger
2 teaspoons minced garlic
*1 bulb **lemongrass***
*2-inch piece of **cinnamon** stick*
1 large red onion, finely minced
2 medium tomatoes, finely chopped
*1 teaspoon **cayenne pepper***
1 teaspoon paprika
*½ teaspoon **turmeric***
½ cup water
1 cup coconut milk
*2 tablespoons **Tamarind Juice** (see recipe, page 203)*
Fresh lemon juice and salt to taste

Directions

Peel, devein, and wash shrimp. Heat oil on medium heat in a large skillet; fry dill, fenugreek, and fennel seeds, and curry leaves until the leaves are crisp and spices pop. Add ginger, garlic, lemongrass, cinnamon, and onion; cook on low heat until onions are light golden brown. Stir in tomatoes and spices, and cook for 2 to 3 minutes. Add shrimp and cook for 2 to 3 minutes, stirring to combine with the spices. Add water, coconut milk, and tamarind juice with salt to taste.

Turn down heat to very low and bring to a gentle simmer. Cook for 8 to 10 minutes. Stir in lemon juice and taste. Season with more salt if needed.

Yields 6 servings

Cured Fish

Any firm-fleshed fish is fine for curing in this manner. My favorite is **ono,** also known as kingfish in many countries. After the fish is cured, it may be refrigerated for a few days. Cured fish may be grilled or broiled. To balance the slightly salty taste of the cured fish, brush with honey or dust with brown sugar when cooking.

1 pound fish fillet

Curing Mix
1 tablespoon cracked black peppercorns
*1 tablespoon crushed **coriander** seeds*
*1 tablespoon **fennel** seeds*
2 tablespoons chopped, fresh dill
¼ cup light brown sugar
¼ cup sea salt
1 tablespoon vegetable oil

Directions
Wipe the fish and place skin side down in a stainless steel pan. In a small bowl, combine ingredients for curing mix and spread mixture over the fish. Cover the fish with a piece of plastic wrap or cheesecloth and place a second stainless pan directly on top of it. Place a 1-pound weight in the top pan. Refrigerate for 24 hours.

When ready to use, remove weight and wash and dry fish with paper towels to absorb excess moisture.

Yields 1 pound

Shrimp with Corn Salad

The shrimp in this recipe, hot with **cayenne pepper,** are balanced by the cheese, the creamy sweet corn, and the tart red wine vinegar dressing. These nuances of flavor get a sprinkling of roasted **cumin** seeds for a crisp, aromatic bite.

1 pound shrimp, peeled and deveined, tails left on
1 teaspoon cayenne pepper
Salt to taste
2 tablespoons vegetable oil

Salad
1 cup fresh corn kernels, from a large ear of corn
2 cups salad greens
2 tablespoons Parmesan cheese, shaved into
    thin slivers
1 small red onion, sliced
1 red bell pepper, seeded and sliced

Dressing
2 tablespoons red wine vinegar
3 tablespoons olive oil
1 teaspoon minced garlic
Freshly ground black pepper and salt to taste

Garnish
1 teaspoon cumin seeds, roasted

Directions
Preheat the oven to 275°F.

Season shrimp with cayenne pepper and salt to taste; mix in oil and set aside. Wrap corn kernels in foil and roast 30 minutes in the oven. Place corn in a medium-size bowl and add salad ingredients. In a smaller bowl, combine ingredients for dressing and add to bowl with greens and corn. Toss lightly. Cook shrimp on a very hot grill for about 1 minute on each side.

Presentation
Spoon salad onto serving plates and place shrimp on the salads. Sprinkle cumin seeds on the plates.

4 servings

Crabmeat and Fruit Salad

This salad is easy to make and can be served as an appetizer in small portions.

1 cup fresh, cooked crabmeat
1/4 cup halved, seeded red grapes
1/4 cup diced, peeled green apples
2 tablespoons chopped fresh dill
2 tablespoons fresh lemon juice
1/8 teaspoon **cayenne pepper**
1 teaspoon Dijon mustard
Salt to taste
2 tablespoons sour cream

Garnish
4 chive leaves

Directions
Combine crabmeat, fruits, and dill with seasonings and salt to taste. In a separate bowl, beat sour cream and then fold into salad.

Presentation
Serve on chilled plates and garnish with chives.

6 servings

Spicy Seafood with Pasta

The poaching liquid for this recipe is aromatized with **cloves** and bay leaves. When they are available, I add a few **curry leaves** in place of bay leaves. The fragrant, seafood-poached liquid acts as a delectable sauce for the freshly cooked pasta. Tomatoes, basil, and Parmesan cheese all infuse their flavors harmoniously into the spice-fragrant sauce.

For instructions on how to clean mussels see page 10, and for instructions on how to prepare squid see page 64.

½ recipe homemade **Pasta** (see recipe, page 170)

Poaching Liquid
1½ cups water
½ cup white wine
1 tablespoon white wine vinegar
3 whole cloves
2 bay leaves
Sea salt to taste

Seafood
2 dozen mussels, cleaned
½ pound cleaned squid, cut into ¼-inch-thick rings
½ pound shrimp, peeled and deveined

Seasonings for Seafood
2 tablespoons olive oil
2 teaspoons minced garlic
1 teaspoon crushed red pepper flakes
2 teaspoons coarse ground **cumin** seeds
1 teaspoon coarse ground **coriander** seeds
Sea salt to taste
1 cup tomato **concassée**
½ cup **chiffonade** of basil leaves
2 tablespoons fresh lemon juice
Freshly ground black pepper to taste

Garnish
2 tablespoons grated fresh Parmesan cheese
1 teaspoon crushed red pepper flakes
4 sprigs basil

Directions
Make the pasta and set aside. Place a pot of water on the stove to cook pasta later.

Place poaching ingredients in a pot with a tight-fitting lid. Bring to a slow simmer. Add the mussels, return cover, and steam for 4 to 5 minutes or until the mussels open. When mussels are cooked, remove from poaching liquid and set aside.

Strain the liquid through a cheesecloth into a clean pan (to get rid of any sand). Prepare squid and shrimp and place aside.

Heat olive oil in a pan, add squid and shrimp, and cook on high heat for 2 to 3 minutes. Add garlic, spices, and the strained liquid. Season with salt to taste. Add the tomato concassée and simmer for 4 to 5 minutes. Stir in the cooked mussels and the chiffonade of basil leaves. Remove from heat. Add lemon juice and freshly ground black pepper to taste.

To cook pasta, bring the water to a rapid boil and drop the pasta in. As it softens, stir gently to keep it from sticking together. Cook for 2 to 3 minutes and drain through a colander.

Presentation
Serve pasta on hot plates, and spoon seafood onto pasta. Sprinkle on the Parmesan cheese and red pepper flakes, and garnish with basil.

4 servings

Oysters in Half Shells with Gotukola Sambol

Oysters are both sexy and showy! They are crowned with caviar and embellished with relishes, vinaigrette, and spices; they are fast-seared, or crusted and deep-fried. Some like to make entire meals out of them, raw or cooked. Today they remain one of the most popular appetizers in restaurants.

There are many types of oysters. The principle types are Pacific oysters, European oysters, Atlantic oysters, and Olympia oysters.

To be good to eat, oysters must be alive. Tight shells that close when shaken indicate they are alive. Strong odor indicates spoilage. Discard any dead oysters. Freshly opened oysters are creamy white, brimming with liquid, and have a very mild, sweet smell. Before shucking oysters, scrub them with a stiff hand brush and rinse under running cold water. To open, hold the oyster in one hand on a towel and insert an oyster knife between the two shells near the hinge. Keep a tight grip on the oyster and twist the knife to break the hinge. Draw the knife edge under the rounded shell and cut through the oyster's adductor muscle. Insert the knife underneath the oyster and cut it away from the flat shell. Quickly rinse oysters in salted water to remove bits of shell. To serve raw, return oysters to their rounded shells with their briny liquid and place on plates with mounds of crushed ice.

The salad of **gotukola**—an Asian pennywort on which the oysters are laid—is unusual. Its dressing is made with lots of lemon juice and a sprinkling of freshly grated coconut. After the juicy morsel is gone in a flash, guests can savor the salad and its lemony dressing as it mingles with the briny juices of the oysters.

Salad

½ cup finely sliced gotukola with stems
1 tablespoon finely chopped yellow onion
Salt to taste
2 tablespoons fresh lemon juice or to taste
Freshly ground black pepper to taste
2 tablespoons freshly grated coconut

18 fresh bluepoint oysters
Freshly ground black pepper to taste

For Presentation

4 cups crushed ice

Garnish

A handful of gotukola with stems
6 lemon wedges

Directions

To prepare salad, mix gotukola with the onion and season with salt, lemon juice, and black pepper to taste. Mix well to combine the greens with the seasonings. Fold in the coconut.

Prepare oysters in their deep half shells.

Pick up each oyster, spoon 1 teaspoon of gotukola salad on the shell, and place the oyster back on the salad. Grind black pepper to taste on the oysters.

Presentation

Embed oysters on a deep platter of crushed ice. To garnish, place gotukola and lemon wedges on the ice.

3 servings

Poached Shrimp with Aioli, Sweet Potato, and Pineapple Relish

This recipe combines the delicate taste of the simply poached shrimp with the sweetness of the sweet potato and the tart flavor of pineapple. The nutty flavor of the black **mustard seeds** cooked in oil gives an exotic flavor to this colorful dish.

1 pound unpeeled shrimp

For Poaching Shrimp

2 cups water
1 tablespoon white vinegar
1 tablespoon chopped yellow onion
1 teaspoon minced garlic
1 bay leaf
1 teaspoon sea salt

For Hot Aioli

5 cloves peeled garlic
A large pinch of salt
2 egg yolks
1 tablespoon water
¾ cup olive oil
1 tablespoon fresh lemon juice
*⅛ teaspoon **cayenne pepper***
Salt to taste

Sweet Potato and Pineapple Relish

*2 small sweet potatoes, peeled and cut into a thick **julienne***
2 cups water
1 tablespoon olive oil
1 white onion, cut into a thick julienne
2 teaspoons black mustard seeds
1 teaspoon crushed red pepper flakes
1 tablespoon sugar
*2 tablespoons **rice wine vinegar***
Salt to taste
¼ pineapple, cut into a thick julienne
1 orange, peeled and segmented (save zest for garnish)

Garnish

1 ounce radish sprouts

1 tablespoon fresh lime juice
½ teaspoon sugar
Salt to taste
1 tablespoon orange zest julienne

Directions

To devein shrimp, make a cut in the shell just above the tail, use a toothpick to pull out the vein, then rinse the shrimp under running water and put aside. (Shrimp deveined this way look neater when cooked.)

Place ingredients for poaching shrimp in a medium-size pan and bring to a simmer. Add shrimp and cook 3 minutes. Cool and peel the shrimp, leaving the tails on, and refrigerate.

For hot aioli, crush garlic and a pinch of salt to a smooth paste. Place in a food processor with egg yolks and 1 tablespoon water, and process for a few seconds. Drizzle in olive oil and beat about 10 seconds. Add lemon juice, cayenne pepper, and salt to taste.

For the relish, cook sweet potatoes in 2 cups simmering water for 8 minutes or until just cooked through. Remove sweet potatoes from the water. Pour olive oil into a sauté pan, place on medium heat, add onions, and sauté a few seconds. Add mustard seeds. When the mustard seeds start to pop, add red pepper flakes, sugar, rice wine vinegar, and salt to taste. Fold in the sweet potatoes and cook on high heat for 3 to 4 minutes. Fold in the pineapple and orange.

Place radish sprouts in a small bowl; add lime juice, sugar, and salt to taste. Toss lightly.

Presentation

Place relish in the center of the plates, with shrimp on top. Arrange garnish by the shrimp. Spoon aioli on the shrimp and sprinkle with orange zest julienne.

4 servings

Crabmeat-Stuffed Mahimahi

Mahimahi, also known as dolphinfish, is a great favorite in Hawai'i. It is moist and flaky when cooked. Other fish such as halibut, pompano, flounder, or black cod may be substituted in this recipe with equally good results.

Lump crabmeat makes a good stuffing. Ginger and **cayenne pepper** give a hint of an exotic accent in the stuffing.

6 ounces mahimahi fillet
Salt to taste
Freshly ground black pepper to taste
1 tablespoon olive oil

For Stuffing

4 ounces cooked crabmeat
2 tablespoons tomato **concassée**
2 tablespoons chopped **tarragon** *leaves*
1 teaspoon minced ginger
½ teaspoon cayenne pepper
1 egg yolk
Fresh lemon juice to taste
Salt to taste
Freshly ground black pepper to taste

For Crust

1 tablespoon white sesame seeds
½ teaspoon crushed **fennel** *seeds*
1 tablespoon fresh white-bread crumbs
1 teaspoon cayenne pepper
1 teaspoon grated lemon rind
1 tablespoon mayonnaise

Garnish

2 sprigs of tarragon
2 lemon wedges

Directions

Preheat oven to 375°F.

Remove skin and cut mahimahi into 2 serving portions. **Butterfly** each portion. Season with salt and black pepper and brush lightly with olive oil. Set aside. Reserve balance of olive oil to use later.

To make the stuffing, place crabmeat in a medium-size bowl and add tomato concassée, tarragon, ginger, and cayenne. Fold gently to combine. Beat egg yolk, add to stuffing, and season with lemon juice, salt, and black pepper to taste. Stuff the butterflied fish with the crabmeat mix.

To make the crust, roast the white sesame seeds and fennel seeds in a skillet on medium heat for 2 to 3 minutes, then remove from heat. Cool and mix into the bread crumbs. Add cayenne pepper and lemon rind. Fold in the mayonnaise.

Heat reserved oil in a baking pan. Place stuffed fish in pan and bake in oven for 8 to 10 minutes.

Remove the fish from the oven and place aside. Spoon the crust mix neatly on each portion of fish. Place under a hot broiler, 6 inches away from the heat, and broil for 2 minutes to brown the tops.

Presentation

Place on hot dinner plates. Garnish with tarragon and lemon wedges.

2 servings

Crab Cakes

Crab cakes are popular items on contemporary restaurant menus. My version is served with a sweet and spicy chutney and a tangy yogurt cucumber salad. A fantastic combination of flavors—sweet, spicy, and sour—meld together perfectly to complement the sweet crab cakes.

1 cup lump crabmeat
¼ recipe **Tomato and Lemon Chutney** (see recipe, page 200)

Seasonings for Crab Cakes
1 tablespoon chopped green onion
1 tablespoon chopped garden mint leaves
1 teaspoon minced ginger
1 teaspoon Worcestershire sauce
¼ teaspoon **cayenne pepper**
1 egg yolk
2 tablespoons mayonnaise
Fresh lemon juice to taste
Freshly ground black pepper to taste
Salt to taste

Crumb Coating
1 egg white, whisked to a froth
1 cup fresh bread crumbs

Yogurt Cucumber Salad
1 small cucumber, peeled
½ cup plain yogurt
1 tablespoon fresh lemon juice
1 teaspoon dill seeds
½ teaspoon cracked black peppercorns
1 tablespoon chopped fresh dill
1 teaspoon sugar
Salt to taste

To Cook Crab Cakes
2 tablespoons **extra virgin olive oil**

Herb Garnish
2 sprigs of Chinese parsley
2 basil leaves
2 sprigs of dill

Directions
Pick through crabmeat and remove any pieces of shell. Make the chutney and place aside.

To mix the crab cakes, add the seasonings, the egg yolk, and the mayonnaise to the crabmeat; season with lemon juice, black pepper, and salt to taste. Using your hands, form into 4 round, flat cakes.

Dip in egg and then toss in the bread crumbs to coat crab cakes.

To make the yogurt cucumber salad, slice the cucumber lengthwise into thin, long ribbons using a peeler; place in a strainer over a bowl and let the liquid from the cucumber drain into the bowl below. Discard the liquid, place the cucumber in a small bowl, and add yogurt, lemon juice, spices, herbs, and sugar, with salt to taste. Toss lightly.

Heat olive oil in a nonstick pan and fry crab cakes on medium heat for 2 minutes on each side or until golden brown.

Presentation
Arrange 2 crab cakes each on 2 warmed plates, spoon cucumber salad and a little chutney by the crab cakes, and garnish with mixed herbs.

2 servings

Seared Scallops with Pear Salad

Scallops add sparkle to this tasty pear salad. Greens with a spicy bite balance the sweet and juicy scallops, pears, and tart dressing.

1 pound large scallops

Pear Dressing

¼ Asian pear
1 peeled and chopped shallot
2 teaspoons Dijon mustard
¼ cup red wine vinegar
2 teaspoons sugar
½ cup olive oil
Salt to taste
Freshly ground black pepper to taste

For Scallops

*2 tablespoons **extra virgin olive oil***
1 teaspoon crushed red pepper flakes
*1 teaspoon ground **cumin***
*1 teaspoon ground **coriander***
Salt to taste

For Salad

1 tablespoon red wine vinegar
*½ cup **mizuna***
½ cup watercress sprigs
1 cup spinach leaves
1 Asian pear, cored and sliced
Fresh lemon juice to taste
Salt to taste
Freshly ground black pepper to taste

Garnish

¼ cup goat cheese

Directions

Trim scallops, wipe to remove any moisture, and set aside.

For pear dressing, peel, core, and dice the pear. Place in a blender with chopped shallots, mustard, vinegar, and sugar, and blend. Gradually add olive oil, and salt and black pepper to taste, and continue to blend until smooth.

To cook the scallops, heat oil in a skillet and season scallops with spices and salt to taste. Add scallops and, on very high heat, sear about 2 minutes on each side. Scallops should be golden brown on the outside and soft on the inside. Remove scallops from skillet and set aside.

Deglaze the skillet on high heat using vinegar. Add the greens, pears, lemon juice, and salt and black pepper to taste. Using tongs, turn the greens and pears around in the skillet for 10 seconds to wilt them partially.

Presentation

Spoon the greens into the center of the salad plates. Place scallops around the greens and spoon the pear dressing on and around the scallops. Break up goat cheese and strew on the salad.

4 servings

Lobster with Honey Butter Sauce, Grapefruit, and Avocado

This lobster dish is refreshing and easy to prepare. Avocado adds richness to the lobster and its accompanying butter sauce. Grapefruit, with just the right bitter tang, brings together the layers of flavors in this dish. When they are available I use the slightly salty **rice paddy herbs** to garnish. Watercress works just as well.

4 lobsters, 1 to 1½ pounds each

For Sauce
¼ cup vermouth
2 teaspoons minced garlic
¼ teaspoon paprika
1 tablespoon honey
2 tablespoons fresh lime juice
½ cup melted unsalted butter
Salt to taste

Garnish
1 ripe avocado, peeled and sliced
1 grapefruit, peeled and segmented
4 sprigs of rice paddy herbs

Directions
Cook lobster in boiling water for 6 to 8 minutes per pound. Remove the lobster from the cooking liquid and allow to cool until it can be comfortably handled.

Pull the claws away from the body and carefully crack them with a mallet without damaging the meat. Pull the meat out of the claws without shredding it. Using kitchen shears, trim away the soft membrane on the underside of the shells. Pull the meat out of the shells intact. Trim the lobster heads and wash to remove any bits and pieces of meat clinging to them. Save the heads for the garnish.

For the sauce, place vermouth, garlic, paprika, honey, lime juice, and salt to taste in a blender. Blend, adding the melted butter gradually until the sauce is emulsified. Spoon ¼ cup of sauce over the lobster meat and leave to marinate for 30 minutes.

When ready to serve, heat up the lobster in its marinade for 3 minutes.

Presentation
Slice the lobster and arrange on plates with the claw meat. Garnish with avocado slices and grapefruit segments. Heat the remaining sauce and pour over the lobster.

Garnish the plates with the lobster heads and rice paddy herbs.

4 servings

Squid Curry with Blackened Coconut

The cooking technique for making this curry is very unique. Roasted coconut and spices, almost black in color, are ground to a silken paste and combined with various other ingredients to produce the hot-and-sour squid curry.

This pungent curry is best served with rice, a vegetable, and salad.

1½ pounds cleaned squid

Blackened Coconut
¼ cup fresh grated coconut
1 peeled and sliced shallot
*½ teaspoon **cumin** seeds*
*1 teaspoon **fennel** seeds*
*1 teaspoon black **mustard seeds***

Curry
2 tablespoons vegetable oil
1 large yellow onion, thinly sliced
*1 bulb **lemongrass***
*1 sprig **curry leaves***
1 teaspoon minced ginger
*¼ teaspoon **turmeric***
*1 teaspoon **cayenne pepper***
1 teaspoon paprika
*2 tablespoons **Tamarind Juice** (see recipe, page 203)*
Salt to taste
1 cup coconut milk
1 teaspoon light brown sugar
Fresh lime juice to taste
*1 teaspoon **garam masala***

Directions
To clean the squid, rinse it under running water. Gently pull away the body sac from the head and set the head section aside. Pull the long, transparent, paperlike quill from the body sac and discard it. Pull out and discard the soft skin covering the body sac. Wash the body sac in running water. Separate the 2 flaps from the body sac. Cut the tentacles from the head and discard it. The head contains the "beak" and the entrails. Wash the body sac, flaps, and tentacles. If it is cumbersome to clean fresh squid, use cleaned, frozen squid.

Cut squid body sacs into ½-inch-thick rings, leaving the flaps and tentacles whole, and refrigerate.

To prepare the blackened coconut, heat a skillet on medium heat, add coconut and shallot, and dry-roast for 3 to 4 minutes or until coconut turns a deep gold color. Add spices to the skillet, and roast until the spice seeds start to splutter; remove from skillet. Using a spice grinder, grind the blackened mixture to a smooth texture.

For curry, heat oil on high heat and add onion, lemongrass, curry leaves, and ginger. Fry 4 to 5 minutes, until onions turn a golden color. Add turmeric, cayenne pepper, and paprika, and fry for 2 to 3 minutes.

Mix in the squid, tamarind juice, and salt to taste; keep mixing for 2 to 3 minutes to combine the seasonings well.

Mix the blackened coconut into the coconut milk and pour into the curry. Cover pan and simmer on low heat for 15 minutes. Season with sugar and lime juice to taste.

Sprinkle on garam masala, cover, and set aside for 5 minutes before serving.

Presentation
Serve in a deep, glass dish.

6 servings

Burst of Flavor

Spicy Oysters on Red Onion, Fennel, and Baby Spinach Salad

This dish has many flavors and textures that meld together harmoniously. Even those who don't like raw oysters will appreciate every mouthful of these satiny oysters in their delicately spiced crust and tangy crème fraîche.

Crème fraîche should be prepared one day ahead. For **Crème Fraîche** recipe, see page 243.

Seasoned Crème Fraîche

4 tablespoons crème fraîche
1 teaspoon chopped red onion
1/2 teaspoon finely diced, seeded, ripe
   jalapeño pepper
1/2 teaspoon grated orange zest
Salt to taste

Oysters

12 Pacific oysters
4 cups water, seasoned with sea salt to taste
1/2 teaspoon **cayenne pepper**
1/2 teaspoon **fennel** seeds
2 tablespoons finely chopped garden mint
3 tablespoons champagne vinegar
Sea salt to taste

To Finish Oysters

1 cup all purpose flour
1/2 teaspoon cayenne pepper
1/2 teaspoon salt
2 large eggs, lightly beaten
1 cup **panko** or white bread crumbs
1 cup peanut oil

Salad

1/4 cup orange juice
2 tablespoons champagne vinegar
3 tablespoons olive oil
1 teaspoon sugar
1 small red onion, peeled and thinly sliced
1 small fennel bulb, thinly sliced
1 cup baby spinach
Salt to taste

Garnish

1 tablespoon beluga caviar
Freshly ground black pepper to taste

Directions

Mix ingredients for seasoned crème fraîche and refrigerate.

Shuck and rinse oysters in salt water. Wipe with paper towels to remove any excess moisture. Add seasoning to oysters, mix, and refrigerate for 20 minutes.

Drain oysters from the seasoning. Mix together flour, cayenne pepper, and salt. Lightly dredge oysters in the seasoned flour, shake off excess flour, dip in egg, and toss in panko. Heat oil in a skillet to 375°F. Deep-fry oysters for 1½ to 2 minutes until light gold.

In a medium-size bowl, whisk together orange juice, vinegar, olive oil, and sugar. Add onion, fennel, and spinach with salt to taste. Toss to coat the vegetables.

Presentation

Place vegetables on plates. Arrange oysters on the vegetables and top with seasoned crème fraîche and caviar. Grind black pepper on the plates.

4 servings

Honey-Glazed, Grilled Cured Fish with Curried Pineapple

Spicy curried pineapple explodes with flavor and is a perfect companion to the robust grilled cured fish in this recipe. The radish salad gives a touch of zing to the dish.

1 pound **Cured Fish** (see recipe, page 52)
½ recipe **Spinach Rice** (see recipe, page 164)

Glaze
1 teaspoon **cayenne pepper**
1 tablespoon chopped garden mint leaves
1 tablespoon honey
1 tablespoon fresh lemon juice

Curried Pineapple
1 tablespoon vegetable oil
1 tablespoon black **mustard seeds**
1 tablespoon **cumin** seeds
2 tablespoons sliced yellow onion
1 sprig **curry leaves**
⅛ teaspoon **turmeric**
½ teaspoon cayenne pepper
1½ cups pineapple, cut into ½-inch cubes
½ cup coconut milk
1 teaspoon country-style Dijon mustard
Sugar to taste
Salt to taste

For Grilling Fish
1 tablespoon vegetable oil

Red Radish Relish
3 red radishes, thinly sliced
¼ red onion, thinly sliced
1 teaspoon snipped chives
1 teaspoon crushed cumin seeds
1 teaspoon seeded, finely sliced **green chili**
Fresh lime juice to taste
Salt to taste

Garnish
1 tablespoon vegetable oil
4 shallots, peeled
4 hard-cooked quail eggs

Directions
Wash the cured fish thoroughly to remove excess salt. Cut fish into 4 portions.

Make the spinach rice and keep hot.

Mix the glazing ingredients and brush on fish; set aside.

To make the pineapple curry, heat oil on medium heat in a **nonreactive** pan and add the mustard and cumin seeds. When they start to splutter, add onions and curry leaves. When they turn golden brown, add turmeric, cayenne pepper, pineapple, and coconut milk. Stir to combine all. Simmer for 10 to 12 minutes. Stir in mustard, season with sugar and salt to taste, and simmer for 5 more minutes.

Place fish on a hot grill, brush with oil, and cook for approximately 3 to 4 minutes on each side.

Toss ingredients for radish relish with lime juice and salt to taste.

For the garnish, heat oil on medium heat in a small pan. Slice shallots and fry to a deep golden color, about 3 minutes. Toss the quail eggs in the hot oil, cook 1 minute, and then cut each egg in half.

Presentation
Mold spinach rice on plates and spoon curried pineapple beside the rice. Place fish by the rice. Arrange relish by the fish. Place fried shallots on top of the rice mold with the quail eggs.

4 servings

Hot and Spicy Fish with Tamarind

A specialty from my hometown in Sri Lanka, *aluth malu* as we call this dish, literally means "new fish." I guess the name came about because it was always made with the freshest fish possible. Fresh fish was plentiful when I was growing up. My mother made the best *aluth malu*, always a family favorite, especially with my brothers.

The red sauce in this dish is spicy and tangy with **tamarind.** I use **goraka** whenever it is available; it gives a deep, dark color to the sauce. Commonly known as fish tamarind, it is the jet-black, dried, fluted skin of an orange-colored sour fruit.

Use any firm-fleshed fish like tuna, kingfish, or swordfish. Serve your choice of vegetable with the fish.

1 pound fish fillet

For Sauce
2 tablespoons vegetable oil
*½ teaspoon **fenugreek** seeds*
*½ teaspoon black **mustard seeds***
*2-inch piece of **cinnamon** stick*

Seasonings for Sauce
½ cup sliced yellow onion
*2 **green chilies,** seeded and sliced*
*1 sprig **curry leaves** or 1 bay leaf*
1 teaspoon minced ginger
2 garlic cloves, peeled and crushed

To Finish Sauce
2 teaspoons paprika
*2 teaspoons **cayenne pepper***
*2 tablespoons **Tamarind Juice** (see recipe, page 203)*
2 cups water
Salt to taste

Wilted Greens
1 teaspoon olive oil
2 cups spinach leaves or greens of your choice
Salt and freshly ground black pepper to taste

Cucumber Salad
1 cucumber, peeled and cut into long slivers with seeds removed
1 tablespoon sliced shallots
1 green chili, seeded and sliced
1 tablespoon coconut milk
Fresh lime juice to taste
Salt to taste

Garnish
8 chives
4 sprigs of chive flowers

Directions
Cut fish into 4 serving portions, and set aside.

Heat oil in a deep, medium-size sauté pan. Add fenugreek, black mustard, and cinnamon, and fry on high heat until seeds start to splutter, about 1 minute. Add seasonings and cook for 2 to 3 minutes or until onions turn a light golden color. To finish the sauce, stir in paprika and cayenne pepper, and cook a few seconds. Stir in tamarind juice and water, and season with salt to taste. Simmer for 15 minutes.

Place fish in the sauce (sauce should cover the fish). Cover pan and simmer for 5 minutes. Remove from heat and let stand for 5 minutes before serving.

Heat oil on medium heat in a pan and put in the greens with salt and black pepper to taste. Turn the greens in the hot pan for 2 to 3 seconds to wilt.

Mix cucumber salad ingredients with lime juice and salt to taste.

Presentation
Serve fish onto plates and spoon sauce over. Place greens and mold saffron rice. Place cucumber salad on the center of each plate, with sautéed vegetables beside the fish. Garnish with chives and chive flowers.

4 servings

Burst of Flavor

Mustard Tuna Salad

This salad resembles a Niçoise salad, which is commonly made with water-packed tuna. I use freshly cooked tuna. Mustard, the vital seasoning ingredient, adds a slight tang, a charming texture, and livens up the whole salad. Back home, we grind our own **mustard seeds** to make our country-style mustard. We use **turmeric** and ground **coriander** to poach fish. These spices combine well with white wine and add fragrance to the fish.

Serve in small portions as a starter to a dinner or in larger portions as a light luncheon salad.

1 pound tuna fillet

For Poaching Fish
2 tablespoons country-style Dijon mustard
⅛ teaspoon turmeric
1 teaspoon crushed coriander seeds
1 cup water
½ cup white wine
2 tablespoons white wine vinegar
Sea salt to taste
Freshly ground black pepper to taste

Dressing
2 tablespoons olive oil
Salt to taste

Vegetables
2 cups water
16 tender green beans, trimmed
1 red tomato
1 yellow tomato
1 red onion
1 cup ice water
*1 cup lettuce, **frisée** and/or **red oak leaf lettuce***

Garnish
*1 tablespoon **capers***
*16 **Niçoise olives** or black olives*
1 medium-size hard-cooked egg, shelled and grated

Directions
Place fish in a **nonreactive** pan. Add the mustard, turmeric, and coriander, and mix to coat the fish. Pour in water, wine, and vinegar, and season with sea salt and black pepper to taste. Cover pan and simmer for 6 to 8 minutes. Cool fish in its cooking liquid, 10 minutes or so. Remove fish from liquid and flake.

For the dressing, strain cooking liquid and whisk in olive oil. Taste and season with salt to taste.

For the vegetables, bring 2 cups of water to a boil. Add the green beans and cook for 3 minutes. Drain the cooking liquid and refresh the beans with cold water. Slice the tomatoes into ⅛-inch-thick slices. Slice the onion and soak in ice water.

Presentation
Place the lettuce, green beans, and tomatoes on chilled plates. Arrange flaked fish on the vegetables decoratively and spoon dressing over generously. Rinse red onion in water and place slices on the salad. Garnish with capers, olives, and grated eggs.

4 servings

Sesame Crusted Fish with Ginger, Coconut, and Yogurt Sauce

The exotic ingredients in this seafood dish—ginger, coconut, black **mustard seeds,** yogurt, white sesame seeds, and **curry leaves**—have an affinity for one another, creating layers of flavor enjoyed in each mouthful.

Use any variety of snapper available. A heavy skillet is essential to cook the fish. The extreme heat in the skillet helps seal in juices and preserve moistness within the crispy crust of the fish.

½ recipe **Saffron Rice** *(see recipe, page 160)*
2 red bell peppers, halved lengthwise
*   and seeds removed*

Ginger and Yogurt Sauce
1 tablespoon chopped ginger
1 tablespoon grated coconut
1 teaspoon vegetable oil
½ teaspoon black mustard seeds
½ cup plain yogurt
1 teaspoon sugar
Fresh lemon juice to taste
Salt to taste
2 tablespoons seeded, chopped tomato

Crusted Fish
1 pound trimmed fish fillet,
*   cut into 4 portions*
Salt to taste
1½ tablespoons olive oil
2 tablespoons white sesame seeds, roasted
2 **green chilies,** *seeds removed*
1 sprig curry leaves or a sprig of garden mint
1 tablespoon sliced shallots
1 tablespoon fresh lemon juice
2 tablespoons water

Garnish
4 sprigs curry leaves or garden mint

Directions
Cook saffron rice and keep hot. Grill bell peppers, about 3 minutes or just long enough to wilt.

For the sauce, grind ginger and coconut into a smooth paste. Pour oil into a small pan and place on medium heat. Add mustard seeds and fry 1 second or until seeds start to splutter. Remove from heat. Stir in ginger and coconut paste, yogurt, sugar, and lemon juice and salt to taste. Fold in tomatoes.

Heat the skillet on the stove. Season the fish with salt to taste and rub in 1 tablespoon oil; set aside. Reserve balance of oil to use later.

For the crust, use a mini-blender to mix the rest of the ingredients to a coarse purée. Season with salt to taste. Coat 1 side of the fish portions with purée. Add the reserved oil to the hot skillet. Place the fish coated side down on the hot skillet and cook for 2 minutes. Turn fish over and cook for 5 minutes more.

Presentation
Fill bell peppers with hot rice and place on hot serving plates. Place fish beside the peppers and drizzle ginger yogurt sauce around the fish. Garnish with sprigs of curry leaves or mint sprigs.

4 servings

Fish in Coconut Sauce

Julia Child still talks about this coconut sauce she first tasted in Sri Lanka. I don't strain the sauce. I simply spoon it over the fish. The slightly sweet and acidic sauce, speckled with rings of shallots, makes the fish incredibly fragrant and flavorful.

*1 pound **opakapaka** or any snapper fillet*

Spice Fragrant Rice
*1 cup **basmati** rice*
1 tablespoon olive oil
1 tablespoon chopped yellow onion
1 teaspoon minced ginger
1 teaspoon minced garlic
*1 teaspoon **cumin** seeds*
*1-inch piece of **cinnamon** stick*
1 bay leaf
2 cups water
Salt to taste

Coconut Sauce
1 cup water
2 shallots, peeled and thinly sliced
*1 sprig **curry leaves***
*1 **green chili,** seeded and sliced*
1-inch piece of cinnamon stick
*⅛ teaspoon **turmeric***
*½ teaspoon **fenugreek** seeds*
¼ teaspoon ground cumin
*¼ teaspoon ground **coriander***

To Finish Sauce
1 cup coconut milk
Peel of ½ lemon
Fresh lemon juice to taste
Salt to taste

Grilled Vegetables
4 mushrooms, trimmed
*4 baby leeks, trimmed and **blanched***
2 yellow squash, each halved lengthwise
4 red apples, sliced

*1 tablespoon **extra virgin olive oil***
*½ teaspoon **cayenne pepper***
*½ teaspoon **garam masala***
Salt to taste

Garnish
*¼ cup **methi** or **pea sprouts***

Directions
Cut fish into 4 serving portions and refrigerate until ready to use.

To cook the rice, wash rice and soak for 20 minutes. Heat oil in a pot and add onion, ginger, and garlic. Cook on low heat until onion turns a golden color. Add cumin seeds and cinnamon. When cumin seeds start to splutter, add the rice drained from the soaking water. Stir to combine with the spices. Add bay leaf, water, and a pinch of salt to taste. Bring to a slow simmer. Cover pan, reduce heat to low, and cook for 25 to 30 minutes. Keep hot until ready to serve.

Place ingredients for sauce in a pan and bring to a slow simmer. Simmer for 4 to 5 minutes. To finish, add coconut milk and lemon peel, stirring continuously. Bring back to a simmer and season with lemon juice and salt to taste. Place fish in the sauce and simmer 4 to 5 minutes; pick out and discard lemon peel.

While fish is cooking, brush the vegetables and apples with oil and cook them on a hot grill for 4 to 5 minutes. Dust with cayenne pepper, garam masala, and salt to taste.

Presentation
Place a mold of rice and a serving of fish on each hot plate. Spoon sauce over and around the fish. Arrange vegetables and garnish with methi or pea sprouts.

4 servings

Baked Fish in Tomato Sauce with Fried Eggplant

Kumu, a member of the goatfish family, is a Hawaiian reef fish with soft white flesh. Once upon a time, it was reserved only for royalty. It was *kapu* (forbidden) to the commoners, a delicious offense punishable by death! I use kumu whenever it is available. The fish averages from ¾ to 2 pounds in weight. I use the smaller, whole kumu in this recipe. Use any snapper in place of kumu.

The mixed spices cooked in oil release their fragrance and give the sauce an extraordinary depth of flavor.

4 whole kumu, gutted, cleaned, and washed

Vegetables
12 pieces dried **morels**
3 cups hot water
4 leeks, white part only

For Sauce
2 tablespoons olive oil
½ teaspoon **coriander** *seeds, crushed*
1 teaspoon **cumin** *seeds, crushed*
1 teaspoon **fennel** *seeds, crushed*
1 medium-size yellow onion, thinly sliced
8 cloves garlic, peeled and thinly sliced
1 cup tomato **concassée**
1 teaspoon crushed red pepper flakes
2 tablespoons red wine vinegar
½ cup white wine
½ cup water
1 teaspoon sugar
24 **Niçoise olives**
Fresh lemon juice to taste
Sea salt to taste

Garnish
Salt to taste
2 long eggplants, cut into ¼-inch diagonal slices
2 tablespoons all purpose flour
¼ cup vegetable oil for frying
6 sprigs of fennel

Directions
Preheat oven to 400°F.

Wipe the fish and refrigerate.

To clean the morels, soak in hot water, and wash in several changes of water to get rid of sand and grit. Set aside with the leeks.

Heat oil in a wide skillet with a fitted lid. Add spices and stir on high heat until they start to splutter. Add onions, garlic, morels, and leeks. Cook until onions turn a light golden color. Add the rest of the ingredients for sauce and season with lemon juice and sea salt to taste. Stir and cook on low heat for 5 to 6 minutes. Lay the fish in the sauce and sprinkle a little sea salt over the fish. Cover skillet tightly with the lid and place in the oven for 15 minutes. Turn fish over once while cooking.

While fish is cooking, sprinkle salt, to taste, on the eggplant and put aside for 5 minutes. Wash eggplant. Using a paper towel, wipe to remove excess moisture and dust with flour. Heat oil on medium heat in a frying pan. Fry eggplant until golden and crisp, about 1 to 2 minutes. Dust lightly with salt to taste.

Presentation
Serve fish on hot plates and spoon a little sauce around. Arrange vegetables and hot-fried eggplant by the fish and garnish with fennel.

4 servings

Millicent's Mustard Fish

Mustard fish is a very popular Sri Lankan dish, but I know of no one who made this better than my mother-in-law, Millicent. She always got raves from her family and relatives. Use **ono,** halibut, swordfish, or **mahi-mahi** in this dish. The **lemongrass** blends well with the ground **coriander.** The coriander has a piquant flavor and is mild enough to give the creamy mustard sauce a veil of fragrance.

Pickled beets are especially good with the fish. Their sweet flavor blends perfectly with the creamy mustard sauce.

½ recipe **Glazed Baby Beets** (see recipe, page 131)
1 pound fish fillet
Sea salt to taste
Freshly ground black pepper to taste
⅛ teaspoon **turmeric**
2 tablespoons olive oil
2 yellow onions, peeled and sliced ¼-inch thick
1 teaspoon sugar
1 cup sliced **portabella mushrooms**

Mustard Sauce

2 teaspoons minced ginger
1 teaspoon minced garlic
1 bulb crushed lemongrass
½ cup white wine
1 cup water
1 tablespoon cider vinegar
⅛ teaspoon turmeric
½ teaspoon ground coriander
Sea salt to taste
Freshly ground black pepper to taste

To Finish Sauce

1½ tablespoons Dijon mustard
¼ cup coconut milk

Garnish

8 sprigs of Chinese parsley

Directions

Make glazed baby beets and set aside.

Cut fish into 4 serving portions. Season fish with sea salt and black pepper to taste, and rub in the turmeric, which gives a nice golden blush to the fish when cooked.

Heat 1 tablespoon of olive oil in a skillet. Sear fish on both sides for about 4 minutes and set aside. Add onions to the skillet, sprinkle in sugar, sauté to a deep caramel color, and set aside. Add the remaining tablespoon of oil to the skillet, sauté the mushrooms, season with salt and black pepper to taste, and set aside. Use the same skillet to make the sauce.

For the sauce, add ginger, garlic, and lemongrass to the skillet and cook a few minutes on low heat. Add white wine, water, and vinegar, and deglaze the skillet. Add the rest of the ingredients for the sauce and season with sea salt and black pepper to taste. Simmer for 4 to 5 minutes.

To finish sauce, whisk in mustard and coconut milk. Place seared fish in the sauce and simmer for 2 to 3 minutes. Place the mushrooms and onion with the fish steaks, cover the skillet, and set aside for 2 to 3 minutes.

Presentation

Place fish on hot plates, and spoon sauce over fish. Place mushrooms, onions, and glazed beets around the fish.

Garnish with Chinese parsley.

4 servings

Steamed Fish Flavored with Spiced Oil

Gray, pink, or red snapper and grouper are good choices for steaming. It takes 30 to 35 minutes to steam a 5- to 6-pound whole fish. Place the whole fish on a platter and then on the steamer rack, allowing the juices to collect on the platter. Spoon them back on the fish before serving.

Steamed fish not only retains most of its nutritional value, but also takes well to flavoring with hot spiced oils, garnishes, and accompaniments.

1 red snapper, 2 pounds, gutted and cleaned
$^1/_8$ teaspoon **turmeric**
Juice of 1 lemon
Sea salt to taste

Garnish
2 tablespoons finely cut ginger **julienne**

Spiced Oil
2 tablespoons mustard oil
4-inch piece of **cinnamon** stick
2 sprigs **curry leaves**
$^1/_4$ teaspoon each **fenugreek** seeds and
   black **mustard seeds**

Directions
Wipe fish dry and rub in turmeric and lemon juice with sea salt to taste. Place on a platter, then in the steamer rack. Cover steamer and steam over boiling water for 20 to 22 minutes.

Presentation
Remove platter with fish from steamer. Strew ginger on the fish. Heat oil in a small frying pan with the cinnamon stick to the smoking point, add curry leaves and spices, and immediately pour on the fish.

4 servings

Seafood with Eggplant

This dish may be made with scallops, clams, mussels, or cut-up lobster in the shell. Spices add fragrance, flavor, and intrigue to the dish. Once cooked in oil, black **mustard seeds** emanate a nutty taste almost like the flavor of hazelnuts, and the **fennel** seeds, sweet, fragrant, and compatible with seafood, create layers of flavor. Serve this delicious seafood and eggplant dish over steaming hot pasta.

16 shrimp
1 cup cooked crabmeat
1 long eggplant
2 tomatoes
1 tablespoon olive oil
$^1/_2$ teaspoon black mustard seeds
$^1/_2$ teaspoon fennel seeds
$^1/_2$ teaspoon crushed red pepper flakes
$^1/_2$ teaspoon paprika
$^1/_8$ teaspoon **turmeric**
1 teaspoon grated ginger
$^3/_4$ cup **Fish Stock** (see recipe, page 46)
$^1/_4$ cup shredded basil leaves
Salt to taste
Fresh lemon juice to taste

Directions
Peel and devein shrimp. Pick through crabmeat and discard bits of shells. Cut eggplant and tomatoes into 1-inch cubes. Heat oil on medium heat; add spice seeds and when they start to pop (careful, seeds might spatter), add spices and ginger. Cook for 2 to 3 minutes. Stir in eggplant. When it starts to color, add stock, cover, and simmer for 5 minutes. Add shrimp and tomatoes, cover, and cook 5 minutes more. Fold in crabmeat, shredded basil, and season with salt and lemon juice to taste.

Presentation
Serve in a deep bowl over pasta.

4 servings

Fish & Shellfish

Spicy Grilled Fish with Fried Potatoes and Basil Leaves

The fragrance of ground roasted spices is different from ground raw spices. Roasting brings out the deep flavor of the different spices, as evidenced in the blend used for the marinade in this recipe. The ingredients in the marinade are so well balanced that no single flavor dominates.

1½ pounds gray or red snapper fillet,
   cut into 4 portions
2 russet or Idaho potatoes, peeled
Cold water for soaking potatoes, (enough to cover potatoes)

Marinade
½ teaspoon **coriander** seeds
¼ teaspoon **cumin** seeds
⅛ teaspoon **fenugreek** seeds
½ teaspoon **cayenne pepper**
1 teaspoon grated ginger
½ cup tomato **concassée**
2 tablespoons **balsamic vinegar**
1 tablespoon fresh lemon juice
Salt to taste
1 tablespoon olive oil

For Frying Potatoes
1 cup vegetable oil

Seasoning and Garnish
Salt to taste
1 teaspoon **garam masala**
1 cup basil leaves

Cucumber and Tomato Salad
1 cucumber, peeled, seeded, and diced
1 tomato, seeded and diced
1 tablespoon each chopped fresh dill and
   green onion
½ cup plain yogurt, whisked
Salt to taste
Fresh lemon juice to taste

Directions
Wipe fish fillet and refrigerate.

Cut the potatoes into medium-size **julienne** and soak in cold water.

For the marinade, roast spice seeds in a skillet on medium heat until crisp, about 4 minutes, and then grind in a spice grinder. Place the ground spices in a blender with the other ingredients for marinade (reserve olive oil) and blend to a purée. Leave fish on a flat pan so pieces do not overlap, and spoon marinade over all. Leave to marinate for 1 to 1½ hours.

While fish is marinating, drain potatoes and dry thoroughly on a towel. Heat oil in a deep pan to 325°F, fry potatoes for 2 to 3 minutes or to a pale golden color. Remove from oil and place on paper towels until ready to fry a second time.

To grill, remove fish from marinade, drizzle the reserved olive oil, and cook over a hot grill for about 3 minutes per side.

Heat the pan of oil to 375°F, fry potatoes again for 3 to 4 minutes or until crisp and golden. Drain on paper towels and sprinkle with the garam masala and salt to taste. In the same oil, fry basil leaves for 10 seconds or until crisp, drain on paper towels, and sprinkle with garam masala and salt to taste.

Mix ingredients for cucumber and tomato salad with salt and lemon juice to taste.

Presentation
Place fish on plates. Place potatoes beside the fish, spoon salad on one side, and garnish with fried basil.

4 servings

Grilled Salmon with Parsnip Puree and Port Wine Glaze

Creamy leeks with just a whisper of **nutmeg** and the port wine glaze with only a faint aroma of **cinnamon** give a subtle background accent to the plain, cooked salmon. The compatible apple relish and horseradish cream give the salmon a refreshing flavor.

1 pound trimmed and boned salmon fillet
1 teaspoon fresh thyme leaves
Freshly ground black pepper to taste
Salt to taste
1 tablespoon olive oil
½ recipe **Parsnip Purée** (see recipe, page 142)

Sautéed Leeks

1 tablespoon unsalted butter
1½ cups sliced leeks, **blanched**
Pinch of grated nutmeg
Salt to taste
Freshly ground black pepper to taste
1 tablespoon full cream

Red Apple Relish

1 red apple, cored and cut into a **brunoise**
3 tablespoons red onion, cut into a brunoise
3 red radishes, cut into a brunoise
1 tablespoon snipped chives
½ teaspoon dill seeds
Fresh lime juice to taste
Salt to taste

Port Wine Glaze

½ cup red port wine
½ cup **balsamic vinegar**
1-inch piece of cinnamon stick

Horseradish Sauce

2 tablespoons plain yogurt or full cream
2 tablespoons freshly grated horseradish
Fresh lemon juice to taste
Salt to taste

Garnish

1 parsnip, sliced very thin, lengthwise
8 sprigs of thyme

Directions

Preheat oven to 275°F.

Cut salmon into 4 portions, season with thyme, and black pepper and salt to taste. Brush with oil and refrigerate.

Save 1 parsnip and make the parsnip purée with the rest. To make sautéed leeks, heat butter in a pan, add leeks, and sauté on moderate heat for 5 minutes. Season with nutmeg, and salt and black pepper to taste. Mix in cream and place aside with the parsnip purée.

Mix ingredients for the apple relish in a small bowl, seasoning with lime juice and salt to taste.

Combine ingredients for the glaze in a **nonreactive** pan and reduce on moderate heat to about 2 tablespoons. Discard the cinnamon sticks.

To make the horseradish sauce, whisk yogurt or cream in a small bowl and add horseradish and seasonings to taste. Whisk to combine.

For the garnish, place parsnip slices on a baking pan and place in the oven for 15 minutes or until the parsnips are crisp. Grill salmon on a preheated hot grill for 3 minutes on each side.

Presentation

Spoon parsnip purée on the plates, and place salmon on the purée. Spoon on sautéed leeks and red apple relish. Drizzle port wine glaze and spoon on creamed horseradish. Garnish with roasted parsnips and thyme.

4 servings

Grilled Sardines with Green Papaya Remoulade and Fried Shallots

When I was a child, deep-fried sardines were one of my favorite appetizers. Fried shallots and red and green chilies were the usual garnish for those crispy sardines. The shallots and chilies were soaked in curd before frying to make them mellow. In this recipe, papaya remoulade gives a new dimension to my favorite childhood appetizer.

16 sardines with heads on, gutted, scales
   removed, and washed
1/2 teaspoon **cayenne pepper**
Salt to taste
1 tablespoon vegetable oil

Green Papaya Remoulade
1/4 cup olive oil
1 tablespoon white wine vinegar
1 tablespoon Dijon mustard
1 tablespoon ketchup
1 tablespoon chopped shallots
1 teaspoon chopped garlic
1 cup shredded green papaya
Salt to taste
Freshly ground black pepper to taste

For Fried Shallots
6 shallots, peeled and sliced into 1/8-inch rings
1 cup buttermilk
2 tablespoons all-purpose flour
1/2 cup vegetable oil
Cayenne pepper to taste
Salt to taste

For Salad Dressing
2 tablespoons fresh lime juice
2 tablespoons **balsamic vinegar**
1 teaspoon Worcestershire sauce
1 teaspoon Dijon mustard
1 teaspoon minced shallots
2 teaspoons sugar
Salt to taste

For Salad
2 cups mixed greens

Directions
Season sardines with cayenne pepper and salt to taste. Add the oil and mix.

To make remoulade, mix all the ingredients together and season with salt and pepper to taste.

Soak shallots in buttermilk and put aside for 20 minutes.

Heat up the grill to grill sardines.

Remove shallots from buttermilk, wipe off excess moisture, and toss shallots in flour. Place the shallots in a strainer and shake off excess flour. Heat oil in a frying pan and fry shallots about 2 minutes or until golden brown. Sprinkle generously with cayenne pepper and salt to taste.

Grill the sardines on the hot grill, about 2 minutes on each side.

In a small bowl, whisk ingredients for salad dressing with salt to taste. Add the greens. Toss to coat evenly.

Presentation
Place dressed greens on plate, and spoon papaya remoulade on the greens. Arrange sardines on the remoulade and top sardines with fried shallots.

4 servings

Fish Steamed in Banana Leaves

The wrapping of banana leaves imparts an earthy flavor to the fish and preserves its natural juices. You may use cabbage leaves or parchment instead, but nothing is as exotic as the banana leaves. *Note well:* The leaves should not be eaten.

4 banana leaves, cut in 10-inch squares
1 teaspoon vegetable oil
1 pound of trimmed soft white fish (snapper or halibut)
1 teaspoon fresh lime juice
Sea salt to taste

Mint Paste

½ cup each garden mint leaves and Chinese parsley
¼ cup fresh grated coconut
2 green chilies, halved and seeds removed
1 teaspoon each sliced shallots and ginger
½ teaspoon ground cumin
2 tablespoons fresh lime juice
2 teaspoons sugar
Salt to taste

Directions

Wash, wipe dry, and warm banana leaves over a stove until they are pliable to help keep them from splitting when folded. Brush oil on leaves. Season fish with lime juice and sea salt to taste. In a blender, blend all the ingredients for mint paste to a smooth texture. Place 1 tablespoon of mint paste on each piece of fish and place paste side down on the leaves. Fold top and bottom edges of leaf over fish and fold sides over to form neat parcels. Steam over boiling water for 8 to 10 minutes.

Presentation

Place the hot fish on a platter and partially open up the banana leaf wrap.

4 servings

Steamed Fish with Mustard Cabbage

Fresh fish and vegetables steamed in one steamer over water infused with **lemongrass** can save both time and the tasty juices. Serve a bowl of rice and a crisp cucumber salad as accompaniments. I often spoon a dollop of chutney on the side of the plate for a bit of added taste.

1 pound snapper fillet
Pinch of turmeric
¼ teaspoon minced ginger
¼ teaspoon minced garlic
Salt to taste
Freshly ground black pepper to taste
1 bulb crushed lemongrass
2½ cups water
1 pound mustard cabbage, cut into ¼-inch strips

Garnish

1 tablespoon sliced green onion

Directions

Cut fish in serving portions, wipe dry, and coat with turmeric, ginger, garlic, and salt and black pepper to taste. Add lemongrass to a saucepan of 2½ cups water and bring to a boil.

Place fish on a plate on a steamer rack and steam for 4 minutes. Uncover, place cabbage on the side of the plate, salt to taste, cover, and steam for 3 minutes more.

Presentation

Arrange fish and cabbage on serving plates and garnish with sliced green onion. Serve hot.

4 servings

Fish & Shellfish

Poultry, Meat . . .

Flavors East and West

I still remember the spice-rich chicken, beef, and mutton curries I enjoyed as a child. Each had its own distinctive blend of spices that gave it a special character. Chicken curry, the family favorite, had a reddish-brown sauce poured over the chicken, which was almost falling off the bone. There were other times when the chicken curry was almost dry and had a dark mahogany color to it. We did not eat beef often, but when we did it was in thick, succulent slices with lots of black pepper and golden brown onion rings.

Sometimes, chicken, beef, or mutton was made into a stew with chunks of fresh vegetables. The stew was always made with crushed spices that added flavor and fragrance. Much of the chicken we consumed had the skin removed before cooking, and the meats were lean or most of the fat was trimmed.

Today's meats are leaner than those of a decade ago, as the desire grows to consume less cholesterol and saturated fat. We do not need to do away with meats completely; in moderation they do provide nutrients and can be a major component in a healthy meal. Serve in small, lean portions and count on flavorful vegetables, lush greens, legumes, and grains to balance the meal.

Sometimes even specially bred hens can have a gamey taste. As a rule, I like to spice them with **garam masala** to counteract the gamey taste and replace it with a spicy fragrance. Robust root vegetables, squashes, and fruits go well with the hens. **Sherried Sweet Potatoes** (see recipe, page 134) and **Curly Kale with Coconut** (see recipe, page 129) make tasty accompaniments to these spicy hens. Sweet potatoes may be made ahead and heated before serving. Kale takes only a few minutes to cook. Have the kale cut up in a plastic bag and ready to cook.

Meats may present health risks other than cholesterol and nutrition. Poultry often carries *Salmonella* bacteria. As a first step, wash poultry inside and out; then wipe it dry. Wash equipment and cutting surfaces, and sanitize. Wash your hands thoroughly after handling poultry to avoid contaminating other foods. To be sure no *Salmonella* survive, poultry must be cooked to an internal temperature of 165°F.

To cook poultry, I rely on an array of cooking elements: spices and herbs, fruits and nuts, vinegars and wines, and yogurt and buttermilk. I use butter and cream in moderation. They are assembled without too much fuss, yet are fancy enough for entertaining special guests.

Rich meats (beef, veal, lamb, and pork) take well to spices. Often I simply roast meats after searing them with spice mixes. Sometimes I simmer them in a broth laced with fragrant **cardamoms,** or I season a roast by rolling it in a mixture of ground or coarse spices. When I season meat with pungent spices, I serve it with a compatible tangy, sweet glaze. I use lots of garlic, black pepper, ground or whole **mustard seeds,** the more exotic crushed **methi** leaves, and browned **neem** leaves to make meat dishes very special. Often, **tamarind** and yogurt or wine go into my marinades. I avoid artificial meat tenderizers and commercial taste enhancers; my marinades tenderize meats and help to thicken the sauces in a healthier, more natural way.

Chicken with Dried Cranberries and Bulgur Pilaf

Crushed **ajowan** seeds have a fragrance much like thyme and are closely related to the **cumin** family. Lemon or lime juice brings out the best in this spice. The tart cranberries and raspberry vinegar used in the sauce helps. Overuse of ajowan can impart a bitter taste to food.

4 boneless, skinless chicken breasts,
   5 to 5½ ounces each
Salt to taste
½ teaspoon ajowan seeds, slightly crushed
1 teaspoon coarse ground black pepper

Bulgur Pilaf
2 tablespoons unsalted butter
2 tablespoons chopped yellow onion
¾ cup **bulgur wheat**
1 pint hot **Defatted Chicken Stock** (see recipe, page 45)
1 bay leaf
Salt to taste

To Cook Chicken
2 tablespoons unsalted butter
2 tablespoons brandy

Sauce
2 teaspoons chopped shallots
1 teaspoon chopped garlic
½ cup dried cranberries
2 tablespoons raspberry vinegar
1 cup defatted chicken stock (from recipe above)
¼ cup buttermilk
Salt to taste

Vegetables
1 tablespoon unsalted butter
1 shallot, peeled and sliced
12 long beans (also known as yard-long beans),
   trimmed and **blanched**
6 cherry tomatoes, halved
Salt to taste
1 tablespoon chopped dill

Garnish
4 sprigs of pineapple sage blossoms

Directions
Wash and wipe chicken. Season with salt to taste and sprinkle both sides of the chicken breasts with ajowan seeds and black pepper. Using a rolling pin, press spices gently into meat and refrigerate.

Heat butter in a saucepan. Add onion and cook to a golden color. Add bulgur and sauté until grains are coated in butter. Add stock, bay leaf, and salt to taste. Bring to a simmer, cover, and cook on low heat for 18 to 20 minutes.

Heat butter in a sauté pan and cook chicken about 3 minutes on each side. Add the brandy and tilt the pan, allowing the brandy to ignite. This procedure should be performed with caution. Shake the pan until the flames die down.

Remove chicken to a platter and keep warm. To the pan, add shallots and garlic, and cook for 1 minute. Add cranberries and raspberry vinegar, and deglaze the pan on high heat. Add chicken stock and simmer 3 to 4 minutes. Whisk in the buttermilk. Taste and season with a dash of salt if desired. Replace chicken in the sauce. Simmer for 3 to 4 minutes on low heat or until chicken is cooked through. Heat butter in a small sauté pan, add the shallots, and cook until wilted. Add long beans and cherry tomatoes to the butter, and season with salt to taste. Stir in chopped dill.

Presentation
Mold pilaf on plates. Arrange chicken on pilaf and spoon sauce around pilaf. Add long beans and cherry tomatoes, and garnish with pineapple sage blossoms.

4 servings

Pistachio-Crusted Chicken

Elegant and lavish north Indian cuisine is a legacy from the Moguls, who came to India in the sixteenth century A.D. It is a cuisine influenced by the subtleties of the Persian flavors the Moguls admired. This dish is an adaptation of the rich north Indian Mogul braised chicken.

2 to 2½ pounds whole broiler chicken, washed
1 teaspoon each ground ginger and garlic
Freshly ground black pepper to taste
Salt to taste

For Crust
*1 teaspoon ground **cardamom** seeds*
*¼ teaspoon **turmeric***
*¼ teaspoon **cayenne pepper***
*½ cup total **blanched** almonds and pistachios*
¼ cup raisins
¼ cup plain, low-fat yogurt

For Basting
¼ cup melted unsalted butter
1 tablespoon honey

Directions
Skin chicken, wipe dry, and rub in ginger, garlic, and black pepper and salt to taste. Leave in the refrigerator for ½ hour. Place all the ingredients for the crust in a blender and blend to a smooth purée. Spoon purée on chicken and refrigerate overnight.

Preheat oven to 375°F. Place chicken on a rack in a roasting pan. Roast in the pre-heated oven for 25 minutes. Mix butter and honey, drizzle on the chicken often, and roast 35 minutes more. Allow chicken to rest for 10 minutes.

Presentation
Carve the chicken, arrange on a platter, and spoon the juices from the roasting pan.

6 servings

Thai-Style Chicken Curry

Thai curry paste is an essential ingredient in this recipe. It is available in Asian groceries and specialty stores. **Kaffir lime** leaves add a fragrance no other citrus leaf can. If these are not available, the second best would be to use fresh lime or lemon leaves. Store kaffir lime leaves in airtight freezer bags in the freezer. Serve this curry on hot jasmine rice.

1½ pounds skinned chicken breasts
1 tablespoon vegetable oil
1 small yellow onion, peeled and chopped fine
1 teaspoon minced ginger
1½ tablespoons Thai curry paste
½ cup water
4 kaffir lime leaves
1½ cups coconut milk
Salt to taste

Directions
Cut chicken in 1-inch-square pieces. Heat oil on medium heat and sauté onions about 5 minutes. Add ginger, curry paste, and water. Reduce heat to low and cook for 3 minutes. Add lime leaves and coconut milk, and sim-mer for 5 minutes. Stir in the chicken, and season with salt to taste. Simmer for 8 to 10 minutes. Remove and discard lime leaves.

Presentation
Spoon the curry on hot jasmine rice.

4 servings

Honey-Glazed Chicken

The chicken in this dish is spiced with **cinnamon** and **cardamom**—both known as warm spices. They blend well with ginger and orange juice. The cooked kale and walnuts add a perfect foil for the honey-glazed chicken. Orange adds a refreshing note, and roasted garlic explodes with flavor in this multifaceted dish. When kale is unavailable, use collard greens.

4 boneless, skinless chicken breasts,
5 to 5½ ounces each

Marinade

1 teaspoon ground dry ginger
¼ teaspoon ground cinnamon
¼ teaspoon ground cardamom
2 tablespoons orange juice
2 tablespoons fresh lemon juice
½ teaspoon cracked black peppercorns
Salt to taste

Garnish

*Zest of 1 orange, cut into a fine **julienne***
1 orange, peeled and segmented
2 cups water
16 garlic cloves, peeled
4 sprigs rosemary

For Basting Chicken

1 tablespoon unsalted butter
2 tablespoons orange flower honey

Greens

1 tablespoon olive oil
2 shallots, peeled and sliced
2 tablespoons chopped walnuts
3 cups shredded kale or collard greens
Salt to taste
Freshly ground black pepper to taste

Directions

Wash and wipe chicken to remove excess moisture. Combine marinade ingredients, mix to coat chicken, and let marinate 1 hour.

For the garnish, **blanch** the orange zest julienne and set aside with the orange segments. Boil 2 cups water, add peeled garlic, and cook on low heat for 10 minutes. Strain and place garlic along with the rosemary on a broiler pan.

Place chicken on a broiler rack and place the rack on the broiler pan. Broil 6 inches away from heat for 5 minutes, basting alternately with butter and honey. Turn chicken over, baste, and broil for 6 minutes more. By now the garlic in the broiler pan should be glazed and the rosemary crispy. Remove garlic and rosemary and place with the orange julienne and orange segments to use later for garnish.

To cook greens, heat olive oil, add shallots and walnuts, and cook for 4 to 5 minutes or until the walnuts are crispy. Add shredded greens, and season with salt and black pepper to taste. Cook 4 to 5 minutes or until greens are wilted.

Presentation

Spoon greens on plates and place chicken on the greens. Top each with a roasted sprig of rosemary, a roasted garlic, and orange zest julienne. Strew the extra garlic, orange zest julienne, and orange segments on the plates.

4 servings

Skillet-Roasted Spicy Chicken with Pomegranate Sauce

The **pomegranate** dates back to the time of the Dravidians in India. King Solomon is believed to have had them in his orchards. Sanskrit literature refers often to the beauty of the pomegranate flowers and seeds. In both Sri Lanka and India, the pomegranate is valued for the medicinal properties in its skin and seeds.

For the purpose of this recipe, bottled or canned juice can be used in place of fresh juice.

2 to 2½ pounds whole broiler chicken, quartered
Juice of 1 lemon
Salt to taste

Marinade
2 tablespoons finely minced yellow onion
4 garlic cloves, minced
*¼ teaspoon ground **cinnamon***
*½ teaspoon **cayenne pepper***
*½ teaspoon ground **cumin***
Freshly ground black pepper to taste

To Cook Chicken
1 pomegranate fruit
1 tablespoon olive oil
½ teaspoon paprika
1 tablespoon dark brown sugar
½ cup Burgundy wine

Roast Vegetables
1 tablespoon olive oil
*2 **endive,** halved lengthwise*
1 red onion, peeled and quartered
Salt to taste
¼ cup hot water
4 large shiitake mushrooms
4 red Swiss chard leaves with the stems
2 cups water

Garnish
*4 green onion leaves, **blanched***
½ cup pomegranate seeds

Directions
Preheat oven to 375°F.

Wash chicken inside and out, and wipe dry; rub in lemon juice and salt to taste. Mix ingredients for the marinade, rub into the chicken, and leave in the refrigerator for 1 hour.

Cut open the pomegranate and remove seeds (set aside ½ cup seeds for the garnish). Use a blender and mix the seeds for 30 seconds on medium speed. Strain through a cheesecloth-lined strainer and reserve the juice.

Heat oil in a wide skillet and add paprika. Add chicken and sear on high heat for 4 to 5 minutes, to give a deep reddish color. Add sugar to the skillet and coat chicken with sugar. Add wine and pomegranate juice. Cover skillet and place in the oven to roast for 30 minutes. Baste chicken with the pan juices 2 to 3 times. Reduce heat to 300°F, remove cover, and roast for another 25 minutes.

To roast vegetables, heat olive oil in a skillet, add endives and onion, and cook 4 to 5 minutes. Season with salt to taste. Add ¼ cup water and place skillet in the 300°F oven; roast for 8 minutes. Add mushrooms and continue to roast for 6 minutes.

Cut the stems of the Swiss chard leaves to about 4 inches long. Boil 2 cups water and add Swiss chard leaves and stems. Cook for 3 minutes; remove and refresh in cold water. Wipe dry. Season leaves with salt to taste. Roll leaves individually around each trimmed stem. Five minutes before chicken is removed from the oven, place leaves in the skillet with the chicken.

Presentation
Place chicken on dinner plates with the vegetables and spoon over skillet juices. Garnish with green onion and the pomegranate seeds.

4 servings

Sri Lankan Chicken Curry

A pioneer in fine cooking and a role model for many of us, Julia Child led a culinary renaissance in America. In World War II she was attached to the war office and was stationed in Sri Lanka, then called Ceylon, where she met her future husband, Paul Child.

When we chat, she never fails to mention Sri Lankan curries she got to know when she was there. Remembering her fondness for our curry, I have included here a recipe for a particularly delicious one.

As with most curries, this one tastes better if you cook it a day ahead and refrigerate. Remove the fat that settles on the surface of the curry and reheat just before serving. For authentic flavor, replace the paprika and **cayenne pepper** with hot chilies, roasted and ground to a fine powder. Serve chicken curry with rice, chutney, and raita.

1 whole chicken fryer

Curry Powder
1 tablespoon **coriander** seeds
2 teaspoons **cumin** seeds
1 teaspoon **fennel** seeds
1 tablespoon paprika
1 teaspoon cayenne pepper

Other Ingredients for Curry
4 tablespoons vegetable oil
1 bulb **lemongrass**
4 sprigs **curry leaves**
1/2-inch piece of **cinnamon** stick
4 **cardamom** pods
2 large yellow onions, peeled and chopped
2 teaspoons minced ginger
2 teaspoons minced garlic
1/4 teaspoon **turmeric**
3 tablespoons **Tamarind Juice** (see recipe, page 203)
1 tablespoon fresh lemon juice
Salt to taste
1/2 cup coconut milk

Directions
Wash chicken inside and out. Skin and joint the chicken. Cut into serving portions, removing the backbone and wing tips (save these for the stockpot).

In a skillet, partially roast coriander; add cumin and fennel, and roast until seeds are crisp, about 3 to 4 minutes. In a spice grinder, grind the roasted seeds to a fine powder. Roast paprika and cayenne pepper in the same skillet for a few seconds and add to the ground spices.

Heat oil on medium heat in a skillet. Sauté lemongrass, curry leaves, cinnamon stick, and cardamom pods until curry leaves turn golden brown, about 2 to 3 minutes. Add onion, ginger, and garlic; sauté for 5 to 6 minutes or until onion turns a gold color. Add roasted spices and turmeric; cook on medium heat for about 5 minutes. Turn down heat and add chicken; mix to coat well with spices. Add tamarind juice, lemon juice, and salt to taste. Stir, cover, and cook on low heat for 40 minutes. Stir in coconut milk and simmer for 5 minutes.

Presentation
Serve the chicken in a deep dish, with rice and chutney in separate dishes.

6 servings

Burst of Flavor

Chicken with Leeks and Mushrooms

The freshly ground **coriander** used in this recipe blends with the wine and vegetables to give the resulting sauce a depth of flavor that is rich-tasting yet light.

4 skinless chicken breasts, bone in,
   5$\frac{1}{2}$ to 6 ounces each

Seasoning
4 garlic cloves, puréed
1 tablespoon coarse-ground coriander
$\frac{1}{8}$ teaspoon **turmeric**
2 tablespoons white wine vinegar
Salt to taste

To Cook Chicken
1 tablespoon olive oil
$\frac{1}{2}$ cup white wine
1 cup **Defatted Chicken Stock** (see recipe, page 45)

Vegetables
4 baby leeks, white parts only
6 sliced shiitake mushrooms
12 red and yellow cherry tomatoes

Garnish
4 sprigs of thyme

Directions
Wash chicken. Mix together and rub in the seasonings. Set aside for 15 minutes. Heat oil in a skillet and sear chicken 3 minutes on each side. Add wine, stock, and leeks. Cover pan and simmer on low heat for 15 minutes. Add mushrooms and tomatoes, and simmer for 2 minutes.

Presentation
Arrange chicken and vegetables on hot plates. Garnish with sprigs of thyme.

4 servings

Chicken and Pineapple Curry

The chicken and pineapple are curried together. The result is a mild, yellow curry. Raw, not roasted, spices are used in the curry to add fragrance without altering the desired yellow color. Serve this curry with hot rice.

1$\frac{1}{2}$ pounds skinless, boneless chicken breasts
2 tablespoons olive oil
2 yellow onions, peeled and minced fine
2 teaspoons minced garlic
2 teaspoons minced ginger
1 teaspoon ground **coriander**
1 teaspoon ground **turmeric**
$\frac{1}{2}$ teaspoon **cayenne pepper**
$\frac{1}{8}$ teaspoon ground **cinnamon**
$\frac{1}{8}$ teaspoon ground **cloves**
$\frac{1}{8}$ teaspoon ground **nutmeg**
$\frac{1}{4}$ cup water
Fresh lemon juice
Salt to taste
1 cup diced pineapple
$\frac{1}{2}$ cup coconut milk
$\frac{1}{2}$ cup unsalted roasted cashew nuts
$\frac{1}{2}$ cup chopped Chinese parsley

Directions
Cut chicken into 1-inch squares. Heat oil and sauté onion on low heat, about 10 minutes or until golden. Add garlic, ginger, and spices, and cook 3 to 4 minutes. Stir chicken in with the spices. Add water and season with lemon juice and salt to taste. Cover and simmer on very low heat for 6 to 7 minutes. Stir in pineapple and simmer 3 to 4 minutes. Stir in coconut milk and sprinkle in cashew nuts and Chinese parsley. Cook for 1 minute and remove from heat.

Presentation
Serve hot with rice.

4 servings

Broiled Chicken with Beluga Lentils

The **tamarind** juice and yogurt in the marinade help to tenderize the chicken, while giving it a deep rich color and taste. Lentils are bland and the infusion of fragrance and flavor from other ingredients is essential to make them palatable. Shallots and garlic are browned in oil. Then in this fragrant oil, black **mustard seeds** and **cumin** seeds are fried until they pop open and release their flavors. This is a common technique used in Sri Lankan cooking to enrich and add fragrance to certain dishes.

4 boneless, skinless chicken breasts,
5 to 5¹/₂ ounces each

Marinade
*¹/₄ teaspoon **cayenne pepper***
¹/₂ teaspoon ground cumin
*1 tablespoon **Tamarind Juice** (see recipe,*
page 203)
1 teaspoon tomato paste
1 teaspoon fresh lemon juice
1 tablespoon plain, low-fat yogurt
1 tablespoon chopped basil
Salt to taste
Freshly ground black pepper to taste

For Lentils
*³/₄ cup **beluga lentils***
3 cups water
1 teaspoon chopped ginger
1¹/₂ tablespoons olive oil
¹/₂ cup sliced shallots
1 teaspoon chopped garlic
¹/₂ teaspoon black mustard seeds
1 teaspoon cumin seed
Salt to taste

For Broiling Chicken
1 tablespoon olive oil

Vegetables
1 teaspoon olive oil
1 teaspoon minced garlic
1 cup trimmed and sliced asparagus
Salt to taste
12 cherry tomatoes, halved
1 tablespoon fresh lemon juice
1 teaspoon chopped dill

Garnish
4 sprigs of basil

Directions
Wash and wipe chicken, mix with ingredients for the marinade, and refrigerate for 1 to 2 hours. Wash and place lentils in a pan with 3 cups water and ginger; cook for 35 minutes. After 35 minutes, the lentils should be cooked and the water dried up. If there is liquid remaining, strain it off. (If lentils are still hard, sprinkle ¹/₄ cup hot water and cook 5 more minutes.)

In a pan, heat olive oil and fry shallots and garlic until golden brown, about 3 minutes on medium heat. Add the spices and fry about 1 minute until the spices start to pop. Add cooked lentils and season well with salt to taste. Keep lentils hot until ready to serve.

Place chicken on a broiler rack over a pan. Brush with olive oil and broil for 4 minutes; turn the chicken over and broil 5 minutes more.

Heat oil in a pan. Add garlic and cook a few seconds on low heat. Add asparagus and salt to taste, cover, and steam for 4 minutes. Add cherry tomatoes, lemon juice, and mix in the dill.

Presentation
Spoon lentils onto plates and place chicken on lentils. Spoon the vegetables beside the chicken and garnish with basil sprigs.

4 servings

Pecan-Crusted Chicken with Mustard Sauce

Spices like **cinnamon** and **nutmeg** work well with rich nuts like pecans. I use the spices to season the chicken before crusting it with the pecans. The accompanying vegetables, with a hint of **rice wine vinegar,** counteract the richness of the chicken.

4 boneless, skinless chicken breasts,
   5 to 5½ ounces each
⅛ teaspoon each ground cinnamon and nutmeg
Salt to taste
Freshly ground black pepper to taste
1 tablespoon olive oil
2 teaspoons Dijon mustard
1 cup coarse-ground pecans
¼ cup **Defatted Chicken Stock** (see recipe,
   page 45)

For Sauce
2 teaspoons chopped shallots
½ cup dry white wine
1 tablespoon white wine vinegar
1 cup defatted chicken stock (from recipe above)
1 tablespoon stoneground Dijon mustard
¼ cup buttermilk
Salt to taste
Freshly ground black pepper to taste

Vegetables
2 cups water
8 baby **bok choy**
1 tablespoon olive oil
1 tablespoon sliced shallots
1 teaspoon grated garlic
1 teaspoon grated ginger
2 tablespoons rice wine vinegar
2 teaspoons light brown sugar
Salt to taste

For Garnish
4 sprigs of rosemary

Directions
Preheat oven to 375°F.

Wash and wipe chicken; season with cinnamon, nutmeg, and salt and black pepper to taste. Heat oil in a sauté pan and sear both sides of the chicken for about 3 minutes. (Keep the sauté pan to use for making the sauce.) Brush the presentation sides of the chicken with 2 teaspoons of mustard and dip the mustard-brushed sides in the ground pecans. Place in a baking pan, pecan-crusted side up. Add ¼ cup stock to the pan and cook in the preheated oven for 8 to 10 minutes.

While chicken is roasting, make the sauce. Heat the sauté pan used for chicken on medium heat, add shallots, and cook to a brown color. Add wine and vinegar, and deglaze the pan. Add stock and simmer until reduced to ½ cup. Whisk in the mustard and buttermilk; season with salt and black pepper to taste. Strain sauce and set aside.

Heat 2 cups water, add the bok choy, and cook for 4 minutes. Drain from the cooking liquid and refresh with cold water. Heat oil in the sauté pan, add shallots, garlic, and ginger, and cook 2 to 3 minutes. Add the bok choy and season with rice wine vinegar, brown sugar, and salt to taste. Cook for 3 to 4 minutes until the vegetables are glazed.

Presentation
Place chicken and vegetables on plates. Spoon sauce over chicken and garnish with sprigs of rosemary.

4 servings

Grilled Chicken and Pineapple on Lemongrass Sticks with Cabbage Salad

The chicken is spiced Thai style and placed on a refreshing tart cabbage salad that adds crunch to the dish. All you need is steamed rice as an accompaniment.

8 stalks **lemongrass**
4 boneless, skinless chicken breasts,
    4 to 5 ounces each
8 large cubes of pineapple

Marinade
1 tablespoon grated yellow onion
1 tablespoon tender lemongrass, minced
2 teaspoons grated ginger
1 teaspoon **chili paste**
1 tablespoon soy sauce
1 teaspoon paprika
¼ cup orange juice
½ cup fresh lemon juice
Salt to taste
1 tablespoon olive oil

Cabbage Salad
1 cup finely shredded head cabbage
1 tomato, cut into thin slivers
¼ cup sliced red onion
1 tablespoon **chiffonade** of basil leaves

Dressing
¼ teaspoon chili paste
2 tablespoons fresh lemon juice
1 tablespoon cider vinegar
2 teaspoons light brown sugar
Salt to taste

Garnish
4 sprigs of basil

Directions
Remove the bulbous bases from the lemongrass stems. Use about 6 to 6½ inches of the stiff tops of the lemongrass as skewers.

Wash and wipe chicken; cut each breast into 4 pieces. Make cuts on the chicken so the pieces can be easily threaded onto the lemongrass skewers. Make similar cuts on the pineapple cubes.

For the marinade, mix grated onion, minced lemongrass, and ginger in a small bowl. Stir in chili paste, soy sauce, and paprika, and season with orange and lemon juice. Add chicken, salt to taste, and coat chicken with the spices.

Thread 2 pieces of chicken and 2 pieces of pineapple on each lemongrass skewer, and brush with olive oil. Set aside for 30 minutes. Grill for 4 minutes on each side or until the chicken is cooked.

For cabbage salad, place cabbage, tomatoes, onions, and basil leaves in a medium-size bowl. Whisk together dressing ingredients in a separate bowl; add to the salad with salt to taste and toss.

Presentation
Spoon salad onto plates and place 2 chicken skewers on each. Garnish with sprigs of basil.

4 servings

Poultry, Meat

Chicken with Wing Beans and Vegetables

Ajowan seeds impart an exciting fragrance to this chicken dish. I use just enough of the spice to enhance, not overpower, the dish. A squeeze of lemon brings out the best in this unique spice.

4 deboned chicken breasts with the stump of
    the wing bones attached, 5½ to 6 ounces each
Salt to taste
Freshly ground black pepper to taste
2½ tablespoons olive oil
1 teaspoon ajowan seeds
1 tablespoon fresh lemon juice

Mirepoix

1 tablespoon diced carrot
1 tablespoon diced yellow onion
1 tablespoon diced celery
1 tablespoon diced leeks

Sauce

½ cup tomato **concassée**
2 cups **Defatted Chicken Stock** (see recipe,
    page 45)
¼ cup red wine
1 tablespoon molasses
2 teaspoons unsalted butter, softened

Vegetables

1 tablespoon olive oil
4 red potatoes, boiled and halved
4 small boiling onions, peeled and boiled
4 wing beans, each cut across into halves
    and **blanched**
Salt to taste
Freshly ground black pepper to taste
2 cups beet greens, coarse stems removed and
    shredded 1-inch thick
4 baby beets, boiled, skin removed, and
    halved lengthwise

Garnish

4 sprigs of **chervil**

Directions

Trim chicken, remove skin, wash, and wipe dry. Season with salt and black pepper to taste. Heat oil on medium heat, add ajowan seeds, and cook 1 minute until they start to pop. Add chicken and lemon juice, and sear about 3 minutes to a side on medium heat. Add **mirepoix** and cook for 4 to 5 minutes. Add tomato, chicken stock, wine, and molasses. Cover pan and **braise** on low heat for 10 minutes. Remove chicken and set aside.

Strain the sauce (about ¾ cup) while pressing on the vegetables. Place the sauce back in the pan on low heat. Whisk butter into the sauce, remove from heat, and place chicken in the sauce.

For vegetables, heat olive oil in a pan, add potatoes and onions, and cook on high heat for 2 to 3 minutes or until vegetables brown lightly. Add wing beans and season with salt and black pepper to taste. Cook 3 more minutes, remove from pan, and place aside.

To the pan, add beet greens and beets, season with salt and black pepper to taste, and cook 3 to 4 minutes or until the greens wilt. Reheat chicken for a few seconds in the sauce.

Presentation

Spoon vegetables and chicken on the plates, and spoon the sauce on the plates. Add the beets and beet greens and garnish with chervil.

4 servings

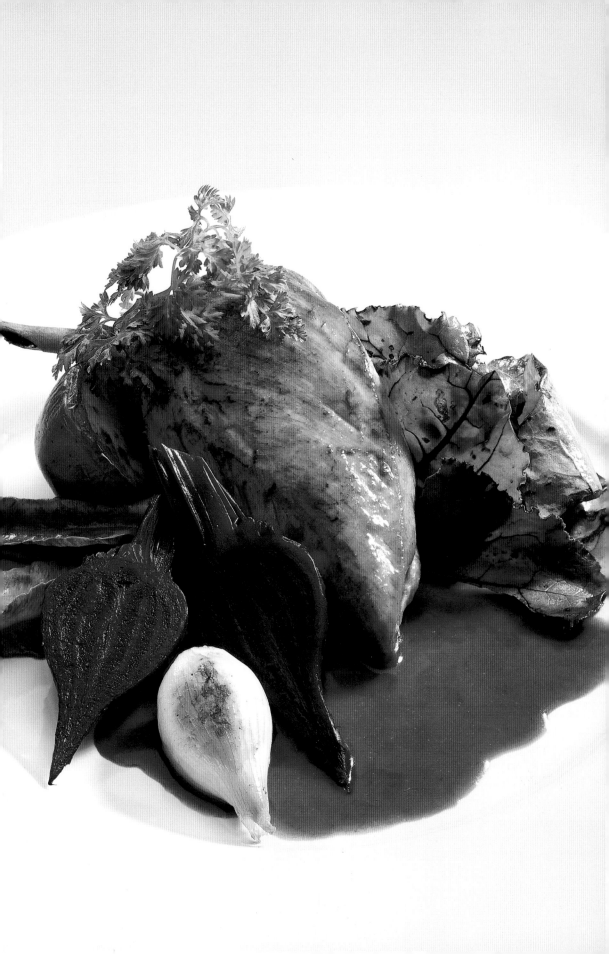

Stuffed Cornish Game Hen

For the marinade I use **garam masala.** It is a roasted and ground blend of aromatic spices such as **cinnamon, cloves, cardamom, mace,** and **nutmeg.** The **turmeric** rubbed on the chicken helps to create a blush on the hens after roasting, and the spices have a tendency to counteract the gamey taste of the birds, which some dislike.

2 Cornish game hens, about 1½ pounds each

Seasonings and Marinade
1 tablespoon garam masala
1 teaspoon salt
1 tablespoon cold, unsalted butter
¼ teaspoon turmeric
1 tablespoon fresh lemon juice

Vegetables
*½ recipe **Butternut Squash and Apple Compote** (see recipe, page 142)*
*20 **haricots verts, blanched***
2 teaspoons unsalted butter
Salt to taste

Stuffing
4 ounces bacon, chopped fine
1 cup chopped yellow onion
2 teaspoons chopped garlic
2 green apples, peeled, cored, and diced
2 tablespoons raisins
Salt to taste
Freshly ground pepper to taste

For Roasting
1 tablespoon unsalted butter

Glaze
*½ cup **balsamic vinegar***
½ cup red port wine
Juice of 1 orange

Garnish
4 orange slices

Directions
Preheat oven to 375°F.

Wash hens inside and out; wipe dry. To season, mix garam masala, salt, and cold butter. Slide your fingers between the skin and the flesh to loosen the skin. Stuff the seasoning between the skin and the flesh of the hen. Rub turmeric and lemon juice on the hens. Leave to marinate 2 to 3 hours in the refrigerator.

Cook butternut squash and apple compote, and keep warm. Place blanched haricots verts in a pan with butter and salt to taste; set aside until ready to serve.

For the stuffing, heat a skillet, add bacon, and cook till bacon is crisp. Remove and discard excess fat. Add onion and garlic to the skillet. Cook for 3 to 4 minutes. Add the rest of the ingredients and cook for 5 to 6 minutes. Cool and stuff the hens. **Truss** the hens. Heat butter in a skillet and sear hens 3 to 4 minutes, place on a rack in a roasting pan, and roast for 45 minutes.

Reduce balsamic vinegar, port wine, and orange juice for 4 to 5 minutes or until glazed. Untie hens and halve them by cutting along the sides of the backbones. Discard the backbones. Trim the leg tips and wing tips. Toss haricots verts on high heat for a few seconds.

Presentation
Place half a trimmed hen and stuffing on each plate with a portion of butternut squash and apple compote. Spoon haricots verts beside the hens and drizzle the glaze on the plates. Garnish each with a slice of orange.

4 servings

Burst of Flavor

Spicy Glazed Cornish Hen

A special breed of chicken, young Cornish game hens are very tender when cooked. A small-boned hen makes a healthy single portion.

4 Cornish hens 1 to 1¼ pounds each

Marinade
*2 tablespoons **Tamarind Juice** (see recipe, page 203)*
2 teaspoons grated ginger
1 teaspoon grated garlic
*2 teaspoons **garam masala***
Salt to taste
Freshly ground black pepper to taste
Juice of 1 orange

To Glaze Birds
1 tablespoon molasses

To Deglaze Roasting Pan
*½ cup **Defatted Chicken Stock** (see recipe, page 45)*
2 tablespoons sherry

Garnish
Handful of green onion

Directions
To bone a hen, cut along both sides of the backbone and remove it. Lay the hen flat on the cutting board, skin side up. Press down with the heel of your hand to break the breastbone. Turn the hen over and pull out the breastbone and ribs so the hen opens out flat. Make a deep cut along each of the insides of the thighbones. (Reserve the bones for the stockpot.) Turn the hen over and tuck the wings behind the breasts. Gently pat down to flatten the hen further.

Season the flattened hens with tamarind juice, ginger, garlic, garam masala, and salt and black pepper to taste; massage seasoning into the hens. Place in a dish, pour orange juice over them, and leave in the refrigerator to marinate for at least 4 hours.

Preheat oven to 475°F. Place hens skin side up on a rack and place in a roasting pan. Place in the oven and roast for 10 minutes. Baste with pan juices and brush with molasses. Roast 18 to 20 minutes more.

Remove the hens and the rack, and place over another pan to collect the juices dripping off the hens. Keep the roasting pan on the stove on low heat, add the chicken stock and sherry, and deglaze the pan. Add any juices collected from the cooked hens. Cook 3 to 4 minutes. Strain.

Presentation
Place the hens on dinner plates and spoon the glaze over the hens. Garnish with green onion.

4 servings

Duck Salad and Wilted Greens in Raspberry Vinaigrette

The sweet and tart vinaigrette balances the rich taste of the spiced, honey-glazed duck. The many pleasurable textures and tastes range from the smooth spicy potatoes to the creamy blue cheese, from the crispy bitter greens to the occasional soft raspberry.

4 boneless duck breasts, 5 to 5½ ounces each
Salt to taste
Freshly ground black pepper to taste
1 tablespoon vegetable oil
*A pinch of ground **cinnamon***
*A pinch of ground **cloves***
*A pinch of ground **nutmeg***
1 tablespoon honey
2 tablespoons raspberry vinegar

For Dressing
2 shallots, minced
2 garlic cloves, minced
2 tablespoons raspberry vinegar
¼ cup red wine
½ tablespoon honey
Salt to taste
Freshly ground black pepper to taste

For Salad
½ red onion, thinly sliced
*½ cup **mizuna** leaves*
*½ cup **dandelion** leaves*
½ cup watercress leaves
¼ cup broken-up radicchio leaves

Garnish
¼ cup blue cheese, crumbled
¼ cup raspberries

Directions
Wash and wipe duck breasts. Score the skins in a diamond pattern. The cuts should not reach the meat. Season with salt and black pepper to taste.

Heat oil in a skillet and place the duck breasts skin side down. Cook on moderate heat for 12 to 14 minutes. Pour out all the fat from the skillet. Turn the duck breasts over. Brush with spices, honey, and vinegar, and cook for 2 minutes on each side. Remove duck breasts from the skillet and keep warm.

For the salad dressing, place skillet back on high heat. Remove duck fat, leaving 1 tablespoon of fat in the skillet. Add shallots and garlic, and cook for 2 to 3 seconds. Add vinegar, wine, honey, and salt and black pepper to taste, and deglaze the skillet.

Add sliced onions to skillet and cook until wilted. Add salad greens and toss to coat with dressing; immediately remove from heat.

Place duck breasts on a carving board and slice thinly.

Presentation
Place salad on plates and lay carved duck on the salads. Crumble blue cheese and strew on the salads with the raspberries.

4 servings

Duck with Sweet Potatoes and Red Cabbage Salad

Sweet potato, naturally sweet, gets a hint of fragrance from the **cinnamon** and pungency from the **nutmeg.** The brandied duck, arranged on cooked apples and surrounded by a crispy red cabbage salad and tart orange glaze, balances many subtle flavors ranging from sweet-and-sour to spicy.

4 boneless duck breasts, 5 to 5½ ounces each

Sweet Potatoes

1 pound sweet potatoes
1 tablespoon vegetable oil
½ teaspoon each ground cinnamon and nutmeg
2 tablespoons brandy
Salt to taste
Freshly ground black pepper to taste

Red Cabbage Salad

4 cups water
2 cups shredded red cabbage
1 tablespoon olive oil
1 tablespoon sliced red onion
1 tablespoon apple cider vinegar
1 tablespoon light brown sugar
2 tablespoons orange juice
Salt to taste
Freshly ground black pepper to taste

For Duck

Salt to taste
1 tablespoon vegetable oil
1 tablespoon brandy

For Glaze

1 green apple, peeled, cored, and sliced
1 teaspoon chopped shallots
½ cup orange juice
½ cup red wine
2 tablespoons cider vinegar

Garnish

4 sprigs of watercress

Directions

Preheat oven to 375°F.

Wash and wipe the duck breasts. Score the skin in a diamond pattern. The cuts should not reach the meat, but should go only through the skin. Wash sweet potatoes and rub with oil. Place in a baking pan and roast in the oven for 45 minutes or until skin is caramelized and the pulp is soft. Remove skin and discard. Place the pulp in a pan. Add spices, brandy, and salt and black pepper to taste. Mix well to combine all the ingredients. Cook for 3 to 4 minutes and keep hot on a double boiler.

Bring 4 cups water to a boil. Add red cabbage and cook for 3 minutes. Strain cabbage from cooking water and set aside. Heat olive oil and sauté onions to a golden brown color. Add cabbage, cider vinegar, brown sugar, and orange juice. Season with salt and black pepper to taste. Cook 2 minutes on high heat.

Season duck breasts with salt to taste. Place a skillet with oil on high heat and place the duck breasts skin side down. Cook on moderate heat for 10 to 12 minutes or until the skin is crispy. Pour out all the fat from the skillet, pour in the brandy, and flambé. Turn over the duck breasts and cook for 4 more minutes. Remove duck from skillet and keep warm. To the skillet, add ingredients for the glaze. Cook for 3 minutes. Remove the apple slices and set aside. Reduce the glaze to ¼ cup.

Presentation

Mold sweet potatoes on the plates. Arrange apple slices on the sweet potatoes, carve the duck breast, and arrange in a fan shape on the apples. Spoon red cabbage around the sweet potatoes. Drizzle glaze on plates and garnish with sprigs of watercress.

4 servings

Burst of Flavor

Roast Duckling with Orange and Apricot Sauce

Cinnamon and **nutmeg** are known as warm spices and are compatible with fruits such as oranges and apricots. Here, these fragrant spices are used to enhance the fruity sauce for this variation of the classic Duck a l' Orange.

2 ducklings, 3 pounds each

Seasoning
Peel of 1 orange
4 garlic cloves, crushed
1 small yellow onion, peeled and thinly sliced
Salt to taste
Freshly ground black pepper to taste

Duck Stock
Chopped duck carcasses
6 cups water
1-inch piece of cinnamon stick
6 black peppercorns
1 bay leaf

For Sauce
¼ cup sugar
¼ cup cider vinegar
1 cup orange juice
¼ cup white wine
½ teaspoon ground cinnamon
¼ teaspoon ground nutmeg
3 cups duck stock
3 dried apricots, finely chopped

Garnish
*1 tablespoon orange zest **julienne***
4 sprigs of watercress

Directions
Preheat oven to 400°F.

Wash ducks inside and out; wipe dry. Remove fat on the inside of the legs, cut off the neck, and save for the stock. Prick the duck all over the skin. Stuff ducks with orange peel, garlic, and onion mixed with salt and black pepper to taste. Place the ducks in a roasting pan, sprinkle with salt, and roast for 30 minutes to color the skin. Reduce heat to 300°F and roast for 1 hour. When ducks are done, set them aside to cool.

Place ducks on a cutting board and carve the legs off, trim away excess fat, and cut off the leg and wing tips. Cut the duck breasts away from the breastbones. Chop the duck carcasses; add ingredients for duck stock and simmer for 45 minutes. Skim off fat while cooking. Strain (need about 3 cups).

To start the sauce, put a heavy-bottomed saucepan on high heat. Add sugar. Without stirring, allow the sugar to get to a deep golden caramel color. Add vinegar, orange juice, and wine. (Keep face away from the pan. The mixture could splatter.) Add spices, duck stock, and dried apricots. Simmer until reduced by half, skimming the sauce often. Strain and keep aside.

Place the carved duck in a roasting pan, place in a 400°F oven, and roast again for 6 minutes or until the skins are crisp.

Presentation
Place a duck breast and a leg on each plate, reheat sauce, and spoon over the duck. Garnish with orange zest julienne and sprigs of watercress.

4 servings

Duck Breasts with Peach Sauce

Here is a recipe for the health-conscious eater. The fatty skins are removed from the duck breasts before cooking. **Cardamom** and **cinnamon** add flavor and richness to the peach sauce. As always, spices counterbalance the rich taste of the meat. **Citrus-Flavored Herbed Rice** (see recipe, page 164) and cooked greens of your choice make fine accompaniments to the duck.

4 duck breasts
¼ teaspoon finely ground cardamom seeds
1 tablespoon red wine vinegar
1 teaspoon grated ginger
Salt to taste
Freshly ground black pepper to taste
1 tablespoon olive oil

Sauce
*2 cups **Defatted Chicken Stock** (see recipe, page 45)*
1 tablespoon red wine vinegar
¼ teaspoon ground cardamom seeds
1-inch piece of cinnamon stick
2 peaches, peeled and sliced
1 teaspoon grated ginger
1 tablespoon red currant jelly
Juice of 1 orange
1 tablespoon brandy

Garnish
4 sprigs of watercress

Directions
Skin duck breast and trim off all the fat. Rub in cardamom, vinegar, ginger, and salt and black pepper to taste. Marinate overnight in the refrigerator.

Brush both sides of duck breasts with olive oil and place on a rack in a broiler pan.

For the sauce, place chicken stock in a saucepan. Add vinegar, cardamom, cinnamon, peaches, and ginger, and place on low heat. Simmer until reduced by half.

Broil duck for 6 minutes on each side (for medium doneness). Place duck breasts on a cutting board to rest for 3 to 4 minutes.

To continue with the sauce, add pan drippings from the roasted duck to the reduced sauce. Place on low heat, whisk in red currant jelly, orange juice, and brandy. Cook on low heat until reduced by half (need about ½ cup).

Presentation
Slice duck breast diagonally into thin slices. Place on dinner plates. Strain sauce and spoon around the duck. Garnish with sprigs of watercress.

4 servings

Filet Mignon, Mashed Potatoes with Black Mustard Seeds, and Date Chutney

This dish is unique and easy to prepare. The accompanying mashed potatoes with black **mustard seeds** are a significant taste element in this dish. The nutty taste of the fried black mustard seeds and the combination of spices in the chutney are subtle, not harsh. They enhance the simply seasoned beef. Tying all these tastes together is the creamy cabbage and the sweetish sauce.

4 beef filet mignon, 4¹⁄₂ ounces each
1 tablespoon olive oil
Salt to taste
Freshly ground black pepper to taste
¹⁄₂ recipe **Mashed Potatoes with Black Mustard Seeds** (see recipe, page 143)
¹⁄₂ cup **Date Chutney** (see recipe, page 202)
1 sprig of thyme

Creamy Cabbage
4 cups water
2 cups thickly sliced head cabbage
2 tablespoons unsalted butter
1 tablespoon chopped shallots
1 teaspoon grated garlic
Salt to taste
Freshly ground black pepper to taste
1 tablespoon country-style Dijon mustard
¹⁄₄ cup full cream

Port Wine Sauce
1 teaspoon unsalted butter
2 shallots, peeled and chopped
¹⁄₂ cup red port wine
2 cups **Defatted Beef Stock** (see recipe, page 44)

Garnish
4 sprigs of thyme

Directions
Wipe the meat, brush with olive oil, and season with salt and black pepper to taste. Prepare the mashed potatoes and keep warm. Prepare date chutney and keep at room temperature.

Heat a skillet until very hot, add the thyme, and sear the beef about 3 minutes on each side. Place the beef in a pan, keep in a warm oven, and reserve the skillet to prepare the sauce.

Bring 4 cups water to a boil. Add cabbage and cook for 2 minutes or until cabbage is wilted. Drain cabbage from cooking water and refresh in cold water.

Heat butter in a pan, add chopped shallots and garlic, and cook 3 to 4 minutes. Add cabbage, and salt and black pepper to taste. Cook 3 to 4 minutes. Beat mustard into the cream and stir into the cabbage.

For the sauce, add butter to the skillet. Add shallots and sauté until golden brown. Add port wine and deglaze the skillet. Add the beef stock and reduce to a glaze, about ¹⁄₂ cup.

Presentation
Mold potatoes on the plate. Using a pair of tongs, pick some of the onions off the potatoes in the pan and heap them on top of the molded potato. Place the beef in the center of the plate and spoon cabbage and the date chutney beside the beef. Drizzle port wine sauce and garnish with thyme sprigs.

4 servings

Spice-Crusted Roast Tenderloin of Beef

On its own, tenderloin of beef can be uninteresting. For the crust, I use a spice blend of **cumin** and **coriander** seeds, black **mustard seeds,** and black peppercorns. These raw spices are crushed to a coarse texture and mixed in with other ingredients to make the textured crust. Cumin and coriander seeds together give a piquant, lemony taste to the crust, and black mustard seeds ground raw give a slightly bitter taste. The peppercorns release their highly volatile oils and further add to the flavor. Paprika gives the deep brown color to the roast beef, and the flour helps to keep the crust together.

2½ pounds beef tenderloin

Vegetables
*2 recipes **Spicy Potato Cakes** (see recipe, page 136)*
*1 recipe **Creamy Saffron Spinach** (see recipe, page 138)*
8 large shiitake mushrooms

To Sear Beef
2 tablespoons olive oil
1 tablespoon each sliced shallots and garlic
2 sprigs each of rosemary and thyme

Crust
2 tablespoons each cumin and coriander seeds
1 teaspoon black mustard seeds
1 tablespoon black peppercorns
¼ teaspoon paprika
1 tablespoon all purpose flour
1 teaspoon salt

Sauce
¼ cup red wine
1 tablespoon red wine vinegar
*1½ cups **Defatted Beef Stock** (see recipe, page 44)*

Garnish
8 sprigs each of rosemary and thyme

Directions
Preheat oven to 375°F.

Trim the beef and refrigerate. Make spicy potato cakes and keep warm. Have ingredients ready for creamy saffron spinach. Trim mushrooms.

To sear the meat, heat olive oil in a skillet, add shallots and garlic, and cook to a golden brown, about 5 minutes. Add rosemary, thyme, and the beef; sauté on high heat, turning as necessary for about 5 minutes or until evenly seared on all sides. Reserve skillet to make the sauce.

For the crust, coarsely crush the spice seeds using a spice grinder. Add the rest of the ingredients and spread on a parchment paper. Place seared meat on the spices and roll to coat evenly. Place meat in a roasting pan and roast in the preheated oven for 25 to 30 minutes; turn over once about halfway through cooking time. Place the mushrooms beside the meat in the roasting pan 5 minutes before it comes out of the oven. Set aside the meat to rest for 8 minutes before carving and reserve the mushrooms.

For the sauce, place the skillet back on high heat, add wine and vinegar, deglaze the skillet, and bring to a simmer. Add stock and reduce to 1 cup. Strain through a cheesecloth-lined strainer. Complete cooking spinach.

Presentation
Place potato cakes on plates. Carve meat in ¼-inch-thick slices and place on the plates along with the spinach and mushrooms. Spoon sauce around the meat and garnish with sprigs of rosemary and thyme.

8 servings

Grilled Flank Steak and Sherried Sweet Potato

Grilled flank steak is a favorite in the Ka'Ikena La'uae Restaurant at the Culinary Institute of the Pacific. The flank steak is a cut of meat from the very edge of the rib of the animal. This piece of meat has long, coarse fibers and stays tender if not overcooked. Flank takes well to spices and seasonings. A single spice, **cumin,** mixed with pineapple and seasonings makes the marinade that tenderizes the steak and gives it a seductive aroma.

2 pounds flank steak

Marinade
2 teaspoons cumin seeds
*3 **green chilies***
4 slices ginger
2 garlic cloves
1 whole green onion
1/2 cup chopped pineapple
*1 tablespoon **balsamic vinegar***
1 tablespoon cider vinegar
1 tablespoon fresh lime juice
Salt to taste

Vegetables
*1 recipe **Sherried Sweet Potatoes** (see recipe, page 134)*

Sauce
1 small, unpeeled red onion, washed
1 teaspoon olive oil
*2 cups **Defatted Beef Stock** (see recipe, page 44)*

To Grill Meat
1 tablespoon olive oil

Garnish
3 pineapple slices, core removed and cut into half rings
5 to 6 sprigs of Chinese parsley

Directions
Trim meat, remove excess fat, and place in a stainless steel or glass container.

Using a blender, blend ingredients for marinade and season with salt to taste. Reserve 1/4 cup of the marinade for the sauce and pour balance on the meat, to coat both sides. Cover and leave to marinate for no longer than 2 hours. Long marination will soften the meat too much.

Preheat oven to 400°F and turn on the grill.

Make sherried sweet potatoes and set aside.

For the sauce, brush onion with oil and roast in the preheated oven for 45 to 50 minutes or until soft. Peel onion and chop fine. Place in a pan with reserved marinade and stock, and reduce to 3/4 of a cup. Taste and season with more salt if desired.

Remove meat from the marinade and brush with olive oil. Cook on preheated grill, on medium heat, for 6 to 8 minutes per side. Set meat aside to rest for 5 minutes.

Reheat sweet potato in the oven; grill the pineapple for 2 minutes per side. Carve meat into thin slices.

Presentation
Place sweet potatoes on plates, fan out carved meat, and place partially covering the sweet potatoes. Garnish with grilled pineapple and sprigs of Chinese parsley. Spoon sauce on the meat.

5 to 6 servings

Roast Carved Rack of Lamb with Pickled Cherries

Lamb is fatty, so as much fat as possible should be removed before cooking. However, without the fat, it has a tendency to dry out while cooking. Take care not to overcook the lamb to avoid drying out the meat. Before searing the lamb, aromatize the searing oil with **neem** leaves by heating the cooking oil on medium heat and frying the leaves in the oil for 2 to 3 minutes. Discard the leaves and use the oil to sear the lamb. Neem is extremely bitter and is believed to have medicinal properties. Here, it gives aroma to the meat.

2 racks of lamb, 8 bones in each, **frenched**
Salt to taste
Freshly ground black pepper to taste

Sauce

1 tablespoon olive oil
1/2 cup chopped yellow onion, carrot, and celery
2 teaspoons sugar
1 cup port wine
3 cups lamb stock or **Defatted Beef Stock**
   (see recipe, page 44)
1/2 cup **Pickled Cherries** (see recipe,
   page 222)
1 pinch of ground **cloves**
1/2 teaspoon ground **cinnamon**

To Sear Lamb

1 tablespoon vegetable oil
3 neem leaves
12 cloves peeled garlic, **blanched**

Vegetables

1 tablespoon unsalted butter
1 cup peeled celery root **julienne**
2 teaspoons fresh lemon juice
Salt to taste
Freshly ground black pepper to taste
2 cups watercress sprigs

Garnish

12 pickled cherries
4 sprigs of rosemary

Directions

Preheat oven to 375°F. Season lamb with salt and black pepper to taste.

For the sauce, heat olive oil in a saucepan and sauté the onion, carrot, and celery for 5 minutes over medium heat, or until the vegetables are golden brown. Stir in the sugar and cook 2 to 3 minutes to caramelize. Add wine, stock, and pickled cherries, and reduce by half. Strain to a clean pan; add the spices and reduce on low heat to 1 cup.

To sear lamb, heat oil on high heat in a skillet. Add the neem leaves, fry 2 minutes, remove from oil, and discard. Sear the lamb in the neem-flavored oil on medium heat until browned on both sides, about 3 minutes per side. Add the blanched garlic cloves to the skillet and place in the preheated oven. Roast for 10 minutes for medium rare. Remove from oven, pick out the garlic cloves, and add them to the sauce. Let lamb rest 5 minutes before carving.

Heat butter in a sauté pan. Add celery root, lemon juice, and salt and black pepper to taste. Cook for 3 to 4 minutes on high heat. Place on dinner plates. To the hot pan, add watercress sprigs. Using the tongs, turn sprigs around until partially wilted. Place by the celery root.

Presentation

Carve lamb and arrange 4 chops by the vegetables on each plate. Spoon sauce around lamb and place roast garlic cloves in the sauce. Garnish plates with pickled cherries and sprigs of rosemary.

4 servings

Minted Rack of Lamb with Onion and Rhubarb Marmalade

Mint is a compatible partner to lamb, and the minty marinade gives an intense flavor to the lamb. Here, the minted lamb is paired with a spicy sweet-and-sour rhubarb marmalade. The spicy marmalade ties all the flavors of the dish together.

1 cup **Rhubarb and Onion Marmalade**
  (see recipe, page 222)
2 racks of lamb, 8 bones each, **frenched**

Marinade
2 teaspoons chopped ginger
1 shallot
2 garlic cloves
2 cups fresh garden mint leaves
1 teaspoon sugar
Juice of 1 lemon
Salt to taste

Sauce
2 cups **Defatted Beef Stock** (see recipe,
  page 44)
½ cup red wine
2 tablespoons **balsamic vinegar**

Vegetables
1 white rose potato
1 lotus root, peeled
1 sweet potato, peeled
1 red potato
1 tablespoon olive oil
Salt to taste
2 baby **bok choy,** halved lengthwise, **blanched**
Freshly ground black pepper to taste

Garnish
4 sprigs of rosemary

Directions
Make the marmalade and set aside.

Place lamb in a stainless steel container. Using a food processor, blend ingredients for the marinade to a coarse paste. Coat the lamb with the paste, making sure the skin side of the lamb is well coated. Cover and marinate overnight in the refrigerator.

Heat oven to 425°F and turn on the grill.

For the sauce, place the beef stock, red wine, and balsamic vinegar in a pan and reduce on moderate heat to a glaze. Set aside.

To prepare vegetables for roasting, slice the vegetables (except bok choy) to ⅛-inch thick pieces. Mix in olive oil and salt to taste. Place in a roasting pan in a single layer and cook in a medium hot oven for 30 to 35 minutes. Season bok choy with salt and black pepper to taste, and cook on a very hot grill.

Place lamb skin side up on a rack in a roasting pan. Roast in the preheated oven for 10 to 12 minutes. Remove from oven and allow the meat to rest for 6 minutes.

Presentation
Layer the vegetables attractively in the center of the plates. Carve and arrange 1 chop and 3 slices of lamb on the vegetables on each plate. Place bok choy on the left of the lamb and spoon the chutney to the right of the lamb. Spoon the sauce around the lamb. Garnish with sprigs of rosemary.

4 servings

Burst of Flavor

Lamb with Spinach

This rich, north Indian lamb dish tastes better a day later, because by then the meat is permeated with the spice flavors. Bring to boiling point slowly before serving.

2 pounds lamb shoulder, fat removed
½ teaspoon **turmeric**
¼ cup vegetable oil
3 yellow onions, peeled and thinly sliced
2 teaspoons each minced ginger and garlic
1 teaspoon **cayenne pepper**
1 teaspoon **cardamom** seeds, ground
1 tablespoon ground **cumin**
½ teaspoon each ground **cloves** and **nutmeg**
¼ cup plain yogurt
Salt to taste
Freshly ground black pepper to taste
1½ cups water
2-inch piece of **cinnamon** stick
1½ pounds spinach, washed, trimmed,
    and shredded

Directions
Cut lamb into 2-inch cubes. Rub in turmeric. Heat oil in a wide, heavy-bottomed pan. Add meat and cook on high heat for 10 minutes until meat turns a brown color. Remove meat from pan and set aside. To the pan, add onion, and cook on medium high heat to a caramel color. Add ginger and garlic, and cook 3 to 4 minutes. Add the ground spices and yogurt, and cook on low heat for 5 to 6 minutes. Fold in the meat and season with salt and black pepper to taste. Add 1½ cups water and cinnamon stick. Cover pan and cook on low heat for 1½ hours.

Fold in spinach and cook 10 more minutes. Taste and season with salt if necessary; cool and refrigerate.

4 servings

Lamb Kabobs

The spices bathe the meat with their aroma, and the yogurt acts as a binder as well as a tenderizer in these silky-smooth minced lamb kabobs served with **Mint Chutney** (see recipe, page 205).

24 bamboo skewers
1 pound ground lamb
1 tablespoon minced yellow onion
2 tablespoons fresh lemon juice
1 tablespoon minced ginger
2 teaspoons **garam masala**
4 tablespoons finely chopped garden mint
2 tablespoons plain yogurt
Salt to taste
Freshly ground black pepper to taste
¼ cup cold water
2 tablespoons olive oil

Garnish
6 sprigs of mint

Directions
Soak skewers in water for 3 to 4 hours. To the lamb, add the onion, lemon juice, ginger, spices, mint, and yogurt with salt and black pepper to taste. Mix thoroughly and refrigerate 3 to 4 hours. Add a little cold water and knead meat to a paste. Divide the meat paste into 24 portions. Dip your hands in cold water and, holding a portion of the meat paste, pass a skewer slowly through the paste. Rotate the skewer with your fingers and mold the paste around the skewer, to about 4 inches in length. Set aside the skewered meat for 30 minutes. Brush with olive oil and cook on a hot grill for 5 to 6 minutes on each side.

Presentation
Garnish the hot kabobs with sprigs of mint and serve with mint chutney.

4 servings

Braised Lamb Shanks with Couscous

I served this dish in a fairy-tale setting. A retinue of maids carried my preparation on priceless antique platters and served Doris Duke in the lavish, Arabian-style "tented" dining room at Shangri-La. Oh, those meaty, fruity, spicy smells! I almost see those aromas wafting up in swirls and disappearing like memories into thin air.

This mildly spiced Moroccan dish should not be greasy. Skim off the fat that has settled on the surface of the braised lamb. If time allows, cook a day ahead, cool, remove the fat, and reheat before adding the raisins and preserved lemon. Simmer 5 more minutes before serving.

6 lamb shanks
Salt to taste
Freshly ground black pepper to taste
2 tablespoons olive oil

Mirepoix
½ cup each diced carrots, yellow onions,
*   and white part of leeks*

For Braising
½ teaspoon ground **cinnamon**
½ teaspoon allspice
½ teaspoon dry ginger
6 cloves sliced garlic
1 whole bayleaf
5 cups lamb stock or **Defatted Beef Stock**
*   (see recipe, page 44)*
½ cup red wine

Relishes
½ recipe **Orange Relish** *(see recipe, page 206)*
½ recipe **Spicy Couscous** *(see recipe, page 165)*

To Finish
¼ cup raisins
4 **Preserved Lemon Wheels** *(see recipe,*
*   page 218)*

Directions
Preheat oven to 375°F.

Scrape the bone ends of the lamb shanks to make an attractive presentation. When the end of bone is scraped, it will be clean looking after cooking. If meat scraps are kept on, they will look untidy, with bits of cooked meat hanging on the bone after cooking. Rub shanks with salt and black pepper to taste, heat oil in a heavy casserole dish, and sear to a golden brown on high heat for 5 minutes. Remove shanks from casserole and set aside. To the fat in casserole, add **mirepoix** and sauté to brown lightly. Place the shanks on the vegetables, add all the ingredients for braising; cover casserole and place in the preheated oven. **Braise** for about 2 hours, until lamb is soft and almost falling off the bone. While the lamb is cooking, make orange relish and **couscous.** Keep couscous warm.

Carefully pick out the lamb shanks and place aside. To the liquid in the casserole, add raisins and preserved lemon. Simmer 5 minutes. Season sauce with salt to taste.

Presentation
Place a serving of couscous in the center of the plate and place a lamb shank leaning on the couscous. Spoon sauce over the lamb shank and orange relish on the plate.

4 servings

Spice-Coated Loin of Lamb
with Pineapple Relish

Rice and grated coconut are often used in Sri Lankan roasted spice blends. Roasted together, they turn a rich mahogany color and impart a delicate aroma. The pineapple relish, sweet and tangy, acts as a sauce and mellows the vigorous flavors of the spice-coated lamb. Wilted **pea shoots** are sweet and make an attractive garnish.

2 lamb loins, 8 to 9 ounces each, trimmed
   and fat removed
1 tablespoon fresh lime juice
1 teaspoon honey
Salt to taste

Dry Roast Spice Mix
2 teaspoons black peppercorns
1 tablespoon uncooked rice
1 tablespoon grated coconut

To Sear Lamb
1 tablespoon vegetable oil
2 **neem** leaves

Relish
1 cup **brunoise** of pineapple
¼ cup brunoise of red bell pepper
2 teaspoons sugar
2 tablespoons fresh lime juice
¼ cup **chiffonade** of garden mint leaves
Salt to taste
Freshly ground black pepper to taste

Vegetables
1 tablespoon unsalted butter
¼ cup water
8 Yukon gold potatoes, cooked
8 steamed baby carrots
Salt to taste
Freshly ground black pepper to taste
1 cup pea shoots

Directions
Season lamb with lime juice, honey, and salt to taste.

To dry-roast the spice mix, place ingredients in a pan on low heat. Stir with a spoon until the peppercorns are crisp and rice and coconut are golden brown, about 6 minutes. Grind to a coarse powder. Roll lamb in the spice mix.

Heat oil in a skillet at moderate temperature and cook neem leaves for 2 minutes or just long enough to impart a fragrance to the cooking fat. Remove neem from skillet and discard. Sear the lamb in the same skillet over medium-high heat. Using tongs, roll to sear all sides of the meat until browned, about 6 minutes. Remove lamb from heat and set aside for 5 minutes.

In a small bowl, mix ingredients for relish and season with salt and black pepper to taste.

Heat butter and ¼ cup water in a pan, and add potatoes and carrots. When vegetables are hot, season with salt and black pepper to taste, cook 2 to 3 minutes, and remove pan from heat.

Presentation
Spoon vegetables onto plates and add pea shoots to the hot pan. Set the pan aside. Carve lamb into ¼-inch-thick slices and place around the vegetables. Strew pineapple relish and wilted pea shoots around the lamb.

4 servings

Burst of Flavor

Veal Chops with Braised Vegetables

These juicy veal chops done just right have an accompanying vegetable-laden sauce redolent with herbs and spices. **Coriander,** ground raw to a powder or a paste, is used in Sri Lankan vegetable preparations. Here it is the leading flavor, and I use it cracked to give texture and infuse the vegetables with its fruity fragrance.

Morels are delicate and spongy, varying in color from beige to brown-black. To use dried morels, soak them for 15 minutes in cold water. Wash in several changes of water and press them dry before use. Dried morels used in this recipe may be replaced with shiitake mushrooms. This dish is simple to make, yet it looks sophisticated.

4 veal chops, 6 ounces each
Salt to taste
Freshly ground black pepper to taste
2 tablespoons olive oil

Vegetables
1 teaspoon cracked coriander seeds
4 shallots, peeled and quartered lengthwise
6 whole cloves of peeled garlic
1 cup white wine
½ cup Madeira wine
8 dried morels, washed in a few changes of water
4 halved red potatoes
2 cups veal stock or **Defatted Beef Stock**
  (see recipe, page 44)
2 sprigs of thyme

2 tomatoes, cored, unpeeled, and cut
  into large dice
1 cup green beans, trimmed and **blanched**
Salt to taste
Freshly ground black pepper to taste
¼ cup shredded basil leaves
1 tablespoon chopped chives

Garnish
8 sprigs of thyme

Directions
Trim veal chops and season with salt and black pepper to taste. Heat olive oil in a sauté pan and sear the chops on high heat about 4 minutes on each side for rare. Remove chops and keep warm.

To the sauté pan, add coriander seeds and fry for 2 minutes. Add shallots and garlic, and fry 2 minutes. Deglaze pan with the white wine and Madeira. Add morels, potatoes, stock, and thyme. Simmer until liquid is reduced by half. Add tomatoes and beans. Season with salt and black pepper to taste, and simmer for 5 to 6 minutes. Mix in the basil and chopped chives.

Presentation
Spoon vegetables with the pan juices onto plates. Place a veal chop on the vegetables and garnish with sprigs of thyme.

4 servings

Pork Vindaloo

History shows that Greeks, Romans, and Chinese all traded for spices. King Solomon's men were among the brave navigators whose search for spices took them to the Malabar coast, an important trading center. Goa, a former Portuguese colony, is north of Malabar on the famous trading route.

Although Goa is unsurpassed for its fiery curries, not all of its native dishes are hot. Its spicy seafood and fish curries are the envy of many cooks around the world. Laden with ground spices and seasonings, flavored with sugar and vinegar, curries from Goa have a very special character, including the fiery hot vindaloo.

Vindaloo is a much-loved preparation in Sri Lanka. It may be made with pork or beef. For marinating, cooking, and storing, use utensils and containers made of stainless steel or glass, which do not react chemically with the high acid content of vindaloo.

Vindaloo tastes better the second day; it allows time for the spices to permeate the meat. Bring it to a slow boil before serving. Serve with rice, vegetables, and a green salad.

2 to 2½ pounds pork shoulder, fat removed

Marinade
6 dried hot red chilies or 2 teaspoons
  cayenne pepper
½ cup cider vinegar
½ cup hot water
3 shallots
1 tablespoon chopped ginger
4 garlic cloves

1 teaspoon freshly ground black pepper
*1 teaspoon **turmeric***
*¼ teaspoon ground **cinnamon***
*¼ teaspoon ground **cloves***
*¼ teaspoon ground **nutmeg***
*1 teaspoon ground **cumin***

For Cooking
3 tablespoons vegetable oil
2 large yellow onions, peeled and finely chopped
1½ tablespoons dark brown sugar
*2 teaspoons **Tamarind Juice** (see recipe,*
  page 203)
Salt to taste

Directions
Cut pork into 1-inch cubes and place in a stainless steel container.

For the marinade, soak chilies in vinegar and hot water for ½ hour. In a blender, blend soaked chilies, shallots, ginger, garlic, and spices to a smooth purée, and pour on the pork. Mix and leave to marinate for 2 to 2½ hours.

For cooking, heat oil in a heavy-bottomed stainless steel pan and add onions; sauté on medium heat to a light gold color. Add sugar and stir until caramelized, about 2 minutes. Drain meat from marinade and add to the caramelized onion. Sear on high heat. Add liquid from the marinade, tamarind juice, and salt to taste. Stir to combine. Turn heat to low, cover pan, and simmer for 45 to 50 minutes. Cool and refrigerate to use a day later.

6 to 7 servings

Vegetables . . .

Simply Seductive

Some memories are feasts for my senses: the vegetable-laden boats on the waters of Kashmir's Dal Lake, displaying baskets of snow-white radishes, bunches of mint, yellow cucumber, and jewel-like red chilies; the floating markets in Bangkok's Chao Phraya River, with wooden pails of light-green onion and bunches of **ong choy** glistening with dew drops in the sunshine; the purple-streaked, small artichokes in the farmer's market in Chartres, France.

Intriguing and enticing vegetables abound in markets everywhere: bittermelon, okra, long beans, sausage-shaped lotus root, and Thai eggplant. Exotic blossoms like **sesbania,** squash, bunches of squash vine tips, and ivy gourd, still with curly tendrils—they all cry for a curious cook's attention.

As a child, I loved snake gourd. It is about six feet long, three inches across, and hollow inside with a few seeds. Pale green, streaked in dark green and chalky white, they were too long to be stored flat, so they were hung from beams in Sunday market stalls in Sri Lanka. My mother simmered them in coconut milk, two-inch pieces filled with a spicy fish stuffing. She took great care to preserve the pale-green color of this beguiling vegetable, cooking it just enough to prevent it from turning a dull green.

My first experience with raw artichoke hearts was in France. Sliced superfine, they looked like curly wood shavings. We dipped them in **virgin olive oil,** grated Parmesan cheese, and ground black pepper. We boiled the large artichokes whole, dipped their leaf bases in a rich hollandaise sauce, savoring the buttery soft hearts last.

Other cultures, too, have developed various ways with vegetables. Some of the world's best vegetable dishes come from India. In a country where vegetarianism flourishes, vegetable cooking is almost a ritual. Indian cooks deftly add, blend, and play with seductive flavors daily, perfecting the art of vegetarian cuisine: vegetables with potatoes or lentils, vegetables with rice, and vegetables with a wide variety of herbs and spices.

To me, vegetables are never monotonous; I cook them in many around-the-world ways. I grill eggplant, first slicing it lengthwise, with the slices still attached to the stem. Then I anoint it with a spice paste and brush it with olive oil while it grills. I stir-fry squash tips the Chinese way to preserve their color and nutrition, then serve them heaped and demurely spilling out of grilled tomato shells. My scooped, baked, golden-nugget, tiny pumpkins with nothing but a spicy chutney in them never fail to amaze my guests. Many detest bitter gourds, but not when I deep-fry them and toss them with tomatoes, fresh herbs, and a tasty lime juice dressing. I **braise** whole **endive** in beef broth and cream so they melt in the mouth, a dish I learned to make in France. (Yes, very rich. I don't serve it often.)

I give daily thanks for the beautiful, versatile bounty of vegetables everywhere. Spiced vegetables are no less nutritious than plain ones; I spice them with a light, loving hand—simply (and not so simply) seductive.

Vegetables

Asparagus Mousse

This dish was made for a dinner hosted by the president of Sri Lanka, Chandrika Bandaranaike Kumaratunge. The chief guest at the dinner for world leaders was Prince Charles of Britain.

Eggs and delicate asparagus benefit by the addition of sweet, aromatic **nutmeg.**

For Asparagus Mousse
8 three- to four-ounce molds
1 tablespoon vegetable oil
1 pound fresh green asparagus
2 cups water
2 tablespoons unsalted butter
1/4 cup white wine
Freshly ground black pepper and salt to taste
3/4 cup whole milk
1/2 cup full cream
2 large eggs
2 large egg yolks
1/8 teaspoon grated nutmeg

For Sauce
1/4 cup peeled, chopped asparagus stems (retained from asparagus used earlier in recipe)
1 shallot, peeled and chopped
3/4 cup white wine
3/4 cup full cream
3/4 cup sweet butter
Fresh lemon juice to taste
Salt to taste

For Garnish
*24 pieces **Tomato Confit** (see recipe, page 219)*
8 asparagus tips
Zest of 1 lemon
1/2 cup water
1 tablespoon unsalted butter
*1 **black truffle,** shaved into slivers*
*1 tablespoon **fennel** leaves*

Directions
Preheat oven to 225°F.

To make asparagus mousse, wipe molds and grease with oil. Trim off coarse ends of asparagus and peel stems (save 8 asparagus tips for garnish and a 1/4 cup white part of stems for sauce). Cut asparagus into 1/2-inch pieces; you need 2 cups asparagus for the mousse. Boil 2 cups water, add asparagus, and cook 3 to 4 minutes; strain. Heat butter in a pan. Add asparagus, wine, and salt and black pepper to taste, and cook 3 to 4 minutes. Place in a blender with milk and blend until smooth. Add cream, eggs, yolks, and nutmeg. Blend 10 seconds. Pour into molds and place in a baking pan. Pour hot water into the baking pan to come halfway up the molds. Cover with foil and bake for 20 to 25 minutes. Remove from oven. Let asparagus molds stand for 10 minutes.

For the sauce, place the chopped asparagus stems, shallots, and wine in a pan. Cook until reduced to a glaze. Add cream, reduce to a 1/2 cup, whisk in butter, and season with lemon juice and salt to taste. Strain the sauce.

For garnish, make cherry tomato confit. Cut each asparagus tip lengthwise into 3 pieces. **Julienne** the lemon zest. Bring 1/2 cup water and butter to a boil. Add asparagus tips and cook 1 minute. Add lemon zest julienne and immediately strain all.

Presentation
Unmold an asparagus mousse onto the center of each plate. Place 3 cherry tomato confit on 3 spots toward the edge of the plate. Place a cut asparagus tip, 2 truffle shavings, a few strands of lemon zest julienne, and fennel leaves by each tomato. Place 3 truffle shavings on the mousse and drizzle sauce around the mousse.

8 servings

Burst of Flavor

Acorn Squash with Honey and Roasted Coconut

A touch of honey added to the squash accents its natural sweetness. **Garam masala,** a blend of roasted spices, and the roasted coconut add a wonderful fragrance to the squash purée. Sri Lankans use grated coconut in spice blends that season squash and pumpkins. You can roast coconut in a moderately hot oven or brown in a skillet on moderate heat.

3 small acorn squash
$^1/_2$ cup water
2 tablespoons honey
$1^1/_2$ teaspoons garam masala
Salt to taste
Freshly ground black pepper to taste
$^1/_4$ cup oven-roasted, grated coconut
2 tablespoons roasted, chopped almonds

Directions
Preheat oven to 450°F.

Wash and halve squash; scrape off seeds with a spoon. Place hollow side down in baking pan, pour water, cover with foil, and bake for 30 to 35 minutes. Test for doneness; the flesh should be soft. Remove from oven. Reduce heat to 300°F.

When cool enough to handle, spoon out pulp, keeping the skin intact. In a medium-size bowl mash pulp; add honey, garam masala, and salt and black pepper to taste; mix well. Heap loosely in shells. Bake for 10 minutes at 300°F.

Presentation
Sprinkle with coconut and almonds, and serve hot.

6 servings

Curried Tomato

This tomato dish is delicious served with Indian breads or rice dishes and as a sauce for grilled meat and fish. The tomatoes blend with the sweet shallots and the nutty black **mustard** seeds, and the bite of the dill seed laced with the creamy sauce help bring out the luscious taste of each ingredient.

Cherish any leftovers; the dish tastes even better reheated a day or two later.

1 pound tomatoes, peeled
2 tablespoons olive oil
$^1/_2$ teaspoon black mustard seeds
$^1/_2$ teaspoon dill seeds
6 shallots, peeled and sliced thin
$^1/_2$ teaspoon grated ginger
$^1/_4$ teaspoon **turmeric**
$^1/_2$ teaspoon **cayenne pepper**
Salt to taste
$^1/_4$ cup full cream or buttermilk

Directions
Cut tomatoes into 1-inch cubes.

Heat oil on medium heat in a sauté pan. Add mustard and dill seeds, and fry until they start to splutter. Stir in shallots and sauté until golden. Add ginger, turmeric, and cayenne pepper; cook, stirring for 2 to 3 minutes, then add tomatoes along with salt to taste. Simmer uncovered for 10 minutes. Stir in cream or buttermilk gradually, to avoid curdling. Remove from heat.

6 servings

Curly Kale with Coconut

Sri Lankans consider greens an essential part of an everyday meal. They shred them fine and cook them with a little grated coconut. The coconut adds a creamy taste to the briefly cooked greens and a dash of **turmeric** gives them a blush of yellow. The beauty of the dish is in the finely shredded greens.

As a child, I was fascinated to watch our household's favorite kitchen help shredding greens for our daily meals. Seated on a low stool, she had a chopping knife propped on a block of wood with the knife handle gripped between her toes, so the knife blade only extended over a flat reed basket. She would gather the greens into a neat, tight bundle in one hand and deftly brush the greens back and forth against the knife. The sheer, green shreds ingeniously fell into the clean reed basket! This style of shredding has almost disappeared, but *mallung* still remains a big part of a Sri Lankan meal.

1 pound curly kale, washed
1 shallot, peeled and thinly sliced
1 fresh chili, seeded and sliced
1/8 teaspoon turmeric
2 tablespoons water
Salt to taste
1/4 cup shredded coconut
Fresh lemon juice to taste

Directions

Trim kale leaves, discarding tough stems and midribs. Shred finely. Place kale, shallot, chili, turmeric, and water in a pan, and add salt to taste. Cover, bring to a simmer, and cook on low heat for 6 minutes.

Uncover, add coconut, and cook until moisture evaporates, 3 to 4 minutes. Stir in lemon juice to taste.

4 servings

Stir-Fried Cauliflower

Plain, steamed cauliflower can look and taste boring. Here the spices transform the crunchy vegetable into a colorful and tasty side dish. The fried spices add a nutty taste and also perfume the cooking oil with their scent. Even nonvegetarians relish this spice-specked, golden-hued dish. **Turmeric** must be used sparingly in vegetable dishes. If it is overdone, it leaves a garish yellow color and a bitter taste.

1 small head cauliflower, about 1 pound
2 teaspoons olive oil
1 tablespoon chopped yellow onion
*1/2 teaspoon black **mustard seeds***
*1/4 teaspoon **cumin** seeds*
1/8 teaspoon turmeric
Sea salt to taste
2 tablespoons water

Directions

Trim cauliflower, wash, and cut into florets. Heat oil on medium heat in a wok. Add onion and stir-fry for 1 minute. Stir in mustard and cumin seeds; when they start to pop, add turmeric and cauliflower. Stir-fry to combine well and season with sea salt to taste. Sprinkle with water, cover, and let steam for 5 minutes.

4 to 5 servings

Vegetables

Balsamic-Roasted Garlic and Onions

These glazed onions and garlic with a hint of **cinnamon** make a marvelous side dish with roasted poultry or game. Strewn around a Christmas turkey or goose, they give the dish a festive look and rich taste to match the meat.

24 pearl onions, peeled
24 garlic cloves, peeled
1½ cups **balsamic vinegar**
Juice of 2 oranges
1-inch piece of cinnamon stick
Pinch of salt

Directions

Preheat oven to 325°F.

Place all the ingredients in a baking pan, and bake for 1 to 1½ hours. Shake the pan twice while roasting. The balsamic vinegar will cook to a glaze.

Remove cinnamon stick before serving.

12 servings

Red Cabbage with Apples

This dish is a tasty and highly compatible vegetable accompaniment to pork and duck. The cider vinegar and green apples with a dash of brown sugar give the cabbage a balanced sweet-and-sour taste. **Cinnamon** leaves a subtle scent in the cabbage.

1 small red cabbage
2 pints water
2 tablespoons cider vinegar
1 tablespoon olive oil
1 yellow onion, peeled and thinly sliced
2 green apples, peeled, cored, and
    sliced ¼-inch thick
1 tablespoon light brown sugar
¾ cup apple cider or apple juice
1-inch piece of cinnamon stick
Salt to taste
Freshly ground black pepper to taste

Directions

Quarter cabbage, remove and discard core, and shred thinly. Cook in 2 pints boiling water for 3 minutes. Strain off water and add vinegar to the cabbage.

Heat oil on medium heat in sauté pan, cook onion and apples until onions are soft, about 5 minutes. Add cabbage and remaining ingredients with salt and black pepper to taste; stir to combine. Cover pan and cook on low heat for 40 minutes, stirring occasionally.

4 to 5 servings

Burst of Flavor

Glazed Baby Beets

Beets are great as a hot vegetable to accompany fish or meat. I serve these spice-specked, glazed beets with **endive** as a warm salad. Instead of grinding the spices, I simply crush them; they add texture to the soft, melt-in-the-mouth beets.

12 baby beets
2 cups cold water
*2 tablespoons **balsamic vinegar***
2 tablespoons red wine
*½ teaspoon crushed **coriander** seeds*
¼ teaspoon cracked black peppercorns
Juice of 1 orange
1 teaspoon sugar
1 tablespoon olive oil
Salt to taste

Directions

Place beets in a pan with cold water. Bring to a simmer, cover pan, and cook 35 minutes. Rub off skins, trim tops and tails, and cut in quarters.

Place vinegar, wine, spices, orange juice, and sugar in a small sauté pan. Cook 2 to 3 minutes to reduce to a glaze, about 3 tablespoons.

Add beets and olive oil, season with salt to taste, and toss to combine well.

4 servings

Creamy Jerusalem Artichokes

Jerusalem artichokes are not starchy and are rather bland if not complemented with butter and cream. I enhance the dish with **turmeric** and **coriander.** These two spices are often used in spice blends for vegetable curries back home. They give color and a lemon fragrance to the vegetables.

1½ pounds Jerusalem artichokes
2 cups water
Juice of ½ lemon
2 teaspoons olive oil
1 teaspoon minced shallots
1 teaspoon minced garlic
⅛ teaspoon turmeric
⅛ teaspoon ground coriander
*¼ cup **Defatted Chicken Stock** (see recipe, page 45)*
Salt to taste
Freshly ground black pepper to taste
2 tablespoons full cream or buttermilk
1 tablespoon unsalted butter

Directions

Peel Jerusalem artichokes, wash, slice thin, and place in 2 cups water with lemon juice. Heat oil on low heat in a pan; add shallots and garlic and cook about 5 minutes. Stir in turmeric and coriander, drain and add artichokes, and mix to combine with the spices. Pour in stock and season with salt and black pepper to taste. Cover pan and cook on medium heat for 3 to 4 minutes or until the cooking liquid reduces to a glaze. Whisk in the cream or buttermilk and butter.

4 to 5 servings

Vegetables

Goat Cheese-Stuffed Squash Blossoms

Ajowan seeds, when cooked, give the fragrance of thyme and blend well with the slight tang of the goat cheese. All the taste elements—creamy, sweet, and tangy—come together harmoniously in this dish.

4 squash blossoms

Stuffing

2 teaspoons olive oil
1/2 teaspoon ajowan seeds
2 tablespoons finely chopped shallots
1 cup goat cheese
2 tablespoons chopped green onion
Salt to taste
Freshly ground black pepper to taste

Garnish

1 yellow beefsteak tomato
1 red beefsteak tomato
1 tablespoon olive oil
1 yellow onion, peeled, sliced, and loosened
  into rings
8 squash vine tips
*2 tablespoons **Vegetable Stock** (see recipe,*
  page 46)
Salt to taste
Freshly ground black pepper to taste

To Cook Stuffed Squash Blossoms

1 1/2 cups vegetable stock
1 tablespoon unsalted butter

Directions

Pluck and discard the sepals of the squash blossoms. Open the petals and remove and discard the stamens.

For the stuffing, heat 2 teaspoons olive oil. Add ajowan seeds and cook on low heat a few seconds until the seeds start to splutter. Add shallots and cook 2 to 3 minutes. Remove from heat and spoon onto the goat cheese. Add green onion and season with salt and black pepper to taste. Mix lightly and cool.

Fill the squash blossoms with the goat cheese stuffing and place in the refrigerator.

To prepare the garnish, peel the tomatoes, seed and cut into small dice, and set aside. Heat olive oil in a pan, add onion rings, and cook on low heat until transparent. Remove onion and set aside. To the pan, add the squash vine tips, tomatoes, and vegetable stock with salt and black pepper to taste. Cook for 2 to 3 minutes until vine tips are wilted, remove from pan, and set aside.

To cook the stuffed squash blossoms, pour vegetable stock into the same pan, reduce to 1/2 cup, and whisk in the butter. Add the squash blossoms and cook 1 minute on low heat. Turn the blossoms over and cook 1 minute more.

Presentation

Place cooked onions in the center of the dinner plates with the squash vine tips on either side of the onion. Spoon the tomatoes around. Place squash blossoms on the onions and spoon the remaining pan juices onto the plates. Grind black pepper on the squash blossoms.

4 servings

Sherried Sweet Potatoes

Sweet potatoes are naturally sweet, but sugar is added in this recipe to create a caramel glaze on them. **Garam masala,** a blend of roasted ground spices, is sprinkled on the dish as a final touch. Sprinkling aromatic, roasted ground spices over cooked food is common practice in Sri Lankan cooking. Here the spices help to tone down the richness of this dish. These delicious sweet potatoes may be placed around roasted birds.

6 to 8 small sweet potatoes, washed thoroughly
1 tablespoon olive oil

Glaze
¼ cup dark brown sugar
¼ cup sherry
Juice and grated rind of 1 orange

Garnish
½ teaspoon garam masala

Directions
Preheat oven to 375°F.

Halve the sweet potatoes lengthwise. Coat with olive oil. Place cut sides down in a roasting pan and roast them in the oven for 40 minutes or until cooked through yet still firm.

Turn sweet potatoes cut side up. For the glaze, mix sugar, sherry, orange juice, and rind, and spoon on the potatoes. Roast 10 more minutes. Remove from oven and sprinkle with garam masala. Serve hot.

6 servings

Roasted Red Potatoes

It doesn't take very long to prepare these aromatic potatoes. Thyme sprigs are added to perfume the oil used to roast them and may be removed before serving. **Ajowan** seeds, added halfway during cooking, remain to give an aromatic bite to the potatoes. Ajowan and thyme have a similar fragrance, and they both lace the potatoes with a subtle aroma.

1½ pounds medium red potatoes, washed
2 tablespoons olive oil
6 shallots, peeled and sliced
2 sprigs of thyme
Salt to taste
Freshly ground black pepper to taste
¼ cup water
½ teaspoon ajowan seeds

Directions
Preheat oven to 300°F.

Place unpeeled potatoes in a roasting pan. Heat oil in sauté pan; add shallots and thyme. Sauté until shallots are light gold. Pour over the potatoes; sprinkle with salt and black pepper to taste. Pour ¼ cup water into roasting pan. Roast in the preheated oven, occasionally moving potatoes around in the pan; if potatoes are browning too fast, cover with foil. Mix in ajowan seeds after potatoes have roasted about 20 minutes.

After 45 minutes, check for doneness by piercing the potatoes with a knife. The water should have evaporated, and the potatoes should be soft inside, crisp and golden in spots on the outside. Serve hot.

4 to 5 servings

Spicy Kabocha Pumpkin

The method I use in this recipe is a common way to cook pumpkin back home in Sri Lanka, but it traditionally calls for coconut milk. Instead of coconut milk, I use buttermilk or cream, which makes the dish taste richer. Use any sweet pumpkin for this recipe. Serve as an accompaniment to roast turkey for a special Thanksgiving dinner.

2 pounds kabocha pumpkin
2 teaspoons grated coconut
2 teaspoons uncooked rice
1 tablespoon chopped yellow onion
¼ teaspoon freshly ground black pepper
1 teaspoon **turmeric**
1 teaspoon grated ginger
1 teaspoon grated garlic
¾ cup water
1 tablespoon Dijon mustard
½ cup buttermilk
Salt to taste

Directions

Peel pumpkin and remove seeds; cut into 1-inch cubes and place in a pan.

In a skillet, roast coconut, rice, and onion to a dark chocolate brown, about 5 minutes; blend in a spice grinder until smooth. Add mixture to pumpkin, with black pepper, turmeric, ginger, and garlic. Add water, stir, cover, and simmer until pumpkin is soft but not mushy, about 25 minutes.

In a small bowl, stir mustard into buttermilk and carefully fold into pumpkin. Season with salt to taste. Simmer for 2 minutes on low heat.

8 servings

Deviled Potatoes

Its name sounds hot, but the seasonings give this dish just the perfect perk. Potatoes have a plain taste that allows them to absorb the flavors of the seasonings and spices. Serve in place of common mashed potatoes for a change.

1½ pounds baking potatoes, scrubbed and washed in cold water
4 cups water
3 tablespoons olive oil
2 medium yellow onions, peeled, halved, and thinly sliced
4 garlic cloves, thinly sliced
1 teaspoon crushed red pepper flakes
⅛ teaspoon paprika
⅛ teaspoon **turmeric**
Salt to taste

Directions

Place potatoes in a saucepan with 4 cups water to cover and cook until soft, about 45 minutes. Peel and cut into 1-inch cubes.

Heat oil in a skillet; add onions and garlic, and sauté on low heat for 5 to 6 minutes. Stir in crushed red pepper flakes, paprika, and turmeric. Cook for 2 minutes.

Mix in potatoes with salt to taste. Cook on low heat for 10 minutes, turning and folding the potatoes with a spatula.

4 to 5 servings

Herbed Potato Purée

Potatoes have a melting effect on flavorings, so I use lots of herbs and a dash of **nutmeg.** Tinted green with puréed herbs, this dish is good to accompany fish, poultry, or meat dishes.

1½ pounds baking potatoes, peeled
4 cups cold water
Salt to taste
8 cloves garlic, peeled
1 cup whole garden mint leaves (reserve picked stems)
1 cup chopped green basil leaves (reserve picked stems)
Freshly ground black pepper to taste
½ cup buttermilk
⅛ teaspoon freshly ground nutmeg

Directions

Place potatoes in a pan with cold water to cover; add salt to taste. Bring to a boil. Add garlic along with picked stems of mint and basil. Cover and simmer about 30 minutes until potatoes are tender when tested with a knife. Remove potatoes and garlic from liquid. Measure and reserve ½ cup of cooking liquid; discard mint and basil stems and the remaining liquid. Return potatoes and garlic to pan; stir over low heat to dry out excess moisture.

Pass potatoes and garlic through a sieve and return to pan. Blanch mint and basil leaves for 5 seconds; purée with reserved cooking liquid. Stir puréed mint and basil into potatoes along with salt and black pepper to taste. Cook on low heat, stirring continuously for about 4 minutes. Stir in buttermilk and nutmeg, and cook 1 minute.

4 to 5 servings

Spicy Potato Cakes

These golden-brown potato cakes, spiked with coarse spices, are great with meat dishes. They can also be served on a vegetable platter.

1 pound baking potatoes
3 tablespoons olive oil
2 shallots, peeled and chopped fine
1 teaspoon cracked black peppercorns
*1 teaspoon **coriander** seeds, coarsely ground*
*1 teaspoon **cumin** seeds, coarsely ground*
Salt to taste

Directions

Preheat oven to 400°F.

Peel potatoes, grate into large shreds, and squeeze out as much water as possible. Place on kitchen towel and wipe dry.

Put 1 tablespoon olive oil in an 8-inch skillet. Add shallots and spices; sauté, stirring for about 3 minutes to brown shallots. Scrape onto the potatoes. Wipe the skillet, add the remaining oil, and place on high heat. Season potatoes with salt to taste, mix well, and add to the hot skillet.

Using a spatula, push down and spread out potatoes into a compact cake. Turn down heat, cook for 4 minutes, and then turn cake over. Press down and cook for another 4 minutes. The potato cake should be brown on both sides but raw inside. Place the skillet with the potato cake in the preheated oven for 10 to 12 minutes. Cut into 4 wedges. Serve hot.

4 servings

Creamy Winter Melon

The sheer bulk of a whole winter melon deters many from buying it, but it is a delicious vegetable. It is now available cut up in quarters in supermarkets. **Turmeric** gives a tempting color to the dish, and a light-handed dash of **coriander** gives a hint of lemony-spice flavor. Mustard and cream are a luscious combination and act as a tangy thickener. The resulting sauce is delicious and just right for grilled spicy beef or chicken.

1 pound winter melon (peeled and seeded
   before weighing)
1/4 teaspoon turmeric
1/2 teaspoon ground coriander
1 peeled and sliced shallot
2 tablespoons **Defatted Chicken Stock**
   (see recipe, page 45) or water
1 teaspoon Dijon mustard
1/4 cup full cream
Salt to taste

Directions

Cut melon into 2-inch squares. Place in a pan with spices, shallot, and chicken broth. Cover and cook on low heat until melon turns translucent, about 15 minutes. There should be no more than 1 tablespoon of liquid.

In a small bowl, mix mustard with cream, add to winter melon, and stir to combine. Season with salt to taste. Simmer on low heat for 1 minute.

4 servings

Tomato and Eggplant

These two vegetables seem to be made for each other. Use purple eggplant and ripe tomatoes for the dish. I use a blend of spices commonly used in Sri Lanka: hot **cayenne** or **pepper, turmeric, cumin,** and **coriander.** In balanced portions they give a subtle spicy flavor to the vegetables. This dish goes well with lamb.

1 pound eggplant, peeled and cut into
   1/2-inch cubes
2 teaspoons salt
2 tablespoons olive oil
1 yellow onion, peeled and thinly sliced
1 teaspoon grated ginger
1 teaspoon grated garlic
1/2 teaspoon cayenne pepper
1/4 teaspoon turmeric
1/2 teaspoon ground cumin
1/2 teaspoon ground coriander
3/4 pound tomatoes, peeled, seeded, and cut
   into 1/2-inch cubes
Salt to taste

Directions

Place eggplant in a bowl, sprinkle with salt, and set aside for 10 minutes. Wash and wipe dry. Heat olive oil in a skillet, add onion and eggplant, and sauté on high heat until eggplant is soft, about 8 minutes. Add ginger, garlic, and remaining spices. Stir to combine.

Add tomatoes; season with salt to taste. Cook for 6 minutes on low heat, shaking the skillet to keep vegetables from sticking to the bottom of the pan.

4 servings

Creamy Saffron Spinach

Cooked spinach often shows up on Sri Lankan tables, but in my family I was the only child who loved it, especially when it appeared with a velvety yellow sauce clinging to the dark green, satiny leaves. Milk from freshly grated coconut provided the creaminess; freshly ground **turmeric** lent the sunny color.

It is hard to surpass a childhood memory, but this version, using **saffron** and cream enhanced with a hint of **nutmeg,** is even better.

2 bunches spinach leaves
Salt to taste
Freshly ground black pepper to taste
Pinch of saffron threads
1 tablespoon hot water
½ cup full cream
Pinch of grated nutmeg

Directions
To trim spinach, remove stems and heavy midribs without breaking leaves apart. Wash in several changes of water, moving spinach around to allow sand and dirt to sink to the bottom. Lift leaves from water, drain in colander, and spin dry.

Place spinach in a sauté pan; cook on high heat for about 2 minutes, turning with tongs. Move spinach to the side and reduce juices partially, about 3 minutes. Stir in salt and black pepper to taste. Add saffron to 1 tablespoon hot water in a cup. Add saffron water and cream to the spinach. Grate nutmeg over the spinach, stir, and bring to slow simmer. Serve hot.

4 servings

Stuffed Baked Tomatoes

The stuffing, creamy and slightly sweet, is lightly seasoned to bring out the best in the tomatoes. Serve them on a bed of **Creamy Saffron Spinach** (see recipe at left).

2 cups water
4 medium-size vine-ripened tomatoes
2 cups ice water

For Stuffing
*1 cup **Paneer** (see recipe, page 242)*
½ teaspoon each grated ginger and garlic
1 tablespoon chopped green onion
1 tablespoon chopped roasted pine nuts
Salt to taste
Freshly ground black pepper to taste

For Baking
1 tablespoon olive oil

Directions
Boil 2 cups water, add tomatoes, cook for 20 seconds, and then place tomatoes in ice water for 5 minutes. Make a cut at the bottom of each tomato and pull the skin up toward the stem ends. Using the skin, form a rose shape around the stem. Cut a slice off each tomato with the rose still intact; set aside to use as the garnish.

Preheat oven to 350°F. Scoop out the pulp of the cut tomatoes; place cut side down on a plate to drain off excess juice. Mix ingredients for stuffing with salt and black pepper to taste; fill tomato shells and place in an ovenproof casserole dish. Drizzle with olive oil and bake in the preheated oven for 10 minutes.

Presentation
Spoon creamy saffron spinach on plates. Place stuffed tomatoes on spinach and top with a tomato skin rose.

4 servings

Grilled Vegetables with Goat Cheese Tart

This dish combines many pleasing textures, from the crunchy vegetables and melt-in-the-mouth goat cheese to the delicate crack of the phyllo pastry. The only spice used is the black pepper in the pastry.

Vegetables

2 yellow squash, halved lengthwise
4 green onions, trimmed
1 long eggplant, sliced lengthwise and halved
1 red bell pepper, sliced and seeded
1 small green zucchini, sliced diagonally
   ¼-inch thick
1 lotus root, peeled and sliced ¼-inch thick

Marinade

2 tablespoons olive oil
1 teaspoon minced garlic
2 tablespoons orange juice
Salt to taste

Tomato Relish

2 tomatoes, peeled, seeded, and diced
1 teaspoon chopped yellow onion
1 teaspoon chopped green onion
1 tablespoon orange juice
1 tablespoon fresh lemon juice
Salt to taste
Freshly ground black pepper to taste

Goat Cheese Tarts

3 sheets of phyllo dough
2 tablespoons unsalted butter, melted
Freshly ground black pepper to taste
4 two-ounce molds
2 medium eggs
½ cup whipping cream
½ cup goat cheese, crumbled
Grated zest of 1 orange
*Pinch of **nutmeg***
Salt to taste

Glaze

¼ cup orange juice
¼ cup balsamic vinegar
¼ cup red wine

Garnish

4 sprigs of rosemary

Directions

Preheat oven to 375°F.

Place the vegetables in a medium-size bowl, add the marinade, and set aside. Turn on the grill. Place ingredients for relish in a small bowl, season with salt and black pepper to taste, toss, and refrigerate.

To make the goat cheese tarts, lay a sheet of phyllo on a cutting board, brush with butter, and grind black pepper to taste over all. Similarly layer 2 more sheets of phyllo, seasoning each with the butter and black pepper. Cut the stack of phyllo sheets into 4 squares. Line the 4 molds with the phyllo squares, letting the phyllo edges stand out of the molds. Place the molds on a baking sheet.

Beat the eggs, cream, goat cheese, and seasonings. Pour into the molds and brush the edges of the pastry with butter. Bake in the preheated oven for 8 minutes.

For the glaze, place all the ingredients in a small sauté pan and reduce to 2 tablespoons.

Grill the vegetables about 3 minutes on each side.

Presentation

Arrange vegetables on a plate, remove goat cheese tarts from the molds, and place on the vegetables. Spoon tomato relish on the plate. Drizzle glaze around the vegetables and garnish with rosemary sprigs.

4 servings

Burst of Flavor

Butternut Squash and Apple Compote

Honey accents the butternut squash, and **garam masala** enriches and weaves together the flavors of the fruits and honey with the squash. Garam masala, a blend of roasted, ground, aromatic spices always takes squash and pumpkin to new heights.

1 small butternut squash, peeled and cut
  into 1-inch cubes
4 cups water
2 green apples, peeled, cored, and cut into
  1-inch cubes
Juice of 2 oranges
Zest of 1 orange
1 cup white wine
2 tablespoons honey
1 tablespoon light brown sugar
1 teaspoon garam masala
Juice of 1 lemon
Salt to taste

Directions
Steam squash for 10 minutes over 4 cups boiling water. Place apples in pan with orange juice, zest, and white wine. Cook on low heat until apples are soft but can still hold their shape (about 6 minutes).

Add squash, honey, sugar, garam masala, and lemon juice with salt to taste. Cook on moderate heat for about 10 minutes to glaze.

8 to 10 servings

Parsnip Purée

Parsnip is a delicious vegetable that is light and delicate. It partners well with salmon. A pinch of **nutmeg** always enhances creamy dishes. It is best to grate nutmeg straight into the purée toward the end of cooking.

5 parsnips, peeled
2 russet potatoes, peeled
6 cups cold water
¼ cup full cream
2 tablespoons butter
Salt to taste
Freshly ground black pepper to taste
Pinch of grated nutmeg

Directions
Peel parsnips and potatoes, wash, and dice into 1-inch cubes. Add cold water to cover vegetables and boil until soft, about 30 minutes.

Drain and purée parsnips and potatoes in a food mill. Place in a pot, add cream and butter, season with salt, pepper, and nutmeg to taste. Cook on low heat for 3 to 4 minutes.

Yields 3 cups

Mashed Potatoes with Black Mustard Seeds

Potatoes have a mellowing effect on added flavorings. They call for more spices than do other vegetables to perk up flavors.

1½ pounds baking potatoes, scrubbed and washed
6 cups cold water
2 tablespoons olive oil
2 yellow onions, peeled, halved, and thinly sliced
1 sprig curry leaves, optional
1½ teaspoons black mustard seeds
½ teaspoon crushed cumin seeds
⅛ teaspoon turmeric
⅛ teaspoon paprika
Salt to taste

Directions

Preheat oven to 375°F.

Place potatoes in a saucepan in 6 cups cold water to cover. Cook on high heat for 45 minutes or until soft. Peel and smash the potatoes. (The potatoes must still remain in large lumps.)

Heat oil in a skillet; add onions and sauté 6 to 8 minutes until onions are a light gold color. Add curry leaves, mustard seeds, and cumin seeds; cook for 2 minutes, until seeds start to splutter. Stir in turmeric and paprika. Cook for 1 minute on medium heat.

Add potatoes with salt to taste. Using a spatula, keep moving the potatoes in the skillet to combine with onions and the spices over high heat for 5 minutes. Transfer all the skillet contents to a baking pan and bake for 20 minutes. When done cooking, the potatoes should still remain lumpy.

5 to 6 servings

Spicy Sautéed Cabbage

This delicious cabbage dish is elegant and easy to make. The shredded cabbage is steam-cooked in spiced oil and is tinted with the light hue of **turmeric.**

1 medium white head cabbage
2 tablespoons olive oil
2 tablespoons sliced shallots
1 teaspoon black mustard seeds
1 teaspoon coarse-ground cumin
½ teaspoon crushed red pepper flakes
⅛ teaspoon turmeric
Salt to taste

Directions

Wash and cut cabbage into quarters. Remove core and shred into ⅛-inch strips.

Heat oil in a sauté pan on medium heat; add shallots and cook for 2 minutes, until wilted. Turn heat to moderate and add mustard and cumin seeds. When they start to pop, add the rest of the spices. Stir and cook for 1 minute. Add cabbage and sprinkle with salt to taste. Turn heat to low, cover pan, and steam 2 to 3 minutes.

4 to 5 servings

Vegetables

Legumes . . .

Legacy from the East

Lentils, beans, and peas are all categorized as legumes. The biblical Esau sold his birthright to Jacob for a potage of lentils, a legume that dates from early Aryan times in India. India remains the greatest legume-consuming country in the world, with an immense repertoire of tasty dishes. Legumes are also widely used in Sri Lanka and are loved by rich and poor, adults and children alike.

Like most Sri Lankan children, I relished legume dishes; legumes were comfort food. They were an integral part of at least one daily meal—breakfast, lunch, or dinner. I loved creamy **pink lentils** simmered with dark-green spinach leaves, gently spiced for exquisite flavor. Other dishes worthy of note were whole **mung beans,** cooked to a velvety smoothness and spiced with a moist paste of ground coconut, mustard, garlic, and shallots; and soft-cooked **chickpeas,** tossed in hot oil flavored by browning sliced shallots, black **mustard** seeds, and whole red chilies. The crispy tidbits speckled the melt-in-the-mouth chickpeas, a delicious breakfast or snack packed with nutrition.

You can cook legumes with lean meats and vegetables and serve them as main dishes. You can also prepare them in spicy sauces and serve them as tasty accompaniments to meats, fish, or rice. Legumes can be used in soups, salads, stews, or made into purées of different textures, ranging from silky to velvety smooth; as purées, they can be used as a side dish to serve with poultry or meat. Milled to a flour, legumes bring character to pancakes, crêpes, and fritters. Sprouted, they are low in calories and easy to digest.

Herbs and spices flavor some of these dishes; fragrant, spice-infused oils further enrich a few. Buttermilk, curds, and yogurt turn a humble potage into an exciting dish. All are a far cry from Jacob's potage of lentils, but close in spirit to Asia's approach to nutritious eating.

Most packaged legumes available in supermarkets and health food stores in the United States are clean and devoid of all foreign material. Some imported varieties need to be picked through and washed clean.

To wash legumes, place them in a colander under cold running water; rub between your fingers for a minute. Repeat process three times.

Soak unhulled legumes like chickpeas, mung beans, and **red kidney beans** at least 3 to 4 hours before cooking. Pour off soaking water and use fresh water to cook.

Cook legumes thoroughly to help break down the starches and aid digestion. If you pressure-cook them, fill cooker not more than halfway to prevent clogging the vent.

One cup of dry legumes makes approximately 2½ cups cooked.

Pickled Onion and Bean Salad with Poached Fish

Three different kinds of onion, pickled in a spicy mix, add zip to the generally bland beans in this salad. Use any firm-fleshed fish you like. Serve this salad with brown bread and butter. Lavosh is a good accompaniment, too.

Pickled Onion

1 yellow onion, peeled and sliced
1 red onion, peeled and sliced
16 spring onions, peeled, tops removed
1 cup white wine vinegar
³⁄₄ cup sugar
1 bay leaf
1-inch piece of **cinnamon** *stick*
Sea salt to taste

For Salad

¹⁄₄ cup **red kidney beans**
¹⁄₄ cup **navy beans**
2 cups cold water
1 red bell pepper
¹⁄₄ cup cut chives, with flower buds
  (1-inch lengths)
1 teaspoon freshly grated horseradish
¹⁄₄ cup garden mint leaves
12 yellow cherry tomatoes
¹⁄₄ cup olive oil
Fresh lemon juice to taste
Sea salt to taste
Freshly ground black pepper to taste

Poached Fish

1 cup water
2 tablespoons white wine vinegar
1 bay leaf
1-inch piece of cinnamon stick
2 teaspoons chopped garlic
Juice of 1 lemon
4 sprigs of garden mint
¹⁄₂ pound fish fillet
Sea salt and freshly ground black pepper to taste

Directions

Place onions and spring onions in a jar. In a **nonreactive** pan, heat up vinegar, sugar, bay leaf, and cinnamon with sea salt to taste. Bring to a boil and pour over onions. Cover jar, cool, and refrigerate for 2 days.

For salad, soak kidney beans and navy beans in cold water overnight. Drain beans and place in a saucepan with 2 cups fresh, cold water. Bring to a boil, lower heat, and simmer for 40 minutes or until beans are soft. Strain from cooking liquid and place in a medium-size bowl.

Cook the bell pepper over a very hot grill until the skin is charred. Peel the pepper; then cut it open and remove the seeds. Cut into thin strips. Add to the beans with chives, horseradish, mint leaves, cherry tomatoes, and olive oil. Toss, adding lemon juice, and sea salt and black pepper to taste. Put aside to marinate.

For poaching the fish, place 1 cup water, vinegar, bay leaf, cinnamon, garlic, lemon juice, and mint in a pan. Place the fish in the liquid, season with sea salt and black pepper to taste, cover pan, and let simmer for 4 to 5 minutes. Cool the fish in the poaching liquid.

Presentation

Pick sliced onions and spring onions from the pickling liquid and add to the salad. Toss gently to combine. Flake the fish and fold into the salad with a spoon of poaching liquid. Arrange on salad plates and serve at room temperature.

4 servings

Mung Bean Salad

Mung beans are also known as green gram beans. When husked, cleaned, and split, they are yellow in color. Husked mung beans cook fast and are easy to digest. When done cooking, they will be crunchy. The black **mustard seeds** fried in oil emanate a nutty aroma and add taste to the beans.

¼ cup husked mung beans
1 cup water
1 cup peeled, sliced cucumber
2 tablespoons chopped Chinese parsley
1 tablespoon chopped green onion
¼ cup grated fresh coconut
1 tablespoon diced red bell pepper
2 tablespoons diced tomato
1 tablespoon olive oil
1 teaspoon black mustard seeds
*1 sprig **curry leaves***
¼ teaspoon crushed red pepper flakes
Salt to taste
Fresh lemon juice to taste

Garnish
4 sprigs of Chinese parsley

Directions
Place mung beans in a pan, add 1 cup water, and cook on moderate heat for 10 minutes. Drain and cool. Add cucumber, parsley, onion, coconut, bell pepper, and tomato. Heat oil on medium heat in a sauté pan; fry mustard seeds and curry leaves. When seeds begin to pop, stir in red pepper flakes and add all to the mung beans. Season with salt and lemon juice to taste. Chill.

Presentation
Spoon onto chilled plates and garnish with Chinese parsley.

6 servings

Pink Lentils with Coconut

This simple but nourishing dish has great serving possibilities. Place grilled beef on a heaping of these lentils. With lentils, the serving portion of beef can be much smaller because lentils are rich in protein-nitrogen compounds.

*1 cup **pink lentils***
1 cup water
1 tablespoon finely chopped onion
2 teaspoons chopped ginger
1 teaspoon chopped garlic
*1 **green chili,** seeded and chopped*
*1 teaspoon ground **cumin***
*1 teaspoon **turmeric***
1 tablespoon chopped almonds
2 tablespoons grated coconut
Salt to taste

Directions
Wash lentils, place in a pan with 1 cup water, and cook until they are soft but not mushy, 15 to 20 minutes. Add onion, ginger, garlic, green chili, cumin, turmeric, almonds, and coconut, and season with salt to taste. Cover pan tightly. Cook on low heat for 5 minutes. Stir to combine. Serve hot.

4 servings

Burst of Flavor

Toor Dal with Spinach

Toor dal, like the other legumes, is naturally bland. In the final cooking stage, it is aromatized and flavor-enriched with spices and onion fried in oil to a rich dark color.

1 cup toor dal
2 cups hot water
2 ½ cups water
½ teaspoon **turmeric**
½ teaspoon ground **coriander**
Salt to taste
1 bunch of spinach leaves, trimmed and washed
½ cup buttermilk
2 tablespoons olive oil
1 teaspoon **cumin** seeds
½ small yellow onion, peeled and
  thinly sliced lengthwise

Directions

Wash toor dal. Place in a pan and cover with 2 cups hot water. Soak 5 hours or overnight. Drain and discard soaking water. Place toor dal in a saucepan with 2½ cups water and the spices. Bring to boil, stirring a few times to avoid lumps. Reduce heat to medium, partially cover pan, and cook until very soft, about 45 minutes. Test by pressing toor dal between a finger and thumb; if not soft enough, add hot water as needed and cook for 10 more minutes. Season with salt to taste, add spinach, cover, and simmer for 3 minutes. Gradually stir in buttermilk and turn off heat.

Heat oil in a separate pan. When very hot, add cumin seeds; when brown (in 2 to 3 seconds), add onions and cook on medium-high heat until onion turns dark golden. Add cooked toor dal. Stir and serve hot.

6 servings

Pink Lentils with Angel Hair Pasta

Lentils and angel hair pasta are combined successfully here. Both are delicate and have only a hint of spices. Serve with a main course of chicken or seafood.

½ cup **pink lentils**
1½ cups water
2 ounces angel hair pasta
1½ cups boiling water
½ teaspoon salt
2 tablespoons olive oil
1 small yellow onion, peeled, halved,
  and sliced lengthwise
1 teaspoon chopped garlic
1 teaspoon ground **cumin**
2 **green chilies,** halved, seeded, and sliced
1 tablespoon coarsely snipped chives
2 tablespoons chopped tomatoes
Salt to taste
Freshly ground black pepper to taste

Directions

Wash lentils. Place in a saucepan with 1½ cups water to cover. Simmer 15 to 20 minutes until cooked through. Lentils should be soft when pressed between finger and thumb. Strain off water and reserve lentils.

Break pasta into 1-inch lengths. Cook in boiling salted water for 3 minutes. Strain off water and reserve pasta.

In a wide sauté or frying pan, heat olive oil. Add onions and garlic, and cook 5 minutes on low heat. Add ground cumin, chilies, chives, tomatoes, lentils, pasta, and salt and black pepper to taste. Toss and cook for 2 to 3 minutes until heated through.

4 servings

Stew of Urad Dal with Vegetables

Like other legumes, **urad dal** can be rather bland on its own. I cook spices and sliced onion in olive oil and, with added liquid, use this mixture as a base to gently stew the vegetables before adding them to the cooked *urad dal*. This process enriches the stew, and the **tamarind** gives the final zing.

Ginger, **fenugreek,** and dill seeds all aid digestion as well as contribute to the flavor. Substitute your choice of vegetables in the stew. Sometimes I add a final handful of cleaned and trimmed fresh spinach leaves.

½ cup urad dal
2 cups water
1 tablespoon grated ginger

To Enrich Dal Stew
3 tablespoons olive oil
*1 teaspoon black **mustard seeds***
1 teaspoon fenugreek seeds
½ teaspoon dill seeds
1 yellow onion, peeled and sliced
*1 sprig **curry leaves***
*½ teaspoon **cayenne pepper***
*⅛ teaspoon **turmeric***

Vegetables
1 red potato, cut into wedges with peel intact
4 baby carrots
½ cup cauliflower sprigs
8 baby whole red onions, peeled
1 cup water
4 wing beans, trimmed and cut into halves
1 large tomato, cut into wedges
Handful of broken-up curly kale leaves

Seasonings
*2 tablespoons **Tamarind Juice** (see recipe, page 203)*
Salt to taste

Directions
Wash urad dal. Place in a medium-size bowl with water to cover and soak for 2 hours. Drain and discard soaking water. Place urad dal in a pan with 2 cups water and ginger, and bring to a boil. Stir a few times to keep urad dal from forming into lumps. Reduce heat to medium, partially cover pan, and cook for 30 minutes. The urad dal should be soft when tested; about 1 cup of liquid should remain in the pan. Turn off heat and keep hot.

Pour olive oil into another pan and place on medium heat; add mustard, fenugreek, and dill seeds. When seeds start to splutter, add onion and curry leaves, and sauté for 2 minutes. Add cayenne pepper and turmeric, stir, turn down heat to low, and cook for 3 seconds.

Add potatoes, baby carrots, cauliflower, baby red onions, and 1 cup water. Cover pan and cook for 12 minutes.

Add wing beans, tomato, and kale. Cover and cook 5 minutes more.

Add urad dal, season with tamarind juice and salt to taste, and bring to a slow simmer. Remove from heat. Serve hot.

4 to 5 servings

Meal in a Dish

Split, husked **mung beans** are the main item here. They are nutritious and cook fast. Make it a day ahead; it takes well to reheating.

For an exotic touch, serve with a bowl of chutney and a green salad.

1 cup split husked mung beans
2 cups water
3 tablespoons olive oil
*1 teaspoon black **mustard seeds***
*1 teaspoon **cumin** seeds*
4 shallots, peeled and chopped
2 cups mixed vegetables (cauliflower sprigs, small diced carrots, tomatoes, red bell peppers, and cooked peas)
*A pinch of **turmeric***
¼ cup water
*¼ cup chopped, **blanched** almonds*
½ cup cooked rice
Salt to taste
¼ cup chopped Chinese parsley

Directions

Cook mung beans in simmering water for 15 minutes; drain off water.

Heat oil on medium heat and fry mustard and cumin seeds; when seeds splutter, add shallots and fry until golden brown. Stir in vegetables and turmeric, and cook for a few seconds. Add ¼ cup water, cover, and steam for 5 minutes on low heat. Add almonds, mung beans, and rice. Season with salt to taste. Stir and cook on low heat for 4 to 5 minutes. Sprinkle with Chinese parsley.

4 servings

Lentil Salad

Sometimes I serve this salad chilled as an appetizer; other times I serve it with grilled fish.

*1 cup **brown lentils***
3 cups water
1 bay leaf
1 slice of yellow onion
¼ pound sliced beef sausages
*1 teaspoon ground **cumin***
3 tablespoons chopped yellow onions
3 cloves garlic, chopped
½ cup chopped sun-dried tomatoes
3 green onions, chopped
¼ cup water
¼ cup chopped parsley
¼ cup fresh lemon juice
*¼ cup **balsamic vinegar***
Salt to taste
Freshly ground black pepper to taste

Directions

Wash lentils and place them in a pan; add 3 cups water, bay leaf, and onion. Simmer on low heat about 40 minutes, until the lentils are tender. Strain lentils, discard onion and bay leaf, and cool the lentils.

Place beef sausage in a skillet and add ground cumin. Cook 2 minutes; add onions and garlic, and cook 5 to 6 minutes. Add sundried tomatoes, green onions, and ¼ cup water, and simmer 4 to 5 minutes. Add to the lentils along with the parsley, and season with lemon juice, balsamic vinegar, and salt and black pepper to taste. Mix to combine well. Remove from heat and spoon into a serving bowl. Serve cold.

4 servings

Chickpeas with Tomatoes

As in other legume dishes, I enhance these with spices. The chickpeas are first cooked with seasonings and spices. The final touch is the **garam masala** sprinkled on the finished dish.

1½ cups dry **chickpeas**
6 cups water
3 tablespoons olive oil
1 large yellow onion, peeled and finely chopped
2 teaspoons grated ginger
¼ teaspoon **turmeric**
1 teaspoon **cayenne pepper**
1 teaspoon ground **coriander**
1 teaspoon ground **cumin**
¼ teaspoon ground **cinnamon**
3 tomatoes, peeled, seeded, and chopped
Juice of 1 lemon
Salt to taste
1 teaspoon garam masala
4 sprigs of Chinese parsley, chopped

Directions

Place chickpeas in a bowl, cover with water, and leave overnight. Drain soaking water, add 6 cups fresh water, and bring to a boil. Cover partially and cook on moderate heat for 45 minutes to 1 hour. Chickpeas should be buttery soft. Test by pressing a pea between a finger and thumb. Drain off water, saving 1 cup of cooking liquid.

Heat oil on medium heat in a pan, add onion, and sauté to a light golden color, about 6 minutes. Add ginger and spices. Cook 3 to 4 minutes. Add tomatoes; simmer for 10 minutes. Add chickpeas and season with lemon juice and salt to taste. Sprinkle in the reserved 1 cup of cooking liquid or 1 cup water and simmer for 20 to 25 minutes. Sprinkle with garam masala and Chinese parsley.

6 servings

Sautéed Peas and Paneer

These fresh peas cooked with **paneer** are delicately spiced. Low-fat ricotta cheese is a good substitute for paneer, and Chinese parsley makes a fine garnish.

¾ cup fresh green peas
2 cups water
1 tablespoon olive oil
1 tablespoon chopped shallots
1 teaspoon minced garlic
1 teaspoon **turmeric**
1 teaspoon **cayenne pepper**
1 cup tomato **concassée**
1 cup **Paneer** (see recipe, page 242), crumbled
1 tablespoon chopped **methi** sprouts
Salt to taste
Fresh lemon juice to taste

Directions

Add peas to boiling water; simmer 30 minutes until soft. Drain. Heat oil in a sauté pan; add shallots and garlic. Cook on low heat for 2 to 3 minutes. Stir in spices; add tomato concassée and cook till combined with the spices, about 5 to 6 minutes. Mix in the peas, turn heat to low, and cook 10 to 15 minutes.

Fold in paneer and chopped methi sprouts. Season with salt and lemon juice to taste. In 1 minute, remove from heat. Serve hot.

4 servings

Lima Beans with Tomatoes

To open the **lima bean** pods, cut a strip along the side edge of the pod. Use your finger to remove the bean seeds. The black **mustard seeds** popped in oil give a nutty flavor and make the dish more colorful.

This dish is a good companion to lamb.

2 cups water
2 cups shelled fresh lima beans
2 tablespoons olive oil
2 shallots, peeled and chopped
1 teaspoon black mustard seeds
1 cup tomato **concassée**
Salt to taste
Freshly ground black pepper to taste

Garnish
½ cup garden mint leaves

Directions
Bring water to a boil, add beans, and cook until soft.

Heat oil on medium heat in sauté pan, add shallots, cook for 1 minute, and add mustard seeds. Allow seeds to pop; it takes 2 to 3 seconds. Add tomato concassée and cook until soft, about 2 minutes. Add beans and season with salt and black pepper to taste. Simmer for 2 to 3 minutes. Fold in the mint leaves and serve hot.

4 servings

Black-Eyed Peas with Tomatoes

Aromatized with spices, the soft-cooked tomatoes blended with the olive oil make this saucy dish very flavorful. A day later, it tastes even better.

1 cup dry **black-eyed peas**
3 cups water
1 cup diced tomatoes
1 teaspoon ginger
1 teaspoon garlic
Salt to taste
1 tablespoon olive oil
½ teaspoon **cumin** *seeds*
½ cup finely chopped red onion
¼ teaspoon crushed red pepper flakes
3 tablespoons plain yogurt, whipped

Garnish
2 tablespoons chopped Chinese parsley

Directions
Wash peas and soak them in 3 cups water for 4 to 5 hours. Drain soaking water; place peas in pan with fresh water to cover and bring to a boil. Turn down heat and simmer until soft, 30 to 35 minutes. Add tomatoes, ginger, and garlic. Simmer for 10 minutes, season with salt to taste, and remove from heat.

Heat oil on medium heat in a small sauté pan and stir in cumin seeds. When they start to pop, add onions and cook until golden, about 6 minutes. Stir in red pepper flakes, cook for 2 to 3 minutes, and pour over peas.

Stir in yogurt, bring to a slow simmer, and remove from heat. Sprinkle chopped Chinese parsley over all.

4 servings

Burst of Flavor

Yellow Split Peas and Vegetables

For a nutritious luncheon, serve this with brown rice and chutney. It is lightly spiced and, as with many other legume dishes, tastes even better when reheated a day later.

$1/2$ cup **yellow split peas**
3 cups water
1 teaspoon each grated ginger and garlic
$1/4$ teaspoon **turmeric**
$1/4$ teaspoon **cayenne pepper**
1 large baking potato, peeled and cut into
  $1/2$-inch dice
1 large carrot, peeled and cut into $1/2$-inch dice
6 string beans, cut into $1/2$-inch lengths
1 cup shredded green cabbage
Salt to taste
2 tablespoons olive oil
1 tablespoon chopped yellow onion
1 teaspoon **cumin** seeds
8 **curry leaves**

Directions

Wash split peas, place in pan, add 3 cups water, bring to a slow simmer, and cook until split peas are soft but not mushy, about 1 hour. Add ginger, garlic, turmeric, and cayenne pepper. Stir well; add potato, carrot, and beans. Cover pan and cook until vegetables are soft, 8 to 10 minutes. Add green cabbage and cook for 4 to 5 minutes. Season with salt to taste.

Heat oil in a pan; when oil is very hot, add onion and stir for a few seconds to brown onion. Add cumin seeds and curry leaves. When cumin seeds start to pop, add cooked lentils and vegetables. Stir gently. Remove from heat.

8 servings

Red Bean Salad

Red kidney beans like many other beans induce flatulence. To minimize this effect, add fresh ginger when cooking the beans. Always remove and discard the scum that floats on the surface of the cooking liquid. Serve this salad in small portions as an appetizer or as a side dish with fish or seafood.

1 cup dry red kidney beans
3 cups water
2 teaspoons grated ginger
2 tomatoes, chopped
$1/4$ cup chopped Chinese parsley
1 tablespoon ground **coriander**
1 tablespoon chopped green onion
$1/2$ cup **chiffonade** of garden mint
$1/4$ cup chiffonade of basil
1 teaspoon grated ginger
1 teaspoon grated garlic
Fresh lemon juice to taste
Salt to taste
Freshly ground black pepper to taste

Directions

Soak beans in cold water overnight. Drain; add 3 cups fresh water to cover and cook until soft, about 1 to $1/2$ hours. Drain and chill the beans. Mix with remaining ingredients, and season with lemon juice, salt, and black pepper to taste. Chill.

6 servings

Grains . . .

Untapped Riches

Grains are the staple food of many countries; the most familiar grains are rice, wheat, and corn.

In Asia rice predominates. Some believe it was first grown in India around 3000 B.C. Others claim that it is a native of China or Thailand. Wherever it originated, more than half of the world's population now eats it as a staple. There are countless varieties in Asia's marketplaces, where it is not unusual to see up to sixty varieties and grades.

Rice was our staple in Sri Lanka. Often our Sunday lunch consisted of "yellow rice," a nationally loved dish. It was cooked in chicken broth, aromatized with **cardamoms, cloves,** and **cinnamon,** and garnished with golden-brown cashew nuts and plump raisins. **Turmeric** gave it the yellow tint. Such rice dishes are the center attraction, surrounded always by curries, pickles, and chutneys.

Exquisite **basmati** rice preparations like North Indian pilaf and Mogul briyani are incomparable. These dishes, loaded with fragrant spices, glow in **saffron** and sparkle with fruits, nuts, and *warak* (edible silver). We ate rich briyanis on special occasions.

Wheat is believed to be the first crop planted by man. People of the Indus valley as well as the Chinese cultivated wheat around 2500 B.C. Today it's as important a staple to the world as rice. There are numerous varieties of wheat; the two cultivated on a large scale are the common wheat and hard wheat.

Wheat flour is milled and refined from a blend of soft and hard wheat, and contains hardly any bran and germ. Flour is enriched with nutrients lost in the milling process, as required by law.

It is recorded that corn, also known as maize, grew wild in southern Mexico about nine thousand years ago. Settlers of the early seventeenth century reported that Native Americans were growing corn in North America but cultivated it widely themselves only after the Civil War. The dried whole kernel or corn is a grain second in importance to wheat. Cornmeal is the coarsely ground whole kernels; corn flour is finer ground than meal.

Underutilized grains like **millet, quinoa** (pronounced *keen-wa*), **amaranth,** and **triticale** are very nutritious. Flavored with exotic spices from the East, they have found a permanent place on my menus.

Basmati Rice with Chives and Black Cumin Seeds

This elegant dish may be served with seafood or poultry. **Cardamom** and **cinnamon** lend a lemony flavor and a sweet, elusive aroma to the cooked **basmati** rice. **Black cumin,** peppery to the bite, leaves a slight hint of it in the rice. Black cumin seeds are sometimes incorrectly referred to as onion seeds. If black cumin seeds are unavailable, use **cumin** seeds as a substitute.

2 cups basmati rice
Water
3 tablespoons unsalted melted butter
6 cardamom pods
1/4-inch piece of cinnamon stick
2 tablespoons chopped yellow onion
2 teaspoons chopped ginger
1 1/2 teaspoons sliced garlic
1/4 teaspoon black cumin seeds
Zest and juice of 1 lemon
2 teaspoons salt
3 1/2 cups cold water
1/4 cup chopped chives

Garnish
1/4 cup sliced onion
Ice water
1/4 cup olive oil
18 chive flowers with 3-inch-long stems
1/4 teaspoon toasted black cumin seeds

Directions
Wash rice, add cold water to cover the rice and soak for 25 minutes. Drain water through a strainer.

Heat butter and add cardamom and cinnamon. Fry on low heat until cardamom pods are puffed, about 2 minutes. Add onion, ginger, and garlic. Cook until onions are transparent, about 3 minutes. Add black cumin seeds and cook 2 minutes on high heat. Reduce heat and add rice, zest of lemon, lemon juice, salt, and 3 1/2 cups cold water. Bring to a simmer.

Add chopped chives, cover the pan, reduce heat to very low, and cook for 20 minutes. Turn off heat and let the rice sit for 5 minutes.

For the garnish, add sliced onion to ice water and set aside for 5 minutes. Drain and wipe the onions with a paper towel to remove any excess moisture. Heat oil, add onion, and fry on moderate heat for 2 minutes until the onions are crisp. Remove onions from oil and drain on paper towels.

Add the chive flowers to the oil and remove instantly. Immerse in ice water; then remove and wipe dry.

Toast the black cumin seeds in a skillet on medium heat for 1 minute.

Presentation
Mold the rice on plates and place fried onions on the rice. Arrange chive flowers on one side and sprinkle black cumin seeds on plates.

6 servings

Saffron Rice

Basmati is India's favorite rice, and the best varieties grow in the foothills of the Himalayas in north India. Many are aged for fifteen years or more. Connoisseurs consider it the best rice in the world. You can find Pakistani basmati, Dehradun basmati, and Patna basmati rice in Indian grocery stores.

To prepare rice, first remove any foreign matter and place the rice in a medium-size bowl. Fill it with cold water, swish the rice around, and pour off the washing water. Repeat this process 4 to 5 times until the washing water runs clear. Washing will remove the excess starch clinging to the grains. Cover the rice with cold water and soak it for 25 minutes. Soaking will soften the rice grains and help expand and elongate them. You may cook the rice in the soaking water or drain water off and cook in fresh water or stock.

Cooked basmati rice exudes a sweet fragrance and the fluffy grains are not sticky to the touch.

Rice is often cooked with **cardamom, cinnamon,** and **cloves.** To add fragrance and a hint of color, use **saffron** or **turmeric.** To enrich the rice, dried fruits and nuts such as almonds and pistachios are added. Serve saffron rice with curries of meat, poultry, or seafood. It also works well with yogurt cucumber salad (see recipe for yogurt cucumber salad in the **Crab Cakes** recipe, page 59) and chutneys.

1½ cups basmati rice
3 tablespoons melted butter
½ small yellow onion, finely chopped
2½ cups water or **Defatted Chicken Stock**
   (see recipe, page 45)
¼ teaspoon saffron threads soaked in
   1 tablespoon of hot water
1 teaspoon salt

For Sachet
8 whole black peppercorns
4 cardamom pods, crushed
4 whole cloves
2-inch piece of cinnamon stick
1 teaspoon crushed ginger

Garnish
1 tablespoon olive oil
¼ cup **blanched** slivered almonds
¼ cup light golden raisins
¼ cup sliced yellow onions

Directions
Soak rice in cold water for 25 minutes and drain off water. Heat butter in a saucepan; sauté onion on medium-high heat until golden. Add rice; stir for about 5 minutes, until grains absorb all the butter. Add water or chicken stock, saffron, and salt.

Tie up peppercorns, cardamom pods, cloves, cinnamon stick, and crushed ginger in a **sachet** and add to rice. Bring to a boil. Stir once and cover with a tight-fitting lid. Turn heat to very low and cook for 25 minutes.

Heat oil in a small sauté pan; add almonds and cook, stirring until light gold. Add raisins and cook a few seconds to plump them. Remove almonds and raisins from the oil and set aside. Add onions to the oil in the pan and cook till golden brown; remove and place with the almond-raisin mix.

When rice is cooked, remove the sachet and discard. Spoon nut-raisin-onion mixture on top. Leave pan covered for 10 minutes. Remove lid; fluff with a fork, combining almonds, raisins, and onions.

6 servings

Sweet Soba Noodles with Spinach, Mushrooms, and Red Pepper Jam

Soba noodles have a nutty flavor and a firm texture when cooked just right. Cook as you would spaghetti, being careful not to overcook. Overcooking makes the noodles mushy.

The red pepper jam and the red pepper flakes in the dressing lend the right amount of spiciness to balance the sweet-and-sour taste in the dish.

For Salad

3 ounces soba noodles
2 cups water
4 cups washed, fresh spinach leaves
1 large **portabella mushroom**
1 tablespoon peanut oil
1 tablespoon chopped shallots
2 teaspoons grated garlic
Salt to taste

For Pepper Jam

½ red bell pepper, unpeeled
2 tablespoons sugar
3 tablespoons water
1 tablespoon white vinegar
Salt to taste

For Dressing

2 tablespoons **rice wine vinegar**
2 tablespoons red wine
1 tablespoon fresh lime juice
1 tablespoon **mirin**
2 tablespoons olive oil
1 teaspoon chopped green onion
1 teaspoon chopped shallots
½ teaspoon crushed red pepper flakes
Salt to taste

Garnish

1 teaspoon toasted black sesame seeds

Directions

Cook noodles in 2 cups boiling water for 2 to 3 minutes, strain, and refresh in cold water. Place in a colander to drain off all the liquid. Wipe the spinach leaves dry, cover, and place in the refrigerator to chill.

Trim and slice the portabella mushroom about ½-inch thick. Heat peanut oil in a skillet, add shallots and garlic, and cook 2 to 3 minutes. Add the mushrooms and cook on high heat for 2 to 3 minutes. Season with salt to taste. Set aside.

For pepper jam, finely chop the red bell pepper. Heat the sugar, water, and vinegar with a pinch of salt to taste. Add the bell pepper and cook on low heat for 5 to 6 minutes until glazed.

For dressing, place rice wine vinegar, red wine, lime juice, and mirin in a small bowl, and whisk. Gradually add olive oil and whisk until emulsified. Whisk in the green onions, shallots, and red pepper flakes. Season with salt to taste.

Presentation

Arrange spinach leaves on salad plate and drizzle on a little dressing. Spoon dressing on soba noodles and arrange on the spinach, alternating with the mushrooms. Place a few spinach leaves on top of the salad and spoon a little pepper jam on top. Sprinkle black sesame seeds over and around the salad.

4 servings

Spinach Rice

This rice is lightly spiced with **cumin** and seasoned lightly with ginger and lemon zest, letting the taste of the spinach stand out. Fresh spinach is used in this recipe. You may substitute a combination of other greens, like **mizuna, dandelion,** and Chinese parsley if you prefer.

1½ cups **basmati** rice
2 tablespoons unsalted butter
½ teaspoon cumin seeds
1 tablespoon chopped yellow onion
1 teaspoon minced ginger
Zest of ½ lemon
2 cups water
2 cups packed spinach leaves
⅛ teaspoon salt

Directions

Wash and soak rice in cold water for 20 minutes, then strain. Heat butter on medium heat in a pan, add cumin seeds, and fry until they start to splutter, about 2 minutes. Add onion and cook until onions turn a gold color. Add ginger, lemon zest, rice, and 2 cups water. Bring to a simmer. Cover pan and cook for 10 minutes.

Remove and discard lemon zest. Add spinach and salt, cover pan, and cook 10 minutes more.

Remove from heat and let rice rest 5 more minutes. Fork rice lightly to combine well with spinach. Serve hot.

4 to 5 servings

Citrus-Flavored Herbed Rice

This lemony rice does well with fish or poultry dishes. The only spice used is **turmeric,** and just enough of it to give a yellow blush to the rice. The herbs add a refreshing note to this citrus-flavored rice.

1½ cups long-grain white rice
2 tablespoons unsalted butter
⅛ teaspoon turmeric
2 cups water
Zest and juice of ½ lemon
Zest and juice of ½ orange
Salt to taste
¼ cup chopped green onion
½ cup chopped Chinese parsley
¼ cup chopped garden mint

Directions

Wash and drain rice. Heat butter in a saucepan on low heat, stir in turmeric, and add rice, 2 cups water, lemon and orange zest and juice with salt to taste. Bring to a fast boil. Stir once, cover with tight-fitting lid, turn down heat to very low, and cook for 25 minutes. Add the chopped green onion, Chinese parsley, and mint. Turn off heat and leave unopened for 10 minutes.

Remove and discard lemon and orange zest. Fluff with a fork and serve hot.

6 to 8 servings

Savory Semolina

Nutritious **semolina** is the main ingredient in this dish, which is speckled with spices and colorful bits of vegetables. Semolina is coarsely ground flour that includes the endosperm of hard wheat such as durum. It makes a simple but superb appetizer. It can also be served as a substitute for potatoes or rice.

1 cup fine semolina
1 tablespoon olive oil
*1 teaspoon each black **mustard seeds** and*
* **cumin** seeds*
1 tablespoon chopped shallots
*⅛ teaspoon **turmeric***
¼ cup small-diced and peeled fresh carrots
¼ cup cooked peas
Salt to taste
2 cups water
Fresh lemon juice to taste
¼ cup chopped pistachio nuts
¼ cup chopped Chinese parsley

Directions

Roast semolina in a sauté pan on moderate heat, stirring constantly with a wooden spoon until grains are crisp and turn a light golden color, about 6 minutes.

Heat oil on medium heat in a medium-size pan and add mustard and cumin seeds. When seeds start to splutter (4 to 5 seconds), stir in shallots and cook for 1 to 2 minutes. Mix in turmeric and vegetables. Season with salt to taste, add 2 cups water, cover pan, and simmer 3 to 4 minutes. Reduce heat to low. With a wooden spoon, gradually stir in semolina. Stir constantly; cooking 10 to 12 minutes.

Season with lemon juice to taste and fold in the pistachio nuts and Chinese parsley. Serve hot.

5 to 6 servings

Spicy Couscous

The secret for good **couscous** is to moisten the grains with water so that they will swell up before cooking. I add spices and herbs to give more flavor to the dish. Serve this spicy couscous with roast lamb or chicken.

2 cups couscous
2 cups hot water

To Season Couscous
2 tablespoons olive oil
1 tablespoon chopped yellow onion
*1 teaspoon crushed **cumin** seeds*
*2-inch piece of **cinnamon** stick*
Salt to taste
¼ cup finely chopped parsley
1 tablespoon unsalted butter

Directions

Place couscous in a bowl. Gradually add hot water and stir, making sure all the grains are soaked with water. Cover tightly and set aside for 10 minutes. Loosen couscous grains with a fork.

Heat olive oil in a pan, add onion, and sauté 2 to 3 minutes. Add cumin and cinnamon stick, cook 1 minute, and stir in couscous. Season with salt to taste. Cover pan and leave on very low heat for 5 minutes.

Remove from heat and fold in the parsley and butter.

4 servings

Sweet and Spicy Pilaf

Although traditional pilaf is served with cooking spices, it is best to remove the whole spices so guests don't bite into them. In the cooking process, the spices lend their fragrance to the rice. When cooking is completed, they settle on top of the cooked rice. It is easy to remove and discard them. However, the remaining **cumin** seeds are delicious to bite into.

1 1/2 cups **basmati** rice
2 tablespoons olive oil
1 teaspoon cumin seeds
1 tablespoon sugar
2-inch piece of **cinnamon** stick
4 **cardamom** pods, bruised
2 1/2 cups hot water
1/8 teaspoon **saffron** threads, soaked in
 1 tablespoon hot water
1/4 cup seedless golden raisins
1/4 cup peeled pistachio nuts
Salt to taste

Directions

Wash rice and soak for 25 minutes. Drain to remove all moisture. Heat oil in a small, heavy-bottomed pot, add cumin seeds, and cook for 1 minute on medium heat. Add rice and keep stirring for 5 minutes to coat the rice with the oil. Sprinkle sugar, stir, and cook for 10 minutes, until rice turns a light brown. Add cinnamon, cardamom, 2 1/2 cups hot water, soaked saffron, raisins, and pistachio nuts with salt to taste.

Bring to a fast boil, stir, turn heat to very low, cover tight, and cook 25 minutes. Remove from heat and keep covered for 5 minutes.

6 servings

Rice Salad

This salad is a quick luncheon or supper dish. Serve the salad in a scooped tomato for a special luncheon or as a garnish for roast lamb.

1/2 cup cooked basmati rice
1/4 cup chopped garden mint
2 tablespoons chopped Chinese parsley
1 tablespoon seeded, chopped **green chili**
1 tablespoon chopped red bell pepper
1 tablespoon chopped pistachio nuts
1/2 teaspoon roasted, crushed **cumin** seeds
1/2 teaspoon grated zest of lemon
1 teaspoon fresh lemon juice
1 teaspoon sugar
1/2 cup plain yogurt
Salt to taste
Freshly ground black pepper to taste

Garnish
4 chives

Directions
Place cold rice in a bowl.

To the rice, add herbs, green chili, bell pepper, and pistachio nuts, and toss lightly. In a small bowl, stir cumin seeds, lemon zest, lemon juice, and sugar into yogurt. Fold into the rice and season with salt and black pepper to taste.

Garnish with chives.

2 servings

Shrimp Pilaf

This spicy shrimp pilaf, redolent with spices and seasonings, is rich in colors and textures. The pilaf is assembled in a casserole, covered tightly, and cooked in the oven in its own aromatized steam. When done cooking, the shrimp nestled in the rice will be plump and juicy. The pilaf may also be the centerpiece on a buffet.

$1^{1}/_{2}$ cups **basmati** rice
2 pounds shrimp
3 tablespoons olive oil
1 medium yellow onion, peeled, halved,
   and thinly sliced
1 tablespoon minced ginger
2 teaspoons minced garlic
1 teaspoon ground **cumin**
2 teaspoons ground **fennel**
$^{1}/_{8}$ teaspoon **turmeric**
2-inch piece of **cinnamon** stick
4 **cardamom** pods, bruised
2 medium-size tomatoes, chopped
$^{1}/_{4}$ cup water
$^{1}/_{2}$ cup low-fat yogurt
Salt to taste
$^{1}/_{4}$ cup sliced green onion
$^{1}/_{4}$ cup chopped Chinese parsley
$^{1}/_{2}$ cup chopped garden mint
2 **green chilies,** seeded and sliced thin
3 cups water

Directions

Preheat oven to 400°F.

Wash and soak rice for 25 minutes.

Peel, remove heads, devein, and wash shrimp. Heat oil in a pan and cook onion, ginger, and garlic for about 5 minutes on moderate heat. Stir in cumin, fennel, and turmeric and cook a few seconds. Add cinnamon, cardamom, and tomatoes and cook for 5 minutes more.

Gradually add $^{1}/_{4}$ cup water and yogurt in small quantities; stir continuously, until the water disappears and the spice mix is moist and oily. Remove from heat. Season with salt to taste and stir in green onion, Chinese parsley, mint, green chilies, and shrimp. Cover, remove from heat, and set aside.

In a pan, bring 3 cups of water to a boil. Drain rice, add to the boiling water, and cook for 8 minutes on high heat, uncovered. Remove from heat and drain rice through a colander to get rid of all the cooking water.

In a casserole or baking pan, arrange the shrimp mix and spread the rice loosely over top of it. Tightly cover with foil and then with a lid. Place in the oven and cook for 25 minutes. Remove from oven and leave unopened for 10 minutes before serving.

Presentation

Fluff the rice pilaf, spoon onto a platter, and serve hot.

8 servings

Grains

Naan Bread

Naan bread is traditionally made in a tandoor —a clay oven heated with charcoal. Flat bread such as naan is slapped onto the sides of this furiously hot tandoor. It is the aroma of the heated clay that gives the flavor to this bread. Naan can also be made in a conventional electric or gas oven; the bread tastes good even without the special aroma. Pizza griddles, clay bricks, or slabs that are available in cookware stores may be heated up in the oven to use for baking naan bread.

2½ to 3 cups all purpose flour
¼ cup lukewarm water
1 ounce dry yeast (1 packet)
2 teaspoons sugar

Egg Mix
1 large egg
¼ cup plain yogurt
2 teaspoons sugar
1 teaspoon salt
¼ cup melted unsalted butter

For Greasing
1 tablespoon melted unsalted butter

Garnish
1 teaspoon melted unsalted butter
*1 teaspoon **poppy seeds***

Directions
Sieve flour into a medium-size bowl, cover, and set aside. Place ¼ cup of warm water in a small bowl, sprinkle in yeast and sugar, and leave in a warm place for 5 to 6 minutes or until it becomes frothy (to see whether the yeast is active). If it does not froth, you will need to start over with a fresh packet of yeast.

For the egg mix, whisk the egg in a medium-size bowl. Add yogurt, sugar, salt, and melted butter, and continue to whisk till smooth. Stir in the yeast mixture. Reserve about ½ cup of flour, add the egg mix to the balance of the flour, and, using a wooden spoon, beat into a smooth dough. Add the reserved flour as needed. As the dough gets stiffer, you need to use your hands to knead. Knead 10 minutes, until the dough is soft and sticky. (The dough can be mixed in a food processor.) Cover dough and place in a warm place until it has doubled in size.

Heat oven to 425°F. Place a large, heavy baking sheet in the oven to preheat.

Grease your hands with melted butter, punch down the dough, and divide into 15 equal portions. Pat the dough balls into flat rounds and pull down one side of each to form teardrop shapes. Brush each with melted butter and sprinkle with poppy seeds. Place on the preheated baking sheet and bake for 8 to 10 minutes, until puffed and dark gold in color. Place under a hot broiler a few seconds, until dark-golden-brown blisters appear on the naan.

Presentation
Place naan in a napkin-lined basket and cover with another napkin.

12 to 16 pieces

Chapati

Chapati, a traditional unleavened flat bread, is easy to make—only flour and water are needed. A touch of salt and melted butter or oil may be added for a softer texture in the bread.

Here is a recipe for chapati made with whole wheat and all-purpose flours. The secret is to knead the dough extremely well for 6 to 8 minutes by hand. A food processor gives better and faster results.

Whole wheat flour is milled from the entire husked kernel of hard wheat and includes the bran, germ, and endosperm. All-purpose flour is white flour that is a combination of both hard and soft wheat flours.

Serve chapati with rich main dishes.

2 cups whole wheat flour
1½ cups all-purpose flour
¾ to 1 cup warm water

Directions

Sift flours separately and reserve ¼ cup of all-purpose flour. Place both flours in the container of a food processor, run the machine, gradually adding water in a slow trickle. As soon as the dough gathers into a mass (about 30 to 40 seconds), add a little more water and run the machine 5 to 10 seconds until the dough forms into a ball. The dough should be smooth and pliable.

Remove, break dough into 2 equal portions, and form into 2 balls. Place balls in a medium-size bowl, cover with a damp kitchen towel, and leave in a warm place (by the stove) for 2 hours.

Dust the work surface with reserved flour; using your hands, roll each ball of dough into a smooth rope about 1 inch in diameter. Cut dough ropes into 1-inch pieces. Form into smooth balls, dust with flour, and keep covered.

Dust the work surface and rolling pin, and roll the dough into thin circles about 6 to 7 inches in diameter; keep covered.

Place a skillet on high heat. When skillet is very hot, place a dough circle in the skillet and cook for 1 minute. Using tongs, turn over and press down with a spatula. Cook for 1 minute or until tiny brown patches appear on both sides. (Pressing down against the very hot skillet helps small blisters to form on the chapati.) Complete cooking all the chapati.

Presentation

Place the cooked chapati in a napkin-lined basket and cover with another napkin.

15 pieces

Pasta

Thomas Jefferson proudly served a special spaghetti dish at a formal dinner. Today, pasta is among America's favorites.

Italian pasta, Chinese egg noodles, Japanese **somen** noodles, and Thai rice noodles are only a small sample of the world of pasta.

Homemade pasta is the best, but many prefer to purchase their pasta fresh or dried for the sake of convenience. It is convenient to use a food processor to make the pasta dough.

3 cups unbleached all-purpose flour
3 medium-size eggs
1 tablespoon olive oil
1/8 teaspoon salt
1/8 cup lukewarm water

Directions

Reserve 1/4 cup of flour and place the balance of the flour in a food processor. Add eggs, oil, and salt. Process gradually, adding a little water, until a soft, smooth ball is formed, about 15 to 20 seconds.

Wrap the dough in plastic wrap and set aside to rest 30 minutes.

Cut dough into 3 portions; dust board with flour and roll each portion to 1/6-inch thick. Cut into strips to preferred size. Place dough strips on a pan dusted with flour and sprinkle more flour to prevent strips from sticking to each other. You may also use a pasta machine to roll and cut the dough.

Yields 1 pound

Herbed Shrimp and Noodles

The glistening, whole red chilies, not to be bitten into, make a lovely garnish. Perhaps it is best to warn your guests.

1 pound shrimp
8 ounces fine-cut noodles
3 cups water
3 tablespoons olive oil
5 whole, dry red chilies
1 teaspoon grated ginger
1 teaspoon sliced garlic
1/2 cup finely sliced green onion
1/2 cup chopped Chinese parsley
1/4 cup **Fish Stock** (see recipe, page 46)
1/2 cup chopped tomatoes
Fresh lemon juice to taste
Salt to taste
2 tablespoons grated fresh Parmesan cheese

Directions

Peel, remove heads, and devein shrimp. Cook noodles in boiling water, drain, and set aside.

Heat oil on moderate heat, add chilies, and cook for 5 seconds. Turn heat down to low, stir in ginger and garlic, and cook for 5 seconds.

Turn heat to high, mix in shrimp, onion, and parsley, and stir to combine well. Add stock and chopped tomatoes, and cook for 2 minutes. Season with lemon juice and salt to taste. Add hot cooked noodles, Parmesan cheese, and toss to combine well.

Pick out and place the red chilies on the top of the pasta and shrimp. Serve hot.

4 servings

Pasta and Crabmeat

Lightly flavored with **cumin** and thyme, and with the blush of the **turmeric,** this dish is perfect for a party.

8 ounces (¹/₂ pound) crabmeat
2 tablespoons olive oil
3 shallots, peeled and chopped
1 teaspoon grated garlic
1 teaspoon crushed cumin seeds
¹/₂ teaspoon crushed red pepper flakes
¹/₄ teaspoon turmeric
3 sprigs thyme
2 tablespoons dry sherry
¹/₄ cup chopped tomato
4 cups water
10 ounces pasta
Salt to taste
Freshly ground black pepper to taste
1 tablespoon chopped green onion

Directions
Pick over crabmeat and remove shell and cartilage.

Heat oil on low heat and sauté shallots for a few minutes. Add garlic and cook about 2 minutes. Stir in cumin seeds, red pepper flakes, turmeric, and thyme leaves (scraped off their stems). In 1 minute add crabmeat, sherry, and tomato, and cook for 3 minutes on high heat. Set aside.

Boil water and add pasta and salt to taste. Simmer 4 to 5 minutes; strain from water, add to cooked crabmeat, and toss with salt and black pepper to taste. Sprinkle green onion over all.

4 servings

Polenta

I use spices to enhance this famous Italian dish. It may be eaten hot as is or chilled, cut up into desired shapes, and grilled or pan-fried.

Cornmeal is available from fine to coarse. Use the finest cornmeal for the best results.

2 tablespoons olive oil
2 teaspoons each minced garlic and shallots
*2¹/₂ to 3 cups **Defatted Chicken Stock***
   (see recipe, page 45)
¹/₂ cup cornmeal
¹/₂ cup whole milk
*Pinch of **nutmeg***
Salt to taste
Freshly ground black pepper to taste
2 tablespoons grated fresh Parmesan cheese

Directions
Preheat oven to 350°F.

Heat oil in a pan on high heat. Add garlic and shallots, and cook until golden brown. Add stock and bring to a boil. Gradually add cornmeal, stirring constantly with a wooden spoon to avoid lumps, and cook for 5 minutes. Beat in the milk and nutmeg, and add salt and black pepper to taste. Spoon into an ovenproof dish. Sprinkle cheese, cover pan, and place in oven for 30 minutes. Open cover and bake 5 more minutes to allow the top to brown lightly.

4 servings

Black Barley Salad

Black barley is the barley grain with only the outer husk removed. It requires long, slow cooking even after soaking. To cut down on cooking time, you may pressure-cook the barley after soaking it.

1 cup black barley
6 cups water

For Salad

1 large red onion, unpeeled
6 cloves unpeeled garlic
1 red bell pepper
1 yellow bell pepper
1 leek (white part only)
2 medium-size tomatoes
2 oranges segmented, cut into ½-inch pieces
1 teaspoon roasted, crushed **cumin** seeds
1 tablespoon chopped basil leaves

For Dressing

¼ cup **rice wine vinegar**
Grated zest of ½ orange
Juice of 1 lemon
Juice of 1 orange
Salt to taste
Freshly ground black pepper to taste

Garnish

2 green onions, cut into 1-inch lengths
4 sprigs of basil

Directions

Soak barley in cold water overnight. Drain barley, place in a pan with 6 cups cold water, and cook for 1½ to 2 hours, until the barley is soft to the bite. Drain the barley and set aside.

Preheat oven to 375°F.

Place the onion, garlic, and bell peppers in a roasting pan and roast in the oven for about 40 minutes. Remove these vegetables from the roasting pan and set aside. Place leeks and tomatoes in the roasting pan and roast for 10 minutes.

Peel the roasted onion and cut into large dice. Peel garlic and chop coarsely. Peel and seed bell peppers, and cut into thin strips. Cut leeks into 1-inch lengths, and peel and chop roasted tomatoes. Place all the prepared salad ingredients in a bowl and add oranges, crushed cumin seeds, and chopped basil. Add the cooked barley and fold to combine all the ingredients.

For the dressing, place rice wine vinegar, orange zest, and lemon and orange juice in a bowl and whisk. Season with salt and black pepper to taste. Pour this dressing on the salad and toss. Taste and season with more salt and black pepper if needed.

Presentation

Spoon salad onto plates and strew green onion over the salad. Top each serving with a sprig of basil.

4 servings

Spicy Couscous Wrapped in Collard Greens

The **couscous** wrapped in collard greens and the vegetables, rich in texture and color, have a tempting aroma of spices. The fragrant couscous, piquant chutney, and vegetables all have exotic Middle Eastern flavors that complement each other.

½ cup **Dried Cranberry Chutney**
  (see recipe, page 205)

For Couscous Mold
½ recipe **Spicy Couscous** (see recipe, page 165)
1 teaspoon olive oil
4 molds (1-cup size)
2 cups water
4 leaves collard greens
1 cup ice water
2 tablespoons sour cream

Vegetables
2 artichokes, whole
2 cups water
Juice of 1 lemon
2 tablespoons olive oil
2 teaspoons minced garlic
1 teaspoon crushed **coriander** seeds
1 bay leaf
2 cups **Vegetable Stock** (see recipe, page 46)
4 pearl onions, peeled
4 baby carrots, peeled and trimmed
Salt to taste
Black pepper to taste
1 cup tomato **concassée**

Directions
Make cranberry chutney and spicy couscous, and set aside.

Preheat oven to 300°F.

Brush olive oil on the inside of the molds.

Boil 2 cups water, add collard greens, and cook for 1 minute. Remove collard greens from the boiling water and place in 1 cup ice water.

Remove collard greens from ice water, place on a kitchen towel, and wipe off excess moisture. Remove the stems and midribs. Line the molds with collard greens, letting the edges of the leaves hang over the edges of the molds. Spoon sour cream into each, pack with couscous, and fold overhanging leaf ends over the couscous. Bake for 10 minutes.

For vegetables, trim and halve artichokes, remove and discard fuzzy centers (chokes), and place in 2 cups water. Add lemon juice and set aside.

Heat oil in a pan and add garlic and crushed coriander. Cook 2 to 3 minutes and add bay leaf and stock. Place artichokes (discard water), onions, and carrots in the pan and season with salt and black pepper to taste. Add tomato concassée, cover pan, and **braise** for 20 to 25 minutes.

Presentation
Turn couscous molds onto plates and spoon in vegetables and chutney.

4 servings

Spiced Quinoa

Quinoa, a light grain, expands to four or five times its size, giving it a good yield. It also cooks in less time than rice. However, it is an underutilized grain. In this recipe I use an array of spices. **Fenugreek** seeds have a forceful aroma and a slightly bitter taste. In combination with **cumin, cardamom,** and **cinnamon,** fenugreek seeds add a complex aroma to this grain many call uninteresting. Here, oil-fried spices bursting with flavor, almonds, and raisins elevate this humble grain to an elegant side dish.

1 cup quinoa
2 tablespoons olive oil
1 tablespoon chopped shallots
½ teaspoon fenugreek seeds
1 teaspoon cumin seeds
4 cardamom pods
1-inch piece of cinnamon stick
½ teaspoon **turmeric**
¼ cup chopped almonds
½ cup raisins
Salt to taste
2 cups water

Directions

Wash and rinse quinoa, and drain to remove all moisture. (It is best to do this an hour before you start cooking so the grains are dry.) Heat a sauté pan, add the grains, and stir with a wooden spoon to toast for about 6 to 8 minutes. Heat oil on medium heat in a saucepan and add shallots, fenugreek, and cumin. Stir 6 to 8 seconds, until the seeds start to splutter. Add toasted grains, spices, almonds, raisins, and salt to taste. Stir 1 minute. Add 2 cups water, bring to a boil, reduce heat to low, cover, and cook 15 minutes. Fluff with a fork and set aside for 5 minutes before serving.

6 servings

Amaranth and Rice with Cashew Nuts

Amaranth, a highly nutritious grain, is edging its way to a prominent place on Western tables. The combination of textures and flavors in this amaranth dish will persuade guests to try it more often. Use it as a stuffing for a roasted bird, make it the centerpiece of a vegetarian meal, or serve it as a side dish for a chicken or meat entrée.

1 tablespoon olive oil
2 teaspoons each minced garlic and shallots
½ teaspoon **turmeric**
½ teaspoon ground **cumin**
1 cup brown rice, uncooked
¼ cup pearled amaranth
Salt to taste
2 cups water
½ cup chopped, toasted, unsalted cashew nuts
½ cup raisins
½ cup cooked peas

Directions

Heat oil in a saucepan and stir in garlic and shallots. Cook 3 to 4 minutes; add spices, rice, amaranth grains, and salt to taste. Stir 2 to 3 minutes. Add 2 cups water, stir, bring to a boil, and cover pan; reduce heat and cook for 45 minutes. Stir in cashew nuts, raisins, and peas. Set aside, unopened, for 5 minutes before serving.

4 to 5 servings

Burst of Flavor

Pink Lentils with Bulgur

Garam masala, a blend of roasted ground aromatic spices, is folded into the cooked lentils and bulgur, giving them a flavorful spark. Serve with roast chicken or meats.

¾ cup **pink lentils**
2 cups water
½ cup **bulgur wheat**
1 cup water
2 tablespoons olive oil
1 small yellow onion, peeled and thinly sliced
1 zucchini cut into a **julienne**
½ red bell pepper cut into a julienne
Salt to taste
Freshly ground black pepper to taste
¼ cup finely cut green onion
¼ cup chopped garden mint
1 teaspoon garam masala

Directions

Wash lentils in 3 to 4 changes of water and place lentils in a saucepan with 2 cups of water. Cook 15 to 20 minutes; they should be cooked through but not too soft. Drain lentils and set aside. Place bulgur wheat and 1 cup of water in a pan over moderate heat and simmer for 20 to 25 minutes, until all of the liquid is absorbed. Remove from heat, cover pan, and use after 10 minutes.

Heat oil in a wide sauté pan and sauté onions for 3 minutes on moderate heat. Add zucchini and bell pepper; cook a few seconds —just enough to wilt. Stir in salt and black pepper to taste. Remove from heat. Add lentils, bulgur wheat, green onion, mint, and garam masala. Toss to combine. Serve hot.

4 to 5 servings

Rice Custard

Custard is a perfect way to use leftover rice. I like to place these rice custards around a roast leg of lamb, elevating a simple, old-fashioned dish to star heights. Grate the **nutmeg** right into the rice mix. As a rule, creamy dishes are enhanced by the exquisite fragrance of freshly grated nutmeg.

2 medium-size eggs
1 medium egg yolk
1 cup cooked rice
1 cup whole milk
¼ cup snipped chives
¼ cup blanched almonds, chopped
Pinch of grated nutmeg
Salt to taste
Freshly ground black pepper to taste
4 four-ounce molds
1 teaspoon unsalted butter

Directions

Preheat oven to 250°F.

Beat eggs and yolk. Mix rice into the eggs and add milk, chives, and almonds. Season with nutmeg, and salt and black pepper to taste.

Grease 4 molds with butter. Divide rice mixture between them. Cover with a piece of parchment paper and place in a **bain marie.** Bake for 35 to 40 minutes.

Remove from the oven and allow the custards to stand for 5 minutes before turning onto plates.

4 servings

Salads . . .

Gardens in the Sun

Nature's finest bounty is a perfect salad—a thing of color, a bouquet of freshness.

Salads played only a minor role in my diet as I was growing up. Vivid in my memory, though, is a cucumber salad, each slice a four-inch cartwheel strewn with wispy rings of red onion and specked with slivers of **green chilies.** It was seasoned only with lime juice, sea salt, and freshly ground black pepper. We did not call such seasonings dressings; we saw no need for oil.

Europe and America opened up to me the rainbow world of salads. In France I first tasted mesclun, tender, cultivated mixed greens of myriad textures, tastes, and colors—bitter and sweet, cool and pungent, sour and mild. These ranged from pale, shy greens to dark, assertive ones, from gentle mauves to punchy reds.

American markets offer the same range to choose from: saw-edged **mizuna,** tiny **totsoi** leaves, edible **chrysanthemum greens, choy sum** with luscious yellow flowers, **pea shoots** with curly tendrils, and pink-tinted **amaranth.** These exotic greens have come to the market forefront and serve beautifully to adorn our salads.

Greens are just the beginning. To the open-minded cook, the whole produce section is a beckoning path of color, form, flavor, and texture. For further inspiration, I meander willingly into a broad highway of other ingredients: herbs, nuts, cheeses, pickles, seaweed, legumes, exotic greens, fruits, and lighter, fragrant dressings.

For me, almost all salad roads lead to fresh herbs. I use the French favorites with appreciation, the Sri Lankan standbys with nostalgia, the local supermarket array with pleasure, and the out-of-the-way treasures with deep thought. At times I bestow a bitter bite upon my salads with **arugula** or **dandelion** greens, **methi** leaves, or tender radish sprouts. Sometimes I get a lemony tang with a sprinkling of **wood sorrel.** For a touch of glamor I strew on edible blossoms: rosemary, chives (white and lavender), and sage.

When it's time for a salad, the options are numerous. Rejoice at the wide variety and make your selections with the discerning eye of a painter, the discriminating taste of a gourmet, and the playful heart of a true adventurer.

Ricotta-Stuffed Mushrooms with Beans and Roasted Red Bell Pepper Vinaigrette

This dazzling salad does well as a starter, too. Spicy ricotta-stuffed mushrooms are full of flavor. The stuffing gets an aromatic crunch from the roasted, crushed **coriander,** an ideal flavor companion to the simple, crunchy beans. The red bell pepper vinaigrette also gets an aromatic crunch from the crushed coriander and spikes up the whole salad. Serve crusty bread as an accompaniment to this dish.

8 medium-size shiitake mushrooms
1 tablespoon olive oil
Salt to taste
Freshly ground black pepper to taste

Spiced Ricotta Cheese
1 cup ricotta cheese
1 tablespoon chopped shallots
1 tablespoon chopped green onion
1 teaspoon seeded and chopped **green chili**
2 tablespoons roasted, crushed coriander seeds
Salt to taste

Vegetables
1 red bell pepper
16 **haricots verts, blanched**
16 yellow wax beans, blanched

Vinaigrette
1 tablespoon Dijon mustard
1 teaspoon chopped shallots
1 teaspoon chopped green onion
1 teaspoon chopped **capers**
1 teaspoon roasted, crushed coriander seeds
2 tablespoons white vinegar
Salt to taste
Freshly ground black pepper to taste
¼ cup olive oil

Garnish
1 medium hard-cooked egg, shelled and grated

Directions
Preheat oven to 400°F.

Remove stems and wipe mushrooms with a wet towel. Heat oil in a skillet and sauté mushrooms for 3 minutes. Season with salt and black pepper to taste. In a small bowl, mix ricotta cheese, shallots, green onion, green chili, and coriander seeds. Season with salt to taste.

Roast the bell pepper in the preheated oven for 15 minutes, leave to cool, and then peel the pepper. Cut open, and remove and discard the seeds. Slice into thin strips. Blanch the beans and place them in a small bowl.

To make the vinaigrette, place the mustard, shallots, onion, capers, coriander, and vinegar in a small bowl. Whisk to combine the ingredients; add salt and black pepper to taste. Add olive oil in a thin stream and continue to whisk until dressing is well emulsified.

Spoon vinaigrette to cover the beans. Mix the vinaigrette with the red bell pepper and set aside until salads are ready to be assembled.

Presentation
Place a mushroom, stem side up, in the center of each plate. Top mushroom with seasoned ricotta and cover each with another mushroom, stem side down. Fan out the haricots verts, keeping the stem end to a point at the base of the mushroom and the tail ends of the haricots pointing toward the rim of the plate. Similarly fan out the yellow wax beans on the opposite side of the plate.

Spoon the red bell pepper on the stem ends of the beans and the balance of the vinaigrette on the mushrooms. Strew the grated egg on the red bell pepper.

4 servings

Sprouts with Sweet Lime Vinaigrette with Basil Seeds

Methi sprouts are my favorite in this mix. They are sprouted from the leguminous spice seed **fenugreek.** Radish sprouts and onion sprouts used in the mix are spicy, while the **pea sprouts** and **mung bean** sprouts add a crunch.

The sweet lime dressing brings out the best in this spectrum of taste and textures. Soaked **basil seeds** have a jellylike coating enclosing their crunchy interiors and give the dressing a fascinating texture.

Cold drinks with soaked basil seeds are popular in Asian countries. As kids, we especially liked a sweet lime juice drink with soaked basil seeds dreamily floating in it. On hot afternoons, this drink was always there for us in a tall glass pitcher. Our elders insisted these drinks had a cooling effect on the system, especially the digestive system.

My childhood memories inspired me to come up with this delicious dressing.

Salad
¼ cup methi sprouts
¼ cup radish and onion sprouts
½ cup each pea sprouts and mung bean sprouts
4 sprigs of basil
*3 handfuls of **mizuna***
2 red onion slices
*4 tablespoons chopped **candied ginger***

Dressing
1 tablespoon basil seeds
¼ cup cold water
*1 tablespoon **rice wine vinegar***
*1 tablespoon **mirin***
*2 tablespoons **fish sauce***
¼ cup fresh lime juice
1 tablespoon chopped green onion
1 teaspoon sesame oil

Garnish
¼ cup purple chive flowers

Directions
Loosen sprouts and arrange in a bowl. Break the basil leaves off the stems, remove mizuna stems, loosen onion slices to get eight onion rings, and add to the salad. Add candied ginger and toss to give an even mix before dressing the salad. Cover and refrigerate.

For dressing, soak basil seeds in a bowl with ¼ cup cold water and set aside for 30 minutes. To the basil seeds, add rice wine vinegar, mirin, fish sauce, lime juice, and chopped green onion. Whisk to combine. Add sesame oil in a slow, steady stream and whisk constantly to emulsify the dressing to a smooth texture.

Presentation
Pour some dressing on the sprouts and toss gently to coat lightly. Arrange on salad plates.

Drizzle a little more dressing around the salads to show off the basil seeds. Strew chive flowers on the plate.

4 servings

Tomatoes with Spiced Baby Mozzarella, Olives, and Basil

The very best ingredients are warranted for this simplest of dishes.

For starters, use the best sun-kissed, vine-ripened tomatoes. Choose them with care to avoid ones with blemishes on their skin. It is also vital to use a soft mozzarella and the best **extra virgin olive oil.** Sweet, licorice-tasting ground **fennel** mixed with **cumin** adds an exotic spiciness to the cheese.

Fitting accompaniments to this elegant salad are roasted whole garlic pods and hot, crusty French bread. To roast garlic, sprinkle olive oil on garlic pods and wrap in foil. Heat oven to 375°F and bake garlic for 45 minutes to 1 hour.

For Cheese with Spices
4 whole baby mozzarella cheeses
½ teaspoon ground, roasted fennel seeds
½ teaspoon ground, roasted cumin seeds
⅛ teaspoon sea salt

Vegetables
1 vine-ripened red tomato
1 vine-ripened yellow tomato
4 red cherry tomatoes
4 Roma tomatoes
*24 **Niçoise olives***

Dressing
2 tablespoons extra virgin olive oil
*2 tablespoons **balsamic vinegar***
Sea salt
Freshly ground black pepper to taste

Garnish
4 sprigs of basil
*1 tablespoon **capers***
12 yellow cherry tomatoes

Directions
Cut the cheeses into halves and dust the cut sides with the ground fennel, cumin seeds, and sea salt.

Slice red and yellow tomatoes and halve cherry tomatoes. Remove a diagonal slice from the stem end of each Roma tomato; scoop and discard seeds and pulp. Slice the bottom of the Romas to enable them to sit on the plate.

Presentation
Place a slice of red and yellow tomato and 2 cherry tomato halves on each plate. Place 1 scooped Roma tomato on each plate and arrange olives in the Romas, letting a few olives spill out onto the plate. Place 2 cheese halves on each plate by the Roma tomatoes.

Drizzle olive oil on the salads and spoon a little balsamic vinegar only on the plate. Sprinkle sea salt and grind black pepper generously on the salads to taste.

Garnish each with basil sprigs, capers, and yellow cherry tomatoes. Serve the salads at room temperature.

4 servings

Burst of Flavor

Okra Salad

Singaporean Fish Head Curry with tender whole okra and other vegetable tidbits has satisfied many an adventurous gourmet. In New Orleans okra is used in Creole gumbos. However, in the United States, it was until recent times categorized as the most disliked vegetable of all.

A native of Africa, okra is one of those vegetables that people either like or hate. Many are put off by its mucilaginous quality, which is its main characteristic.

Okra is a much-loved vegetable in India and Sri Lanka, where pods are simmered in coconut milk and spices, stuffed with spices and deep fried, or sliced and deep fried to a delicious golden brown to strew over rice.

Pick small okra that are not discolored. The thick, large okra with seeds protruding from under their skin are coarse and fibrous.

To keep okra from turning slimy, cook it in acidulated water as I do to prepare this salad. Additionally, use lime juice or lemon juice as a seasoning.

This salad has red pepper flakes in the vinegary dressing, which helps to cloak the viscosity of the okra.

³/₄ pounds tender whole okra
2 teaspoons lime juice
3 cups water
2 kale leaves
1 cup ice water
2 tomatoes, cored and cut in wedges
*1 small red onion, cut into a **julienne***
2 tablespoons chopped green onion
*1 **green chili,** seeded and sliced*

Seasoning for Salad
¼ teaspoon crushed red pepper flakes
2 tablespoons white wine vinegar
*2 tablespoons **virgin olive oil***
Lime juice to taste
Salt and freshly ground black pepper to taste

Garnish
8 quail eggs

Directions
Add okra and lime juice to 3 cups of boiling water; simmer for 6 minutes. Drain okra from cooking water and chill. Trim the kale leaves and discard the stems. Break the leaves into 2-inch pieces. Boil the remaining cup of water, add kale, and cook for 2 minutes. Drain kale from cooking water and place in 1 cup ice water to chill.

Place tomatoes, red onion, green onion, and green chili in a bowl. Toss to combine the ingredients evenly.

Drain okra and kale leaves, wipe off excess moisture, and add to the tomatoes. Add red pepper flakes, white wine vinegar, and olive oil and season with lime juice, salt, and black pepper to taste.

While the salad is chilling, prepare the garnish. To hard cook quail eggs, place them in a saucepan and cover with cold water. Bring to a gentle simmer and cook for 5 minutes. Cool eggs in cold water. Peel and halve eggs.

Toss lightly to combine the ingredients with the seasonings. Leave in the refrigerator for 10 to 15 minutes.

Presentation
Spoon salad onto chilled plates and garnish with halved quail eggs.

4 servings

Exotic Greens with Sweet and Spicy Dressing

Asian greens are easily available in the West. Open markets carry a wide range, as do supermarkets, though their selection is more limited.

The more recent varieties available in the markets are red-tinted **amaranth, rice paddy herbs,** and **pea shoots.** Our familiar favorites, **totsoi,** red and green mustard, **mizuna** leaves, and **choy sum** have been around for a while.

All these Asian greens are ideal in mixed salads. When you choose what to include, pick the freshest greens. Tender greens are ideal in salads; they are mild and delicate. The more mature greens do well when cooked, as in stir-fries and soups.

Once a selection is made, greens should be thoroughly washed and then dried by absorbing the excess moisture with paper towels or by putting greens in a salad spinner.

Green salads should be dressed only at the point of serving. Needless to say, these delicate Asian greens need to be dressed *lightly* to bring out their flavors.

Salad
¼ cup choy sum with flowers
½ cup amaranth
½ cup totsoi
½ cup mizuna
½ cup pea shoots
*4 **African coriander** leaves*

Dressing
*1 tablespoon **mirin***
*1 tablespoon **rice wine vinegar***
1 tablespoon fresh lime juice
*1 tablespoon **fish sauce***
½ teaspoon finely chopped grated ginger
½ teaspoon chopped shallots
½ teaspoon chopped green onion
A pinch of chili powder
1 tablespoon sesame oil

Directions
Snip and remove stems, wash choy sum flowers, cover, and place in the refrigerator.

Wash all the greens and dry with paper towels or spin dry to remove excess moisture. Place in a bowl, cover, and refrigerate.

For the dressing, place mirin, rice wine vinegar, lime juice, fish sauce, ginger, shallots, and green onion with a pinch of chili powder in a bowl. Whisk to combine. Add sesame oil in a slow stream and whisk to emulsify the dressing to a smooth texture. Pour dressing on the greens and toss gently.

Presentation
Arrange greens on chilled plates and place choy sum flowers decoratively on the greens. Drizzle a little more dressing around the salads on the plates. Serve immediately.

4 servings

Roasted Pumpkin, Glazed Shallots, and Garlic with Honey Mustard Vinaigrette

Pumpkin is full of vitamins and low in calories. Inexpensive and abundant, with a sweet buttery texture, pumpkins shouldn't end up only as grinning faces.

Select pumpkins with hard, unblemished rinds. I use kabocha pumpkin in this salad. It is a variety of sweet Japanese pumpkin, easily available in supermarkets. This salad elegantly displays its golden-orange flesh glistening with its natural sugars. The luscious flavors of the sweet roasted shallots and garlic work in harmony with the pumpkin.

The honey mustard vinaigrette and the final dusting of spices tie all these exotic flavors together.

1 small kabocha pumpkin
2 tablespoons **extra virgin olive oil**
Salt to taste
Freshly ground black pepper to taste
A sprig of rosemary, crushed
8 shallots, peeled
8 cloves of garlic, peeled
12 walnut halves

Glaze
1 tablespoon honey
½ tablespoon apple cider vinegar
Pinch of **cayenne pepper**
Pinch of ground **cinnamon**

Dressing
2 tablespoons country-style Dijon mustard
2 tablespoons honey
2 tablespoons white wine vinegar
3 tablespoons extra virgin olive oil
Salt to taste
Freshly ground pepper to taste

Garnish
4 sprigs of rosemary
¼ teaspoon ground cinnamon
⅛ teaspoon ground **nutmeg**
⅛ teaspoon ground **cloves**

Directions
Preheat oven to 325°F.

Halve the pumpkin lengthwise; remove and discard the seeds. Cut into wedges ½-inch thick (you need 20 wedges). Peel the remaining pumpkin and prepare about 1 cup of pumpkin finely diced.

Mix pumpkin wedges and diced pumpkin with olive oil, salt and black pepper to taste, and crushed rosemary. Place in a roasting pan, add shallots, garlic, and walnuts, and roast in the preheated oven for 12 minutes.

Remove the roasting pan from the oven. In a small bowl, mix honey, vinegar, cayenne pepper, and cinnamon. Brush shallots and garlic with the glaze, turn them over, and brush with glaze again.

Turn over the pumpkin wedges. Put roasting pan back in the oven for 15 minutes more; then remove from the oven and discard the rosemary.

In a small bowl, whisk ingredients for dressing. Season with salt and black pepper to taste.

Presentation
Arrange diced pumpkin and pumpkin wedges on plates. Spoon shallots, garlic, and walnuts among pumpkin wedges and drizzle dressing over salads. Garnish with rosemary and dust the plates with spices.

4 servings

Burst of Flavor

Zucchini and Tomato Salad with Honeyed Garlic Cloves

Garlic is believed to have been around in India since Aryan times, but respectable people did not eat it.

According to Waverly Root, before he left the United States in 1927 to live in Europe, you were looked down upon if you ate garlic. When he returned in 1940, you were looked down upon if you didn't.

Garlic is the most pungent member of the onion family. Fresh garlic has a subtle flavor and is ideal in salads. Look for fat, round, hard bulbs when buying garlic.

As a child, I ate roasted garlic pods drizzled with bees' honey. This treat usually came once a month; we children enjoyed it with my mother in her canopied four-poster bed. Much later I learned mother ate it for its medicinal values (to overcome menstrual cramps, not gastronomical ones). Today I like to delight my garlic-loving friends with another favorite: spiced honeyed garlic cloves, which I use in this recipe.

Adjust the garlic in this recipe to suit your taste. It's milder than you might expect; the marinating takes away the bitterness.

Spiced Honeyed Garlic Cloves
16 whole garlic cloves
2 cups water
2 tablespoons honey
1 tablespoon cracked black peppercorns
1 teaspoon cracked **coriander** *seeds*
1 tablespoon fresh lime juice

Salad
2 small zucchini
1 small red onion
1 tablespoon **extra virgin olive oil**
12 cherry tomatoes
1 teaspoon crushed fresh thyme leaves

Dressing
2 tablespoons white wine vinegar
¼ cup extra virgin olive oil
Salt to taste

Garnish
4 butter lettuce leaves
4 radicchio leaves

Directions
To prepare honeyed garlic, carefully skin the garlic cloves. Bring 2 cups water to a boil, add garlic, and cook for 12 to 15 minutes. Drain and place garlic in a bowl. Add honey, black peppercorns, coriander seeds, and lime juice. Mix and leave to marinate for 24 hours.

To prepare salad, cut each zucchini lengthwise into 4 pieces. Cut these 4 pieces into 2-inch chunks. Peel onion and cut into large dice. Heat oil in a sauté pan, add zucchini and onion, and sauté on very high heat for 1 minute. Add tomatoes and remove from heat immediately (the heat of the vegetables will wilt the tomatoes slightly).

Place vegetables in a bowl, add marinated garlic with its marinade, and toss in thyme leaves.

Whisk vinegar and oil with salt to taste and pour on the salad. Toss to combine all and leave to marinate for 1 hour in the refrigerator.

Presentation
Spoon salad onto chilled plates. Garnish with butter lettuce and radicchio.

4 servings

Red Potato Salad

This salad is very easy to prepare. The freshly fried spices in combination with the mint add a touch of the exotic and lift the potatoes to new heights. Serve hot as a side dish with fish, poultry, or meat.

8 medium-size red potatoes
3 tablespoons olive oil
3 shallots, peeled and sliced thin
2 teaspoons crushed **coriander** seeds
2 teaspoons crushed **cumin** seeds
1 teaspoon crushed red pepper flakes
1 tablespoon fresh lemon juice
1 teaspoon grated ginger
½ cup chopped garden mint leaves
Salt to taste
Freshly ground black pepper to taste

Garnish
4 lettuce leaves
4 sprigs of garden mint

Directions
Boil potatoes until soft (do not peel) and cut into 1-inch dice. Heat oil in skillet on medium heat; add shallots and sauté to light golden. Add coriander and cumin; sauté for 10 seconds. Remove from heat and add potatoes and all remaining ingredients, with salt and black pepper to taste. Combine, transfer to a dish, and refrigerate for 30 minutes.

Presentation
Place lettuce leaves on plates, spoon potato salad over lettuce, and garnish with mint.

4 servings

Salted Salmon Salad

This salad is made in the style of the Hawaiian *lomi lomi* salmon. Ice cubes in the salad help to cut down on the salt and keep the salmon moist and juicy. **Ogo** is a type of seaweed. You may skip the garnish; the salad will still be tasty.

5 ounces salmon fillet
2 tablespoons sea salt
3 cups cold water
2 tablespoons thinly sliced green onion
2 Roma tomatoes, cut into small dice
4 ice cubes

Garnish
4 Roma tomatoes, sliced
1 small red onion, peeled and thinly sliced
1 red **chili pepper,** chopped
¼ cup ogo, trimmed and washed
1 teaspoon black sesame seeds, roasted
1 tablespoon **chili pepper water**

Directions
Coat salmon with sea salt, place in a **nonreactive** pan, cover with 3 cups cold water, and refrigerate for 2 days.

Drain off water, remove skin and bones from salmon, and wash away excess salt in 2 or 3 changes of water. Chop salmon and mix with green onion and diced tomatoes. Add ice cubes and refrigerate.

Presentation
Arrange sliced tomatoes and onion on plates. Sprinkle chopped red chili pepper over tomatoes and onion; spoon over salted salmon salad. Top with ogo. Sprinkle sesame seeds over the salad and drizzle chili pepper water on the plate.

4 servings

Green Papaya Salad

Papain, an enzyme extracted from papaya, acts as a tenderizer when added to meat, a practice still very common in Asian countries. As a child I relished picking slices of cooked green papayas off my beef curry. Green papaya salad is even better; it is crisp, crunchy, and elegant.

The most enjoyable part is the lashing of chili on the tongue. No papaya salad is complete without this exotic heat.

1 green papaya, peeled, seeded, and grated
   into long shreds (about 2 cups after grating)
1 tomato, halved lengthwise and thinly sliced
¼ cup thinly sliced red onion
1 tablespoon **chili paste**
4 tablespoons **fish sauce**
2 tablespoons brown sugar
Fresh lime juice to taste
¼ cup broken-up garden mint leaves
¼ cup broken-up sweet basil leaves

Garnish
1 tablespoon roasted, chopped peanuts

Directions
Place green papaya, tomato, and onion in a bowl. Toss with the chili paste, fish sauce, brown sugar, and lime juice to taste. When well combined, fold in mint and basil leaves.

Presentation
Spoon onto chilled plates and top with chopped peanuts.

4 servings

Herb Salad Doris

Unconventional though it may be, I made this luncheon salad for Doris Duke one hot day in her New Jersey "Duke Gardens." I used a variety of herbs and greens brought in a big basket by a hothouse *jardinière*. She loved my creation and immediately ordered an herb patch close to the mansion. Within three days, as many as fifteen varieties of herbs sprang up in the pots.

She asked for this salad often in summer, and I named it after her.

½ cup watercress leaves
1 cup each torn **field salad** and
   limestone lettuce
¼ cup parsley, leaves only
¼ cup each torn basil and **dandelion** leaves
¼ cup each **chervil** and **burnet** leaves
¼ cup broken-up dill sprigs
¼ cup each **lemon balm** and **sweet cicely** leaves

Dressing
3 tablespoons **extra virgin olive oil**
2 tablespoons white wine vinegar
1 tablespoon Dijon mustard
Salt to taste
Fresh lemon juice
Freshly ground black pepper to taste

Directions
Wash and spin dry all greens and herbs, and place in a bowl.

Whisk ingredients for dressing in a small bowl with salt, lemon juice, and black pepper to taste. Drizzle dressing and toss gently to coat the greens.

Presentation
Serve on chilled salad plates.

4 servings

Spinach and Avocado Salad with Honey Vinaigrette

The honey vinaigrette makes a perfect match for the buttery richness of the avocado. The thymelike fragrance of the **ajowan** seeds that laces the vinaigrette complement this salad of many flavors and textures.

1 bunch spinach, leaves trimmed
1 ripe avocado, peeled, pitted, and sliced
2 ripe beefsteak tomatoes, cored and sliced
2 red onion slices

Honey Vinaigrette

2 tablespoons white wine vinegar
1 tablespoon fresh lemon juice
1 teaspoon chopped garlic
2 tablespoons honey
3 tablespoons **extra virgin olive oil**
1/8 teaspoon roasted, crushed ajowan seeds
Salt to taste
Freshly ground black pepper to taste

Garnish

1 hard-cooked egg, shelled and grated

Directions

Wash spinach leaves, then dry with paper towels or spin dry to remove the excess moisture.

Presentation

Arrange spinach leaves in a fan shape on large salad plates. Place avocado slices on spinach, keeping the fan shape and leaving a margin to show off the spinach. Place 2 overlapping tomato slices on base of fan. Loosen onion slices and pull out rings. Place 2 onion rings each on the tomato slices.

In a small bowl, whisk together ingredients for dressing, drizzle over the salad, and garnish with grated egg.

4 servings

Asparagus Vinaigrette

You may serve this refreshing salad as a starter, too. The vinaigrette has texture and layers of flavors that enliven every mouthful of asparagus. This recipe works well for tender beans and can be served hot or cold.

4 cups water
1 1/2 pounds peeled, trimmed asparagus
4 cups ice water

For Vinaigrette

3 tablespoons **rice wine vinegar**
2 teaspoons Dijon mustard
1 teaspoon crushed **cumin** *seeds*
1 teaspoon chopped garlic
1 tablespoon chopped shallots
1 tablespoon grated orange zest
1 tablespoon chopped parsley
1 teaspoon chopped **capers**
1 teaspoon sugar
1/4 cup **extra virgin olive oil**
Salt to taste
Freshly ground black pepper to taste

Directions

Bring 4 cups water to boil and add asparagus. Cook until tender, 2 to 3 minutes. Shock in 4 cups ice water. Drain from water and refrigerate.

Whisk together ingredients for the vinaigrette. Season with salt and black pepper to taste.

Presentation

Arrange asparagus on plates and spoon on the vinaigrette.

6 servings

Burst of Flavor

Marinated Beets with Watercress Salad and Goat Cheese

The sweet-and-sour beets, the spicy watercress, and the creamy goat cheese complement one another. The various textures in the salad are well balanced. The lemony crunch of the briefly oil-fried, crushed **coriander** seeds adds an exotic accent to this delightful salad.

Marinated Beets

16 baby beets
3 cups cold water
*1 tablespoon **extra virgin olive oil***
½ tablespoon crushed coriander seeds
*1 tablespoon **balsamic vinegar***
1 tablespoon white wine vinegar
Juice of 1 orange
1 tablespoon light brown sugar
Salt to taste
Freshly ground black pepper to taste

For Watercress Salad

2 cups watercress sprigs
1 tablespoon fresh lemon juice
1 tablespoon fresh lime juice
1 teaspoon crushed red pepper flakes
Salt to taste

Garnish

½ cup (2 ounces) goat cheese

Directions

Place beets in a pan with 3 cups of cold water and cook for 30 minutes on high heat. When cool enough to handle, peel and trim tops, keeping about 1 inch for presentation.

Heat oil, add coriander seeds, and fry on medium heat for 1 minute. Add remaining ingredients and the beets. Cook 3 minutes. Remove from heat, cool, and refrigerate.

Place watercress in a medium-size bowl, add lemon and lime juice, red pepper flakes, and salt to taste, and toss lightly.

Presentation

Arrange watercress on salad plates, place marinated beet on the watercress. Sprinkle goat cheese on the beets.

4 servings

Chutneys, Relishes . . .

Jewels in the Crown

Today's finest cooks—from professional chefs to busy mothers—share one main goal: simplify. There are many reasons; the main one is an interest in healthy eating. Uncomplicated recipes using short cooking times and simple cooking methods (poaching, steaming, broiling, grilling) not only eliminate or reduce fat and salt intake and preserve nutrients, but also cut down on labor and time.

Customers, guests, and family are now getting more pure, honest, and undisguised food. But many still yearn for more flavor—zip, surprise, mystery—without reverting to the heavy and complicated sauces of yesteryear. Thus we witness, along with the growing use of exotic spices and herbs in Western dishes, the increasing appearance of chutneys, relishes, sambols, pickles, and preserves on Western tables.

Chutneys, pickles, relishes, sambols, and preserves are a few of my favorite things. When I was growing up, we had at least two of these items on the table at every meal.

Chutneys and pickles were nearly always available. They have long shelf lives. On the other hand, sambols could be whipped up in a jiffy.

Pickles can last as long as ten to twelve years. In fact, pickles improve with age. My mother always had a few glass jars of gorgeous, dark brown, sun-dried lime pickles. I consider pickles a culinary treasure. Piquant and pleasing, these jewels add zest and act as complementary and delightful partners to whatever dishes they accompany. You'll enjoy them as much as I do if you take them seriously—as palate teasers that stimulate the appetite, enrich a menu, and aid digestion. I often include several on an Indian menu. Their nuances of flavor—from sweet to sour, from mild to hot, from subtle to spine-tingling—blend into each other like the colors of a vanishing rainbow.

Chutneys, relishes, and pickles should be prepared in **nonreactive** pans.

Mango Chutney

What I remember best about the home where I grew up in Sri Lanka are the five mango trees. As kids, we plucked green mangoes, peeled and sliced the flesh, and put it into a mortar with whole dried red chilies, whole black peppercorns, vinegar, sea salt, and a sprinkling of sugar. We pounded this spicy mango mix with a pestle. This childhood repast of green mangoes was great. For our family mango chutney, we use half-ripe mangoes. They are sweeter and turn a golden color when cooked. This chutney is piquant, sweet, and spicy—all the flavors well balanced.

2 packed quarts mango, peeled, seeded, and
    sliced into ¼- by 2-inch pieces
1 cup dark seedless raisins
4 cups sugar
4 cups cider vinegar
1 yellow onion, minced
4 tablespoons each minced ginger and garlic
2 teaspoons crushed red pepper flakes
1 teaspoon grated **nutmeg**
1 teaspoon ground **cloves**
2-inch piece of **cinnamon** stick
6 pods **cardamoms**
Salt to taste

Directions
Wipe mangoes dry of all moisture; set aside with raisins. Place remaining ingredients in a **nonreactive** pan and simmer over low heat for 15 minutes. Add mangoes and raisins. Simmer until mangoes turn transparent and chutney is thick, about 2 to 2½ hours. Cool, ladle into sterilized jars, cover, and refrigerate. Keeps up to 3 months.

Yields 2 quarts

Tomato and Lemon Chutney

Tomato and lemon zest, two colorful partners, bring out the best in each other. In this recipe, spices are used whole rather than ground; fried in oil, they give texture and a haunting aroma to the soft, glazed tomatoes. The sharp **cumin** and the sweet licorice **fennel** add a mild aroma. The more assertive **fenugreek,** a small legume used as a spice, emanates a pungent charred flavor when cooked in oil, and black **mustard seeds** give a nutty flavor. **Poppadom** accompany the chutney especially well.

2 tablespoons olive oil
½ teaspoon whole cumin seeds
½ teaspoon fennel seeds
¼ teaspoon fenugreek seeds
½ teaspoon black mustard seeds
½ teaspoon crushed red pepper flakes
4 cloves garlic, peeled and thinly sliced
1 tablespoon finely shredded ginger
½ cup sugar
½ cup white vinegar
Salt to taste
1½ pounds ripe tomatoes, cut into small dice
Zest of 2 lemons, cut into a fine **julienne**

Directions
Heat oil in a **nonreactive** pan and, on medium heat, fry cumin, fennel, fenugreek, and mustard seeds. When mustard seeds start to pop, add red pepper flakes, garlic, and ginger. Stir over low heat for a few seconds. Add sugar, vinegar, and salt to taste; bring to a slow simmer. Stir in tomatoes and cook on low heat for 45 minutes. Add lemon zest julienne and simmer until chutney is thick. Cool, pour into sterilized jars, cover, and refrigerate. Keeps up to 1 month.

Yields 1 pint

Burst of Flavor

Peach Chutney

The fragrant spices lend a refined accent and flavor to the soft-textured peaches cooked in a sweet vinegar base.

Peach chutney is especially good with Thanksgiving roast turkey and Christmas ham. It may also be a substitute for sauce with roast pork and poultry.

3 cups sugar
3 cups cider vinegar
½ cup minced yellow onion
¼ cup minced ginger
1 teaspoon **cayenne pepper**
1 teaspoon ground **cloves**
1 teaspoon ground **cinnamon**
Salt to taste
2 quarts of peeled, seeded, and sliced peaches
1 cup raisins

Directions

Place all the ingredients except the peaches and raisins in a **nonreactive** pan. Cook on low heat for 30 minutes. Add peaches and raisins. Continue to simmer on medium heat until peaches turn transparent and the chutney is thick, about 1 hour. Ladle into sterilized jars, cool, cover, and refrigerate. Use within 1 month.

Yields 2 quarts

Date Chutney

Dates have natural sweetness and, in this recipe, cook down to a sweet, sour, and spicy glaze. The chutney is lavish with ginger, but when done cooking only an elegant hint remains.

Date chutney is an uncommon yet refined accompaniment to meats and game.

1½ pounds seeded dates
½ cup raisins
1 cup cider vinegar
½ cup dark brown sugar
1 tablespoon ground ginger
2 teaspoons ground garlic
2 cups minced yellow onion
2-inch piece of **cinnamon** stick
¼ teaspoon **cayenne pepper**
½ cup white wine
Salt to taste

Directions

Cut dates into even dice and place aside with raisins.

In a **nonreactive** pan, combine vinegar, sugar, ginger, garlic, onion, cinnamon, cayenne pepper, and wine. Cook on low heat until the mixture comes to a slow boil.

Add dates and raisins and season with salt to taste. Continue to cook on low heat until chutney is thick and glazed, about 40 minutes.

Cool and ladle into sterilized jars. Cover tightly and refrigerate. Use within 1 month.

Yields ¾ pint

Tamarind Chutney

The tree commonly known as **tamarind** is native to India. It also grows profusely in Sri Lanka. It has shaded many a weary traveler. Children delight in playing under its enormous bowers and in eating its pods and leaves, valued for their medicinal properties throughout Asia.

Tamarind is naturally fruity yet also sour. Added sugar brings out these flavors' contrasts. Raisins intensify its sweet flavor. This recipe is also spiked with **cumin,** ginger, and red pepper.

Tamarind chutney may be substituted for sauces with a sweet-and-sour note.

¼ pound seedless tamarind
1½ cups warm water
¾ cup dark brown sugar
1 teaspoon roasted cumin seeds, coarsely ground
2 teaspoons finely grated ginger
½ teaspoon crushed red pepper flakes
¼ pound seedless raisins
Salt to taste

Directions

Soak tamarind in 1½ cups water. Crush, strain, and place juice in a **nonreactive** pan with sugar, cumin, ginger, and red pepper flakes. Simmer on low heat until syrupy, about 5 minutes.

Add raisins; season with salt to taste. Simmer for 5 minutes. Cool, place in a sterilized jar, cover, and refrigerate. Keeps well for up to 2 weeks.

Yields 2 cups

Tamarind Juice

Ripe **tamarind** has a tangy, sweet-sour flavor. The chocolate-brown juice adds color and a sophisticated taste to soups, seafood, and meats. It adds color and texture when used in marinades and leaves behind a rich hue after cooking.

You can find packaged dry-block tamarind with or without seeds in health food stores, gourmet stores, and ethnic markets. You can also find instant tamarind pretty easily (it has suddenly become very popular). Once a package of dry tamarind has been opened, it should be stored in the refrigerator.

¼ pound seedless tamarind
2 cups hot water

Directions

Place tamarind in a **nonreactive** bowl, pour 2 cups hot water over, cover, and leave for 2 hours. Crush with a wooden spoon and strain into another bowl, using the back of the spoon to push out pulp in the strainer. Discard fibrous membrane and pith. Store juice in a covered glass jar. Keeps well for 2 weeks in the refrigerator.

Yields 1½ cups

Chutneys, Relishes

Green Tomato Chutney

Green tomatoes in this chutney are accented with ginger, garlic, and fried black **mustard seeds.** These fried, nutty-tasting seeds add to the appearance of the chutney and give it a flavorful bite as well. **Turmeric** gives a glow to the cooked tomatoes.

Green tomatoes are available in many ethnic markets in larger cities. The small varieties of green tomatoes are the best. Green tomato chutney can replace a sauce in fish, seafood, poultry, or meat dishes.

To peel tomatoes, place them in boiling water for 1 minute, remove, and place them in cold water for 5 minutes. Using a knife point, loosen the skin at the flower end of the tomato and pull up toward the stem end.

2½ pounds green tomatoes, peeled
1 cup cider vinegar
1 cup sugar
⅛ teaspoon turmeric
1 teaspoon crushed black mustard seeds
1 tablespoon grated ginger
1 tablespoon minced garlic
1 teaspoon **cayenne pepper**
2-inch piece of **cinnamon** stick
Salt to taste

Directions

Slice tomatoes ¼ inch thick and reserve. Place remaining ingredients in a **nonreactive** pan and simmer on medium heat until syrupy, about 30 minutes. Add tomatoes and cook on low heat until glazed and thick, about 30 to 40 minutes. Cool; pour into sterilized jars and cover tight. Place in refrigerator. Keeps well for 3 months.

Yields 1 pint

Gooseberry Chutney

Gooseberry chutney has a preservelike finish to it. This tart berry chutney gets its fragrance from a mix of whole spices fried in oil.

Here in Hawai'i, I use a purple variety of gooseberry that few know about unless, like me, they have a friend who has a tree in her backyard. The green variety works just as well. Gooseberries are highly acidic and you may need to add more sugar than the recipe calls for. I use gooseberries with skin and seeds in the chutney. It can be tedious to peel and de-seed these berries.

2 pounds gooseberries, stemmed and washed
1 tablespoon olive oil
¼ teaspoon **fenugreek** seeds
½ teaspoon **fennel** seeds
½ teaspoon **cumin** seeds
½ teaspoon black **mustard seeds**
2 garlic cloves, sliced thin
2 teaspoons grated ginger
½ teaspoon **cayenne pepper**
1 cup cider vinegar
1 cup sugar
Salt to taste

Directions

Wash berries, place in a colander, and let all moisture dry out.

Heat oil in a **nonreactive** pan, add spice seeds, and cook on low heat until they start to pop. Add garlic and ginger; cook a few seconds. Add cayenne pepper, vinegar, and sugar, and bring to slow boil. Add berries, season with salt to taste, and simmer on medium heat until berries are soft and chutney is thick and shiny, about 35 minutes. Cool, pour in sterilized jars, cover, and place in the refrigerator. Keeps well for 3 months.

Yields 1 pint

Dried Cranberry Chutney

Dried cranberries are cooked into a chutney with a base of sweetened red wine vinegar and red wine. To keep the color theme, red onions are added, which turn a luscious, glazed burgundy. The chutney is mildly enlivened with fruit-friendly spices—**cinnamon** and **cloves**. Dried cranberry chutney goes well with poultry, especially game birds, lamb, and pork. It adds zip to cooked grains.

½ cup dried cranberries
¼ cup finely chopped red onion
1 cup sugar
1 teaspoon grated ginger
1 teaspoon grated garlic
½ cup red wine vinegar
½ cup red wine
½ teaspoon crushed red pepper flakes
1-inch piece of cinnamon stick
⅛ teaspoon ground cloves
1 bay leaf
Grated zest of ½ lemon
Salt to taste

Directions
Place all ingredients in a **nonreactive** pan and place on low heat. Simmer about 40 minutes, to a glaze. Season with salt to taste.

Yields 1 cup

Mint Chutney

This emerald green–hued preparation is an uncooked chutney. It is pungent and pesto-like, but the coconut provides a creamy taste. The preparation is simple and the result is an exotic, tasty chutney.

3 cups garden mint leaves
½ cup freshly grated coconut
1 shallot, peeled and sliced
2 teaspoons grated ginger
*1 **green chili**, halved, seeded, and chopped*
2 tablespoons lime or lemon juice
2 teaspoons sugar
¼ cup water
Salt to taste

Directions
Place all ingredients in a food processor and blend until smooth. Taste and adjust seasoning. Spoon into a small glass bowl. Cover and refrigerate. Keeps for 2 days.

Yields 1 cup

Pineapple Relish

Relishes, also called fresh chutneys, are usually uncooked. Most relishes must be used shortly after preparation—some immediately, others within a couple of days. Often the freshest ingredients are used and they are seasoned, not spiced.

This relish is sweet, rich, and exploding with flavor when made with a fresh, ripe pineapple. Serve with fish or seafood, lamb, and pork.

1 cup diced fresh pineapple
½ cup diced red bell pepper
½ cup diced red onion
1 tablespoon toasted black sesame seeds
¼ cup chopped Chinese parsley
1 tablespoon light soy sauce
¼ teaspoon freshly ground black pepper
¼ teaspoon crushed red pepper flakes
1 tablespoon sugar
Salt to taste
Lemon juice to taste

Directions

Mix all ingredients in a small stainless steel bowl, seasoning with salt and lemon juice to taste. Serve immediately.

4 servings

Orange Relish

The sweet, tart orange juice mixed with herbs in this relish are particularly refreshing. Roasted, crushed **cumin** seeds help to create an exotic Middle Eastern flavor.

It complements seafood, fish, and lamb dishes.

2 oranges
Juice of 1 orange
1 tablespoon white vinegar
½ cup shredded garden mint
¼ cup shredded Chinese parsley
¼ cup broken-up dill leaves
¼ teaspoon cracked black peppercorns
¼ teaspoon crushed red pepper flakes
1 teaspoon grated garlic
1 teaspoon roasted, crushed cumin seeds
1 teaspoon ground cumin seeds
1 tablespoon lemon juice
Salt to taste
Sugar to taste

Directions

Peel and cut oranges into segments. Remove pith and seeds. Combine with remaining ingredients in a stainless steel bowl with salt and sugar to taste.

Leave to marinate at least 30 minutes in the refrigerator and serve.

6 servings

Burst of Flavor

Mango and Papaya Relish

Hot, sweet, and sour, this relish may also be served partially frozen as an intermezzo.

2 partially ripe mangoes, peeled, seeded, and diced
1 small papaya, peeled, seeded, and diced
Juice of 1 lemon
1 teaspoon chopped **jalapeño pepper**
1 teaspoon sliced green onion
1 teaspoon grated ginger
1 tablespoon white wine vinegar
1 tablespoon sugar
Salt to taste
Freshly ground black pepper to taste

Directions

Mix all ingredients in a small stainless steel bowl with salt and black pepper to taste. Leave to marinate for at least 30 minutes in freezer before serving.

8 servings

Cooked Papaya Relish

This briefly cooked relish of ripe papaya is left with a delectable sweet-and-sour sauce coating it.

Serve this relish warm with grilled fish or seafood.

1 ripe papaya, peeled and seeded
1 tablespoon olive oil
1 small red onion, cut in $\frac{1}{2}$-inch cubes
1 teaspoon grated garlic
1 tablespoon cracked black peppercorns
$\frac{1}{2}$ cup white wine
$\frac{1}{4}$ cup white wine vinegar
1 tablespoon **fish sauce**
1 teaspoon crushed red pepper flakes
Sugar to taste
Salt to taste

Directions

Cut papaya into $\frac{1}{2}$-inch cubes.

Heat oil in sauté pan on medium heat and sauté onion until wilted. Add garlic and pepper, and cook 1 minute.

Stir in wine, vinegar, fish sauce, and red pepper flakes. Simmer a few minutes.

Add papaya; move around in pan. When well combined, season with sugar and salt to taste. Remove from heat and serve warm.

6 servings

Avocado Relish

This saladlike relish is refreshing. Herbs, ginger, and **green chili** add a spark to the buttery avocado.

With a basket of **poppadom,** it makes a light appetizer, or it can be served with fish or seafood. For a salad, top crisp greens with this relish.

1 small avocado, peeled and seeded
1 orange, peeled and segmented
2 tablespoons shredded Chinese parsley
1 tablespoon shredded basil leaves
1 tablespoon **balsamic vinegar**
1 teaspoon grated ginger
1 teaspoon seeded, chopped green chili
Salt to taste
Freshly ground black pepper to taste
Lemon juice to taste
Sugar to taste

Directions

Cut avocado into medium dice and place in a small glass bowl. Remove pith and seeds from orange segments and discard. Add segments to avocado. Add Chinese parsley and basil, and toss.

Add balsamic vinegar, ginger, green chilies, with salt, black pepper, lemon juice, and sugar to taste. Toss to combine all. Serve within 1 to 2 hours.

4 servings

Vegetable Relish

This relish has many textures and flavors. It is mildly spiced with freshly ground **coriander,** which gives the relish an earthy flavor.

To serve this attractive relish, spoon a portion on a plate and top with cooked seafood, fish, chicken, or meat.

1 yellow bell pepper, seeded and cut into
    a **julienne**
½ red onion, cut into a julienne
1 tomato peeled, seeded, and cut into a julienne
1 cup basil leaves, shredded
½ cup chopped parsley
¼ cup garden mint leaves, shredded
½ cup iceberg lettuce, shredded
½ teaspoon ground coriander
½ teaspoon freshly ground black pepper
Salt to taste
Lemon juice to taste

Directions

Mix all the ingredients in a medium-size stainless steel bowl and season with pepper, and salt and lemon juice to taste.

Marinate in the refrigerator for 1 hour and serve.

4 servings

Ogo Relish

Ogo is a type of seaweed. Once tossed, serve it immediately; otherwise, it loses its crunch.

Seafood kabobs are perfect with this relish.

1 cup fresh ogo
3 Roma tomatoes, cut into small dice
1 cucumber, peeled, seeded, and cut into
*   small dice*
1 tablespoon chopped green onion
1 tablespoon chopped garden mint leaves
*1¼ cups **rice wine vinegar***
*1 tablespoon **fish sauce***
1 tablespoon soy sauce
1 teaspoon crushed red pepper flakes
*1 tablespoon **mirin***
Salt to taste
Lemon juice to taste

Directions

Trim, wash, and cut ogo into 1-inch lengths. Mix all ingredients in a small stainless steel or glass bowl, seasoning with salt and lemon juice to taste. Serve immediately.

Yields 1½ cups

Tomato Relish

The sweet taste of the tomatoes stands out in this very light relish. Use wine-ripened red or green tomatoes for best results.

Serving possibilities are endless here. The relish may be part of an appetizer or a salad. It can be an accompaniment to seafood, fish, or meat. It can also act as a sauce.

2 tomatoes, cut into small dice
1 tablespoon chopped Chinese parsley
1 tablespoon chopped garden mint
2 tablespoons white wine vinegar
1 teaspoon cracked black peppercorns
Salt to taste
Lemon juice to taste

Directions

Mix all ingredients in a small stainless steel bowl; season with salt and lemon juice to taste. Refrigerate for 1 hour. Serve with seafood or fish.

4 servings

Seeni Sambol

Sambols are great favorites in Sri Lanka and are nearly as popular in Singapore and Malaysia. As a rule they are hot and spicy, often made of dried shrimp, pickled fish, or grated coconut, fresh or roasted. Cooked sambols keep a week if refrigerated; uncooked ones should be refrigerated and used within a day or two. Still others must be enjoyed as soon as they are made

In Sri Lanka this caramelized onion sambol, a cooked sambol, shows up often with special rice and curry meals. Traditionally, it contains **Maldive fish,** though I leave it out for my vegetarian guests.

1 tablespoon vegetable oil
2 pounds yellow onions, thinly sliced
1 piece **lemongrass** bulb
1 sprig **curry leaves**
2-inch piece of **cinnamon** stick
4 whole **cardamoms,** crushed
1/4 teaspoon **cayenne pepper**
2 teaspoons paprika
1 tablespoon sugar
1/4 cup **Tamarind Juice** (see recipe, page 203)
Salt to taste

Directions

Heat oil in sauté pan; add onion, lemongrass, and curry leaves. Cook on moderate heat until onions turn deep gold, about 10 minutes. Stir in spices and sugar, and cook for 5 minutes. Add tamarind juice and salt to taste. Cook 20 minutes on moderately high heat, stirring occasionally to avoid burning. Remove lemongrass and cinnamon stick. Cool. Store in a glass container and refrigerate. Use the next day; serve at room temperature. Keeps well for 3 to 4 days if refrigerated.

8 to 10 servings

Coconut Sambol

This sambol is hot and spicy, sweet-and-sour, and the creamy taste of the coconut provides the counterbalance for this luscious sambol. This sambol keeps well for a day or two. Bring it to room temperature to serve.

You may leave out the **Maldive fish.** Maldive fish is cured bonito. The curing process involves boiling, smoking, and drying the fish.

1 cup grated fresh coconut
1 tablespoon coarse-ground Maldive fish
1 teaspoon chopped shallots
1/8 teaspoon **cayenne pepper**
1 teaspoon paprika
1 tablespoon fresh lemon juice
Salt to taste

Directions

Put all ingredients into a food processor. Pulse a few times. Taste and adjust seasoning with more salt or lemon. Spoon into a small glass bowl and serve.

4 servings

Tomato and Onion Sambol

This tomato sambol can accompany most entrées. The juices of the thoroughly mixed sambol make a tasty sauce for the dish it partners. *Note well:* The sambol must be used up by the end of the meal or discarded.

1 tomato, cored, halved, and seeded
½ red onion, sliced fine and soaked in
*   ice water for 10 minutes*
½ cup shredded basil leaves
½ teaspoon cracked black peppercorns
½ teaspoon crushed red pepper flakes
1 tablespoon cider vinegar
1 tablespoon fresh lemon juice
Salt to taste

Directions
Slice tomato very thin. Drain water from the onions, wash in fresh water, squeeze out excess water, and place with tomatoes in a small glass bowl. Add basil leaves, spices, vinegar, and lemon juice; season with salt to taste and mix well to combine. Serve immediately.

6 servings

Parsley and Coconut Sambol

This is a delicious and refreshing sambol that can be served as an appetizer or as an accompaniment to seafood and fish. It should be used up within a day or two.

2 cups parsley leaves, washed
½ cup grated fresh coconut
*2 **green chilies,** halved, seeded, and chopped*
¼ teaspoon freshly ground black pepper
2 limes, juiced and strained
Salt to taste
½ teaspoon sugar

Directions
Place all ingredients in food processor and blend until smooth. Taste; adjust seasoning by adding more lemon juice, salt, or sugar. Spoon into a glass bowl. Serve chilled.

4 servings

Blachan

Though Malayan in origin, this blachan is a favorite of many ethnic groups in Sri Lanka. It's used in Sri Lanka's famous lumprais, a savory rice wrapped in banana leaves and baked. You may also serve blachan with rice and curries.

½ cup dried shrimp, without shells
¼ cup grated coconut
2 shallots, peeled and sliced
2 teaspoons grated ginger
1 teaspoon grated garlic
1 teaspoon **cayenne pepper**
¼ cup coconut milk
1 teaspoon sugar
Salt to taste
Lemon juice to taste

Directions

Roast shrimp in skillet on medium heat; when partially roasted, add coconut and roast until coconut turns dark brown. Remove coconut and shrimp from the skillet. Blend all ingredients in a food processor to a smooth purée, seasoning with salt and lemon juice to taste. Turn onto a small serving dish, patting into a hamburger shape. Serve with rice and curries.

8 servings

Eggplant Sambol

As always, eggplant is a great accompaniment to lamb and as a dip for pita bread. The roasted eggplant is left to marinate so it can absorb much of the seasonings. Use this sambol within a day or two.

1 round eggplant, about 1 pound
1 teaspoon olive oil
1 tomato, chopped
¼ cup chopped yellow onion
1 **green chili,** *seeded and chopped*
½ teaspoon crushed red pepper flakes
½ teaspoon ground black peppercorns
1 tablespoon white vinegar
Lemon juice to taste
Salt to taste

Directions

Preheat oven 400°F.

Using a sharp knife, make 3 cuts 2 inches long and 1 inch deep in the eggplant. Rub skin with oil and place in a baking pan. Roast in the oven until soft, about 1 hour. Cool. Peel and discard skin, and chop pulp.

Place in a small glass bowl with remaining ingredients, adding lemon juice and salt to taste. Marinate in the refrigerator for 1 hour before serving.

4 to 5 servings

Sweet Mint Dip

Sweet-and-sour, this dip may be served as a dressing for salad or as a dip for vegetables.

1 cup sugar
1 cup cider vinegar
½ cup water
*1 teaspoon crushed **fennel** seeds*
1 cup broken-up fresh garden mint sprigs
*Pinch of **cayenne pepper***
Salt to taste

Directions
Place all the ingredients in a stainless steel saucepan. Place on low heat and simmer for 20 minutes.

Cool, strain, and chill before serving.

Yields 1 cup

Citrus Pickle

Use strips of pickled lemon and lime and a halved kumquat to accent some entrées like grilled hens. To accompany curry and rice, chop the pickle coarsely (seeds removed, of course) and serve.

6 unblemished lemons
6 unblemished limes
6 unblemished kumquats
1 tablespoon coarsely grated ginger
*2 teaspoons **cumin** seeds*
1 teaspoon cracked black peppercorns
2 tablespoons salt
8 to 10 large lemons, juiced and strained
½ cup sugar
1 tablespoon crushed red pepper flakes
*6 whole **cloves***
*2-inch piece of **cinnamon** stick*

Directions
Wash fruit and wipe dry with kitchen towels to remove moisture. Quarter the lemons and limes, cutting to about ¼ inch from the stem end so the quarters remain attached to the base. Mix ginger, cumin, peppercorns, and salt. Stuff the cut fruits, press to original shape, and place carefully in a sterilized jar. Add kumquats and pour in lemon juice. Cover jar with cheesecloth and tie at neck. Place in the sun or a warm spot and let stand for 1 week.

At the end of the week, strain juice into a **nonreactive** pan. Add sugar, red pepper flakes, cloves, and cinnamon. Simmer on low heat until sugar dissolves, about 5 minutes. Add fruits and simmer on gentle heat for 10 to 15 minutes. Place in a sterilized jar; cool. Cover jar tightly and let stand in a cool place for 4 weeks before using. It keeps well for 6 to 8 months. Once opened, refrigerate.

Yields 2 pints

Pickled Lemons

These lemons are pickled in lightly spiced salt and lemon juice. Make larger quantities when lemons are in season. Pickled lemon wedges are good with roast lamb and boiled beef.

Limes are equally good pickled this way.

6 large lemons
4 tablespoons salt
*2 tablespoons **cumin** seeds, crushed*
½ teaspoon cracked black peppercorns
*2-inch piece of **cinnamon** stick*
6 lemons, juiced

Directions

Wash and dry lemons with a kitchen towel. Make 4 cuts lengthwise on each lemon, leaving the wedges still attached at the stem end. Mix salt, cumin, and peppercorns. Stuff the lemons and gently press the wedges back together. Place in a sterilized glass jar and sprinkle in any leftover salt. Drop in cinnamon stick and cover jar.

Leave in a warm place, preferably in the sun, for 3 days.

Bring lemon juice to a boil and pour over the lemons. Let cool and cover the jar tightly.

Set jar in a warm place. Invert the jar every 2 to 3 days to mix the flavors. Use after 1 month.

Yields 1 pint

Pickled Whole Garlic Cloves

I love to sauté these pickled garlic cloves and strew them among grilled vegetables accompanying grilled fish. Sometimes I sauté them lightly to garnish a steak, or mash them in a salad dressing to give that extra delicate whiff. Another option is to sprinkle a few on a chicken during the final stage of roasting for unexpected sparkle.

1 pound garlic, peeled
1 tablespoon whole black peppercorns
*¼ teaspoon **turmeric***
*1 tablespoon **cayenne pepper***
*2 tablespoons **fennel** seeds*
*1 tablespoon **garam masala***
*1-inch piece of **cinnamon** stick*
*1 sprig **curry leaves** or 1 bay leaf*
1 teaspoon salt
1½ pints olive oil

Directions

Dry garlic with a kitchen towel to remove moisture. Place in sterilized pickling jar; add spices, curry or bay leaves, and salt. Add enough oil to cover garlic; stir. Cover jar with cheesecloth and tie at neck.

Place jar in the sun. If you don't have a sunny spot, put it by the stove. Keep it there for 4 days, shaking once a day. Remove cheesecloth and cover with sterilized lid. Use after 1 month. It keeps well for 3 to 4 months. Once opened, refrigerate.

Yields 2 pints

Pickled Fruit

This fast pickle should be used within two days. I offer these with sliced ham, not forgetting the mustard.

2 pounds seeded, peeled watermelon
$\frac{1}{2}$ small honeydew, halved and seeded
1 small cantaloupe, halved and seeded
2 cups sugar
1 cup water
$\frac{1}{2}$ cup white vinegar
$\frac{1}{2}$ cup white wine
5 whole **cloves**
1 bay leaf
5 crushed **cardamoms**
2-inch piece of **cinnamon** stick

Directions

Using a melon-baller, cut watermelon, honeydew, and cantaloupe into balls; reserve in glass or stainless steel container.

Cook remaining ingredients in a pan on moderate heat for 20 minutes. Cool; strain liquid onto the fruits, discarding all spices except the cinnamon stick. Put cinnamon stick with the fruits. Refrigerate overnight. Remove cinnamon stick before serving.

6 to 8 servings

Pickled Vegetables

This healthy standby is easy to prepare. I use it in salads, with crisp greens, sprinkling a little of the juice from the pickle on the greens. Take it on a picnic to accompany barbecued meats or poultry.

1 cup peeled shallots
2 carrots, peeled, sliced $\frac{1}{8}$ inch thick
8 string beans, cut in $1\frac{1}{2}$-inch pieces
12 wax peppers
1 head cauliflower, cut in florets
$\frac{1}{2}$ cup Dijon mustard
1-inch piece of **cinnamon** stick
2 pints white vinegar
1 teaspoon crushed red pepper flakes
1 teaspoon freshly ground black pepper
$\frac{1}{2}$ teaspoon **turmeric**
$\frac{1}{2}$ teaspoon ground **cumin**
1 teaspoon chopped ginger
1 tablespoon sugar
Salt to taste

Directions

Blanch all vegetables for 1 minute and leave in colander to drain off all moisture.

Combine remaining ingredients in a medium-size bowl. Add vegetables and mix with a sterilized spoon to combine well. Fill sterilized jars, cover tightly, and refrigerate. The pickled vegetables are ready to use in 3 days. Keeps well for 2 weeks.

Yields 2 pints

Vegetable Platter with Mustard Pickles

To delight vegetarians, serve these pickles with a platter of vegetables. They're equally delicious as a garnish for a roast. I serve these mustard pickles in a bowl along with a bowl of Dijon mustard to accompany a baked ham.

½ cup finely chopped dried apricots
½ cup pitted dates
½ ripe pineapple, peeled, cored, and cut
    into large dice
1 carrot, cut into ½-inch cubes
1 small red onion, peeled and cut into large dice
1 cup white wine
1 cup cider vinegar
1 tablespoon Dijon mustard
2 tablespoons sugar
2 teaspoons grated ginger
¼ teaspoon **turmeric**
Salt to taste
Freshly ground black pepper to taste

Vegetable Platter for Four

2 sweet potatoes
1 beet
2 wing beans
1 lotus root
1 red apple
1 **endive**
1 small cucumber
¼ red bell pepper

Directions

To make the mustard pickles, place all fruits and vegetables in a large glass bowl. Mix remaining ingredients into fruits and vegetables until well coated. Cover and leave in refrigerator to marinate for 2 days before use. Keeps well for 2 weeks.

To prepare the vegetable platter, preheat oven to 375°F. Roast the sweet potatoes and the beet for 40 minutes. Cool, peel, and cut into wedges.

Blanch wing beans, refresh in cold water, and cut each in half.

Peel and slice lotus root ⅛ inch thick. Place in a baking pan and roast in the oven for 8 minutes.

Slice apple, endive, and cucumber. Cut red bell pepper into a thick **julienne.**

Presentation

Place a bowl of mustard pickles on a platter and arrange the vegetables around it.

Yields 3 pints of pickles

Burst of Flavor

Pickled Green Papaya and Long Beans

Pickles have a long shelf life.

Make and store pickles in sterilized glass containers. For those that require cooking, as in this recipe, use a stainless steel pan. Use these pickles as an accompaniment to grilled fish, meat, or chicken. For a change, serve these pickles on a vegetable platter.

1 small green papaya, peeled, seeded, quartered, and cut into ½-inch slices
1 pound long beans, cut into 2-inch pieces
1 carrot, peeled and cut into ⅛-inch slices
¾ pound whole shallots, peeled
Salt to taste
4 cups white wine vinegar
½ cup country-style Dijon mustard
½ cup sugar
2 cloves garlic, crushed
1 tablespoon grated ginger
1 teaspoon ground **cumin**
1 teaspoon crushed red pepper flakes
¼ teaspoon **turmeric**

Directions

Add papaya, beans, carrot, and shallots to boiling, salted water. Cook for 2 minutes and drain. Cool vegetables; combine with remaining ingredients.

Put into jars, cover, and refrigerate for 3 days.

Yields 1 quart

Preserved Lemon Wheels

I use these preserved lemon wheels to garnish broiled or roast chicken and roast veal. The lemon wheels have only a hint of spices after they are cooked.

4 lemons, sliced ⅛ inch thick, seeds removed
2 cups cold water
1 tablespoon salt
¾ cup sugar
½ cup honey
2 cups water
8 whole **cloves**
½-inch piece of **cinnamon** stick
4 **cardamoms,** crushed

Directions

Place lemons in a bowl, cover with 2 cups cold water, sprinkle with salt, and set aside for 25 minutes.

Place sugar, honey, and 2 cups water in a stainless steel saucepan. Tie up cloves, cinnamon, and cardamoms in a **sachet.** Add to saucepan and bring to slow boil. Lower heat and simmer 10 minutes.

Drain lemon slices, wash in fresh water, and add to syrup. Simmer for 20 minutes on low heat. Discard sachet. Put into a sterilized jar. Cool and refrigerate. Keeps for 1 month.

Yields 1 pint

Burst of Flavor

Tomato Confit

Although it could be tedious to peel these cherry tomatoes after cooking them, the end result will make it all worthwhile.

These tomatoes, cooked in oil with a hint of **cinnamon,** have many uses, but they are stunning as a garnish.

1 cup olive oil
½ cup sugar
½ cup white wine
1-inch piece of cinnamon stick
1 bay leaf
2 cloves crushed garlic
Pinch of salt
32 to 36 cherry tomatoes

Directions

Place oil, sugar, wine, cinnamon, bay leaf, and garlic with pinch of salt in a pan. Place on low heat and bring to a simmer. Add tomatoes and cook on very low heat for 30 minutes.

Cool and refrigerate. Peel tomatoes and use as needed.

Yields 1 pint

Spicy Winter Melon Preserve

You will need to buy about 3 pounds of melon to net 2 pounds of flesh. It is cooked in a spiced tangy syrup that results in glazed, translucent winter melon, fragrant with the spices.

For festive occasions, I garnish roast birds with these preserves. Unusual yet elegant, it never fails to thrill my guests.

2 pounds peeled and seeded winter melon
*2-inch piece of **cinnamon** stick*
*6 whole **cloves***
*6 **cardamoms,** crushed*
2 cups sugar
2½ cups water
½ cup white vinegar
½ cup white wine

Directions

Prick winter melon with a fork, wrap in a tea towel, and roll to squeeze out as much liquid as possible. Cut in 1-inch cubes.

Tie cinnamon, cloves, and cardamom in a **sachet;** place in a pan with sugar, water, vinegar, and wine. Simmer on low heat for 10 minutes. Stir in melon; continue to cook on low heat for 40 minutes. Remove from heat and leave out overnight. Simmer again for 40 minutes; remove and discard sachet. Cool, place in sterilized jars, and refrigerate. Keeps well for 2 to 3 weeks.

Yields 2 pints

Chutneys, Relishes

Preserved Spicy Oranges

Oranges need only a hint of spices. The spices in this recipe are in the syrup in which the oranges are simmered. They leave only a veil of fragrance on the oranges.

Instead of serving a whole orange wedge, you may serve the wedges cut finely into strips as a garnish for roast birds, lamb, or pork.

3 oranges
Water
4 tablespoons salt

For Syrup
1 cup sugar
1½ cups water
½ cup cider vinegar
4 whole **cloves**
5 crushed **cardamoms**
3-inch piece of **cinnamon** stick
1 blade of **mace**
2 teaspoons shredded ginger

Directions
Cut each orange into 8 wedges. Cover with water and sprinkle with salt. Leave overnight. Drain oranges and rinse in fresh water.

Place ingredients for syrup in a **nonreactive** pan and bring to a simmer on low heat; add oranges and simmer for 1 hour. Remove from heat and leave out the oranges in the syrup overnight.

The next day, cook the oranges in syrup on low heat for 1 hour, until the oranges are glazed. Store in sterilized glass container.

Yields 1½ pints

Spicy Kumquat Preserve

Before adding kumquats into the spicy syrup, prick them with a pin in five to six spots. This process enables the syrup to seep into the fruit and keep them plump when preserved. Kumquats cooked in the mildly spiced syrup retain only a hint of the spices.

To use the preserved kumquats, press out the seeds and chop, dice, or cut them into strips. They are good in sauces, as garnishes, and in compound butter.

1 pound kumquats
2 cups water
4 tablespoons salt

For Syrup
1 cup sugar
2 cups white wine vinegar
2 cups water
1-inch piece of **cinnamon** stick
4 whole **cloves**
4 **cardamoms**
1 blade of **mace**
1 bay leaf

Directions
Place kumquats in 2 cups water, add salt, and leave overnight. Wash and refresh with cold water. Prick each kumquat in 5 or 6 spots using a sharp knifepoint.

Bring ingredients for syrup to a boil. Add kumquats and simmer on low heat for 15 minutes. Leave kumquats out in syrup overnight.

Drain and set kumquats on the side. Boil drained syrup, add kumquats, and simmer 2 minutes. Pour into sterilized jars. Use after 2 weeks.

Yields 1½ pints

Onion and Rhubarb Marmalade

For the sake of color continuity, I use red onion in this recipe whenever possible. The red port wine adds sweetness and works together with the red wine vinegar to keep the red color in the marmalade.

2 tablespoons unsalted butter
1 large red onion, thinly sliced
2 rhubarb stems
½ cup sugar
2 teaspoons grated ginger
¼ cup red port wine
¼ cup red wine vinegar
3 whole **cloves**
2-inch piece of **cinnamon** *stick*
Salt to taste
Cayenne pepper *to taste*

Directions
Heat butter in a **nonreactive** pan on medium heat and sauté sliced onion until golden brown and caramelized.

Remove the outside stringy peel from the rhubarb, slice the stem ½ inch thick, and add to onion.

Add sugar, ginger, port wine, and red wine vinegar, and simmer on low heat for 3 to 4 minutes. Add cloves and cinnamon stick, and season with salt and cayenne pepper to taste. Continue to cook on low heat for 40 minutes to the consistency of a marmalade. Store in a sterilized glass container.

Yields 1 cup

Pickled Cherries

The aromatic spices used in the pickling mix give the cherries only a hint of their fragrance. These gorgeous cherries, with their festive aroma, are an ideal addition to the larder during Christmas time. They come in handy to put in sauces, to use as a garnish, or to add to an hors d'oeuvre tray.

2 pounds cherries unstoned and with stems on

Pickling Mix
1 cup white wine
1 cup white wine vinegar
1 cup water
2 cups sugar
1 teaspoon whole black peppercorns
2-inch piece of **cinnamon** *stick*
4 whole **cloves**
4 **cardamoms**
Peel of 1 orange
¼ blade of **mace**

Directions
Sort cherries and place in sterilized jars.

Place all the pickling mix ingredients in a **nonreactive** pan and bring to a slow simmer. Simmer for 10 minutes.

Remove and discard orange peel. Pour the mix over cherries, cool, cover jar, and refrigerate for 3 weeks before use.

Yields 1½ pints

Preserved Peaches

When peaches are plentiful, they are at their best. It is important to pick the best ripe peaches for preserving. These peaches are spiced, but they are equally good in desserts.

6 ripe peaches
2 cups water
4 cups ice water

For Syrup
2 cups water
1 cup sugar
*6 whole **cloves***
*3-inch piece of **cinnamon** stick*
1 cup brandy

Directions
Place peaches in 2 cups of boiling water for 1 minute and drop in 4 cups of ice water. Peel the peaches. The skin should drop off easily.

For syrup, place 2 cups water and sugar in a pan and bring to a slow simmer. When sugar is melted, add cloves and cinnamon. Add the peeled peaches and simmer 15 minutes. Place peaches in a sterilized jar and pour syrup over. Pour the brandy in jar and seal. Keeps up to 3 months.

Yield 1 pint

Apple and Lemon Marmalade

The spices give only a hint in the background, keeping the lemony-glazed apples standing on their own. This marmalade is delicious with seafood; it perks up the food it accompanies. It is best to use tart green apples in this recipe. To avoid discoloration, dice and place apples in a bowl of cold water with the juice of a lemon.

6 large green tart apples
3 cups cold water
Juice of 1 lemon

For Syrup
¾ cup sugar
¼ cup water
1 cup dry white wine
Juice of 2 lemons
*⅛ teaspoon ground **mace***
*⅛ teaspoon ground **cinnamon***
*⅛ teaspoon ground **cardamom** seeds*
*⅛ teaspoon **cayenne pepper***
2 teaspoons grated lemon zest
Salt to taste

Directions
Peel, core, and cut apples into small dice. Place the apples in a bowl with 3 cups cold water and the lemon juice. For the syrup, place sugar, water, wine, and lemon juice in a **nonreactive** pan. Place on low heat and simmer for 3 minutes. Strain the apples and add to the syrup. Add the spices, lemon zest, and salt to taste. Stir frequently and cook for 30 minutes or until the marmalade is thick and glazed. Cool. Pour into sterilized jars and refrigerate. Keeps up to 1 week.

Yields 3 cups

Chutneys, Relishes

Desserts . . .

Perfectly Fabulous

Those were the days! Our afternoon tea was almost a ritual. Lavariya was a sweetmeat we loved for weekend afternoon teas. Its steamed, fine, rice-flour strands enclosed a moist coconut and treacle filling. Delicately scented with crushed **fennel** seeds, it was shaped like a half-moon. Sago, another favorite treat, was cooked with thick coconut milk, whole **cardamom** pods, treacle, and served in a large silver bowl. Yes, such desserts were possible with plenty of help in the kitchen.

My mother always believed in giving the finishing touches to any preparation she fed her family. She was an authority on spicing. She often made aggala—nothing more than roasted rice, finely ground almost to a gossamer gold dust. This powder was ground again with palm sugar, freshly ground coconut, and a few peppercorns. How many? I don't know, but she made sure she was there to count them before grinding them. What I do know and relish is that breath of black pepper in the aggala; the flavoring was so well balanced, it tugs at my heart even now.

Growing up in multiethnic Sri Lanka, we joined in many of its ethnic celebrations. I remember celebrating many a Dipavali with my friends. We had sweetmeats, rich and delicious, with ghee and spices. I remember their haunting, spicy fragrance.

We often celebrated Ramadan. Sweetmeats were served enriched with cream and eggs, raisins and pistachios, and spices for that ultimate touch of elegance.

Since childhood I have grown to appreciate many tastes from many countries. I duplicate the aromatic, silky carrot pudding, although I rarely lay the gossamer silver sheet on the pudding as the Muslims do when they serve it at every Ramadan feast. I reserve the silver sheets for very special occasions.

Millicent, my mother-in-law, like many others of her generation in Sri Lanka, was an expert at making desserts and sweetmeats. Her Christmas table always had pink roses of winter melon preserves among other delicacies. It was amazing how she twirled the thin strips of hot pink–tinted winter melon preserves with two forks to form perfect roses. She set aside these roses to let the sugar crystallize.

From my English guru, George Charman, I learned the intricacies of making fabulous desserts and pastries. His crème anglaise and puff pastry are yet to be surpassed. I won many hearts, and a reputation for desserts, with his chocolate gâteau, which I duplicated when I was the chef at The Willows. In this chapter, you will encounter the theme of fragrance with a burst of flavor—an enchanting way to end a meal.

Desserts

Cinnamon Ice Cream with Jaggery Sauce

Ice cream with **jaggery** sauce is one of Sri Lanka's most popular desserts. Jaggery is derived from the sugars of various palms or sugarcane. It tastes like caramel and molasses with a whisper of mocha. If jaggery is unavailable, serve a caramel sauce with the ice cream.

For Cinnamon Ice Cream
2 cups whole milk
6 large egg yolks
1 cup sugar
2 teaspoons freshly ground **cinnamon**
1 cup full cream

For Cashew Nut Brittle
1 tablespoon vegetable oil
1 cup cashew nuts
1¼ cups sugar
¼ cup water

For Jaggery Sauce
¾ cup crushed jaggery
3 tablespoons water

Garnish
6 four-inch sticks of cinnamon

Directions
To make ice cream, place milk in a saucepan on low heat and bring to a slow simmer. Remove from heat and place aside.

Place egg yolks and sugar in a medium-size bowl and beat until light and creamy. Pour half of the hot milk over the eggs and whisk to combine. Pour back in the saucepan with the rest of the milk. Whisk in the cinnamon and place on low heat. Stirring constantly, cook until the mix is thick. Remove from heat and set aside to cool for a few min-utes. Add cream, place in an ice cream freezer, and freeze according to the manufacturer's instructions.

For cashew nut brittle, grease a baking sheet with the oil and set aside to use later. Place cashew nuts in a skillet and leave on moderate heat for 5 to 6 minutes. Place sugar and ¼ cup water in a saucepan and boil until sugar reaches 248°F, about 6 to 8 minutes. Add cashew nuts and stir with a wooden spoon. After 1 minute, remove from heat and stir until the sugar turns grainy.

Place the saucepan with the cashew nuts back on medium heat and cook for 3 to 4 minutes, stirring constantly until sugar is melted. Cook until sugar turns a dark cara-mel color, pour cashew nut mixture onto the greased baking sheet, and cool for 1 hour. Break up the brittle, place in a food processor, and process to a coarse-ground texture.

For jaggery sauce, crush jaggery into smaller pieces; this may be done using a heavy rolling pin. Place jaggery and 3 tablespoons water in a pan. Stirring constantly, cook over low heat for 5 to 10 minutes until jaggery is melted. Set aside. (The jaggery should be warm when served.)

Using 2 serving spoons, mold ice cream into large **quenelle** shapes.

Presentation
Place 2 quenelles of ice cream on each chilled plate, pour warm jaggery sauce over top, and sprinkle crushed cashew nut brittle gener-ously over ice cream. Top each serving with a cinnamon stick. (Save extra brittle in an air-tight container.)

6 servings

Burst of Flavor

Coconut Ice Cream in Lemon Tuille Cups

Palm honey and creamy coconut are a heavenly combination. Sometimes referred to as treacle, palm honey is made with the boiled-down sap of coconut palms. It is available in Asian grocery stores. In this recipe, palm honey is used as a garnish for coconut ice cream.

Coconut Ice Cream
2 cups whole milk
1 vanilla bean, split open lengthwise and
  pulp scraped
6 large egg yolks
3/4 cup sugar
1 cup coconut milk
1/4 cup grated coconut

Lemon Tuille
Nonstick oil spray
2 egg whites
1/4 cup sugar
2 tablespoons unsalted butter, melted
1/2 cup sifted all-purpose flour
1 teaspoon grated lemon zest

Almond Brittle
*3/4 cup **blanched,** whole almonds*
3/4 cup granulated sugar
1/8 cup water
2 tablespoons unsalted butter

Garnish
4 tablespoons palm honey

Directions
Place milk and vanilla bean pulp in a saucepan and bring to a boil. Remove from heat, cover saucepan, and allow to infuse for 10 minutes.

Place egg yolks and sugar in a bowl, and beat to a ribbon stage. Place the infused milk back on the heat and bring to a slow boil. Remove the vanilla bean and pour a little of the boiling milk on the creamed egg yolk and sugar. Beat briskly. Pour back into the milk and stir to combine. Cook on low heat, stirring constantly until the custard is thick, about 5 to 6 minutes. Strain the custard and fold in the coconut milk and grated coconut. Let the mixture cool. Place in an ice-cream maker and freeze according to the manufacturer's instructions.

Preheat oven to 400°F. For the tuille, spray a baking sheet with nonstick oil spray. Whisk egg whites stiffly, add sugar, and beat thoroughly. Gradually add butter with the sifted flour and whisk gently. Mix in grated lemon zest. Spread out in heaped teaspoonfuls on the greased baking sheet, making sure there is enough room for the tuilles to spread out as they bake. Place in the oven and bake 5 to 6 minutes. Quickly lift each tuille with a spatula and drape over a cup turned upside down to form a cup shape with a slightly frilly edge.

To make almond brittle, place almonds in a roasting pan and warm them slightly in the oven. Place sugar and 1/8 cup water in a pan and boil until sugar reaches 248°F, about 6 to 8 minutes. Add the nuts and remove from heat. Using a wooden spoon, stir until the sugar starts to crystallize. Put the sauce pan back on medium heat and cook for 3 to 4 minutes. Cook until the sugar starts to caramelize to a dark golden color. Mix in 1 tablespoon of the butter. Brush a baking sheet with the remaining butter and pour on the nut mix. Cool for 1 hour. Break the brittle into small pieces. Grind them to a coarse texture in a food processor.

Presentation
Place a tuille cup on each plate and place 2 scoops of ice cream in each cup. Sprinkle almond brittle generously on the ice cream and around the tuille cup. Drizzle with palm honey.

8 to 10 servings

Burst of Flavor

Hazelnut Meringue Cake with Raspberries

This cake is another favorite English dessert of mine. Instead of raspberries, you may use sliced strawberries, apricots, peaches, or mangoes. A good substitute for crème fraîche in the filling is sour cream lightly whisked with brown sugar and a pinch of freshly grated **nutmeg.** Crème fraîche takes a day and a half to prepare.

This cake keeps well in an airtight container in the refrigerator for a few days.

For Cake
1 tablespoon oil
1 tablespoon sugar
4 egg whites
1 cup sugar
¼ teaspoon almond extract
*¼ teaspoon ground **mace***
1 cup roasted ground hazelnuts

Filling
*1 cup **Crème Fraîche** (see recipe, page 243)*
1½ cups raspberries

For Dusting
¼ cup powdered sugar
¼ teaspoon freshly grated nutmeg

To Finish
*1 cup **Berry Sauce** (see recipe, page 232)*

Directions
Preheat oven to 375°F.

Prepare 2 eight-inch sandwich cake pans. Apply oil on the sides of the pans, and dust with sugar. Line the bottom with a disk of parchment paper.

Beat egg whites till foamy. Gradually add sugar, almond extract, and mace. Beat until peaks form, then fold in the hazelnuts.

Divide the batter between the 2 pans and bake for 40 minutes. Invert cakes in the pans onto a rack and allow to cool overnight. Remove cakes from pans the next day.

On first cake, spread crème fraîche and then place raspberries on top. Top with second cake and press down gently to make it compact. Place in refrigerator 3 to 4 hours.

Presentation
Mix powdered sugar and freshly grated nutmeg and sieve on the cake. Cut into wedges and place on the dessert plates. Drizzle berry sauce on the plates.

10 to 12 servings

Hot Fig Gratin

The addition of **cinnamon,** a sweet fragrant spice, lends an exotic spicy note to this fig dessert. It helps to prepare figs, place them in a gratin dish, and then pour on the sour cream mix beforehand. The last step does not take too long. Crème fraîche takes a day and a half to prepare.

12 ripe red figs
½ cup sour cream
4 tablespoons dark brown sugar
1 tablespoon fresh lemon juice
3 tablespoons **Crème Fraîche** (see recipe, page 243)

For Topping
½ teaspoon ground cinnamon

Directions
Peel and halve figs lengthwise, arranging cut side up in a gratin dish. Whip sour cream with 1 tablespoon brown sugar and lemon juice, and pour on the figs. With a wooden spoon, lightly move the figs as necessary to ensure that the sour cream seeps to the bottom of the gratin dish. Spread crème fraîche on the figs.

For topping, mix remainder of sugar with cinnamon and sprinkle over figs.

Presentation
Place under the broiler a few minutes to let the surface bubble and caramelize. Serve immediately.

6 to 8 servings

Marinated Guava

Gorgeous coral pink is the color of this beautiful, marinated guava dish. Partnered with a spoonful of vanilla ice cream, it is exquisite. For best results, use the seedless, fleshy guava or guava that has very few seeds.

3 ripe guavas

Syrup
3 tablespoons sugar
½ cup dry white wine
Pinch of **mace**
1 tablespoon fresh lemon juice
1 **rose geranium** leaf, crushed

Garnish
4 rose geranium leaves

Directions
Peel and halve guavas lengthwise. Scoop out the centers with the seeds; reserve shells.

For syrup, place peel, pulp, sugar, wine, mace, and lemon juice in a stainless steel pan. Simmer on low heat about 4 minutes. Strain syrup into a glass bowl.

Slice guava shells lengthwise into ⅛-inch strips and add to the hot syrup with the crushed rose geranium leaf. Cover and set aside until the syrup is cooled. Remove and discard rose geranium leaf. Place the guava in refrigerator.

Presentation
Place a scoop of vanilla ice cream on each plate; spoon guava over the ice cream. Garnish with a rose geranium leaf.

4 servings

Watermelon Compote

There are times when we get tired of fresh watermelon. Occasionally, watermelon compote is most welcome. Spoon watermelon compote on individual portions of fruit salad or over ice cream. Watermelon compote may be used in ways other than in desserts. Serve in place of a sauce with a hot and spicy grilled chicken or as a dip for spicy grilled chicken kabobs.

3 pounds watermelon

For Syrup
1 cup watermelon juice
¼ cup white wine
2 tablespoons white wine vinegar
¼ cup sugar
*4 whole **cloves***

Garnish
6 sprigs of mint

Directions
Remove seeds from watermelon and, using a melon-baller, scoop the melon and place it in a glass dish. You need about 1½ cups unbroken melon balls. Peel the remaining watermelon, discard the seeds, blend watermelon flesh, and strain the juice. You need 1 cup of juice.

For syrup, in a stainless steel pan, simmer watermelon juice, wine, vinegar, sugar, and cloves for 6 minutes. Cool. Pour cooled syrup on watermelon balls and chill in refrigerator for 2 hours. Remove and discard cloves before serving.

Presentation
Place a scoop of ice cream on each plate; spoon watermelon compote on and around the ice cream. Garnish with sprigs of mint.

6 servings

Poached White Figs

Three poached white figs per guest topped with a spoon of **Crème Fraîche** (see recipe, page 243) make an elegant dessert. Crème fraîche takes a day and a half to prepare.

The hint of spicy fragrance in the figs is intriguing.

12 white figs

For Syrup
¾ cup sugar
1½ cups white port wine
*2-inch piece of **cinnamon** stick*
*4 whole **cloves***
Juice of 3 lemons

Directions
Trim stems and wash figs. Place sugar, wine, spices, and lemon juice in a **nonreactive** pan. Bring to a slow simmer.

Add figs, reduce heat to very low, cover pan, and cook 8 to 10 minutes, until figs are soft. Cool. Place in a glass jar or container, cover, and refrigerate. Remove and discard spices before serving.

4 servings

Rice Pudding

Every mouthful of this simple dessert is delicious. The spice-infused milk imparts fragrance to the soft-cooked rice.

2 cups whole milk
6-inch piece of vanilla bean
*4 crushed **cardamoms***
*1-inch piece of **cinnamon** stick*
½ cup short-grain white rice
Zest of ½ lemon
1 cup water
3 tablespoons sugar, or to taste
¼ cup heavy cream, whipped to a soft peak
½ cup chopped pistachio nuts
*½ tablespoon chopped **candied ginger***
*1 cup **Berry Sauce** (see recipe at right)*

Garnish
1 cup fresh berries (any kind)
5 sprigs of mint

Directions
Place milk in a saucepan. Split vanilla bean, scrape it, and add the pulp to the milk. Add spices and bring to a simmer. Remove from heat, cover, and let infuse for 10 minutes. In a separate pan, boil the rice with lemon peel and 1 cup water for 5 minutes. Strain off water, discard lemon peel, and put rice back in the pan. Strain milk into the rice. Cook on low heat, stirring constantly for 35 minutes, until the rice is soft. Stir in sugar and cook 4 to 5 minutes. Remove from heat, fold in cream, pistachio, and candied ginger. Pour into a medium-size bowl, cool, and refrigerate.

Presentation
Spoon rice pudding onto plates and drizzle on berry sauce. Garnish with berries and mint.

4 to 5 servings

Berry Sauce

Strawberries, raspberries, and blackberries are all good in this sauce. You can use more than one kind of berry when berries are plentiful. If berries are tart, add more sugar to taste. Frozen berries do make a good sauce.

1 pound berries
5 tablespoons powdered sugar

Directions
Place berries and sugar in a food processor and purée for 4 to 5 seconds. Pass through a strainer, pressing out as much of the pulp as possible.

Yields 1 cup

Peach Sorbet on Grilled Peaches, Laced with Champagne Sabayon

When peaches are at the end of their season and you are tired of fresh peaches, try this recipe with the ripest peaches you can get. The rich, yet light sabayon has a hint of sweet fragrant **mace** in it.

Peach Sorbet
4 peaches, peeled, stoned, and sliced
½ cup sugar
1½ cups water

Champagne Sabayon
3 large egg yolks
¾ cup champagne
½ cup granulated sugar
Pinch of ground mace

Broiled Peaches
4 peaches, peeled, halved, and stoned
1 tablespoon unsalted butter
3 tablespoons light brown sugar

Garnish
4 sprigs of mint

Directions
For the sorbet, process the sliced peaches in a food processor and pass through a strainer; you need 1½ cups of peach purée.

Bring sugar and water to a simmer. Continue to simmer on low heat for 10 minutes, then set aside to cool.

Mix with peach purée and freeze in an ice-cream maker according to the manufacturer's instructions.

For the champagne sabayon, place egg yolks, champagne, sugar, and mace in a double boiler. Cook over simmering water. Whisk for 8 minutes. Remove from heat and transfer mix to a medium bowl. Using an electric beater, beat on medium speed for 6 to 8 minutes.

Reduce speed to low and beat for 2 to 3 minutes. The mixture should be light and fluffy. Hold the sauce at room temperature.

For broiled peaches, place peaches cut side down on a baking sheet and brush with butter. Heap the brown sugar on the buttered peaches and place under a broiler for 4 to 5 minutes or until the sugar melts to a glaze. Put aside for 5 minutes.

Presentation
Arrange the 8 broiled peach halves on 4 plates and spoon a scoop of peach sorbet on each. Lace with champagne sabayon and garnish with mint.

4 servings

Grilled Fruit Salad with Green Peppercorn Vinaigrette

This simple fruit salad, which is easy to make, blends many taste sensations. You may use any fruit in season. I use **chenna,** a home-made fresh cheese curd, to garnish this dessert, and it is big part of the dish. Ricotta is a good substitute for chenna. It is simple to make. Whole milk treated with an acid product such as lemon juice helps the milk proteins coagulate to form soft curd. I further garnish the salad with sprigs of **green peppercorns,** but a sprinkling of readily available loose green peppercorns works just as well.

Green Peppercorn Vinaigrette

1 tablespoon olive oil
1 tablespoon white wine vinegar
1 tablespoon white wine
2 tablespoons fresh lemon juice
1 tablespoon bruised green peppercorns
1 tablespoon honey
1 tablespoon grated orange zest
Salt to taste

Fruit

2 plums
6 thin wedges of peeled Persian melon
½ pineapple, peeled
1 orange, peeled
2 apricots

Garnish

*½ cup **Chenna** (see recipe, page 242)*
*1 tablespoon crushed **rock candy***
4 sprigs of green peppercorns
Handful of rosemary flowers

Directions

Place ingredients for vinaigrette in a small bowl and whisk to combine. Season with salt to taste.

Slice the plums thinly, avoiding the stone. Cut across the melon wedges. Cut pineapple into half rings. Slice oranges and apricots. Grill the fruits on a very hot, oiled grill. It takes about 5 to 6 minutes to grill all the fruits. Using a spatula or a pair of tongs, turn the fruits over (after about 3 minutes). Grill 3 more minutes. Fruits should have grill marks.

Arrange fruit on plates and drizzle with vinaigrette. Sprinkle chenna and strew rock candy on the fruit. To bruise the green peppercorns, place them on a cutting board and lightly run a rolling pin over them. The object is not to crush them but to slightly crack them open or "bruise" them. Place a sprig of green peppercorns on the fruit salad and rosemary flowers around the fruit salad.

4 servings

"Two Leaves and a Bud"
(Ceylon Tea Sorbet with Pineapple Compote)

When tea leaves are harvested, they are plucked with two leaves and a bud. Try this recipe with **Ceylon tea,** which is among the best teas in the world. You may have tea strong or mild to your taste.

The flavors of the aromatic mint and sharp **green peppercorns** meet together to complement beautifully the sweet pineapple compote with the crown of tea sorbet.

Tea Sorbet
2 cups water
1½ cups sugar
1 cup freshly brewed Ceylon tea
Fresh lemon juice to taste

Pineapple Compote
1 small pineapple
1 cup water
½ cup white wine
½ cup sugar
2 sprigs of mint
½ teaspoon green peppercorns

Garnish
4 fresh tea leaf sprigs ("2 leaves and a bud"
on each sprig) or 4 sprigs of mint

Directions
To make tea sorbet, place water and sugar in a saucepan. Place on low heat; simmer for 10 minutes. Cool.

Add tea and lemon juice to the syrup to taste.

Place in an ice-cream freezer and freeze according to the manufacturer's instructions.

Peel pineapple and cut into ¼-inch-thick slices. Remove the core using a sharp cutter. Cut each pineapple ring into 4 equal quarters.

Place water, wine, and sugar in a pan on low heat, and simmer for 8 minutes. Add pineapple, mint, and green peppercorns. Simmer on very low heat for 5 to 6 minutes. Remove from heat, pick out and discard the mint sprigs, and chill.

Presentation
Spoon the pineapple compote onto 4 chilled plates and evenly distribute the green peppercorns. Using 2 serving spoons, make sorbet into **quenelle** shapes and place 2 on the pineapple on each plate.

Garnish each plate with "2 leaves and a bud" or fresh mint sprigs.

4 servings

Chewy Gooey Warm Chocolate Mold with Crème Anglaise

You will want more of this decadent chocolate mold. The best part is that it is easy to make.

8 four-ounce soufflé cups or metal molds
1 tablespoon sweet butter
*½ recipe **Crème Anglaise** (see recipe, page 243)*

For Chocolate Mold Mix
¾ cup sweet butter
2 cups semi-sweet chocolate
4 large eggs
1 tablespoon sugar
1 tablespoon all-purpose flour
*⅛ teaspoon freshly ground **mace***

Garnish
¼ cup semi-sweet chocolate
16 whole strawberries
2" x 2" block of semi-sweet chocolate
  at room temperature
1 tablespoon powdered sugar

Directions
Preheat oven to 425°F.

Grease molds with butter and place on a sheetpan. Make the crème anglaise and allow to chill.

In a double boiler, melt butter and chocolate over low heat. Place eggs and sugar in a large bowl and place the bowl over simmering water. Beat with an electric hand mixer. When the eggs start to thicken and the mixture is lukewarm, remove the bowl from the hot water. Continue to beat the mixture until it is light and fluffy, and has doubled in volume.

Using a spatula, gradually fold in the flour, mace, and melted chocolate.

Fill the molds and place in the oven for 15 minutes. Remove and set aside to cool for about 20 minutes before serving.

For the garnish, melt chocolate in a double boiler and place aside for a few minutes. Dip 8 strawberries in the chocolate (1 at a time) and coat them; place on greaseproof paper and refrigerate. (Reserve the melted chocolate.)

Cut the other 8 strawberries into halves. Using a sharp vegetable peeler, peel the block of chocolate into curls and refrigerate.

Presentation
Run a knife around the sides of the chocolate soufflé cups to loosen the chocolate molds and turn them onto plates. Spoon crème anglaise around the chocolate molds and place 1 chocolate-dipped strawberry and 2 strawberry halves beside each. Spoon a little of the reserved melted chocolate over each mold and arrange the chocolate curls on top. Dust lightly with powdered sugar.

8 servings

Black Plum Soup with Lemon Ice Cream and Lemon Curd

This lovely summer dessert has many compatible flavors and colors. The lemon curd in the soup takes the plum.

Lemon Ice Cream
2 cups whole milk
6 large egg yolks
1 cup sugar
Grated zest of 2 lemons
1 cup full cream

Lemon Curd
½ cup sugar
4 tablespoons sweet butter
Grated zest and juice of 1 lemon
2 small eggs

Plum Soup
4 ripe black plums, halved, pitted, and sliced (save the pits)
1 cup water
½ cup sugar
1 ripe black plum, halved, pitted, and thinly sliced
1 cup Sauternes

Garnish
¼ cup water
1 tablespoon sugar
1 tablespoon lemon zest julienne
1 ripe green plum, halved, pitted, and thinly sliced
1 tablespoon chiffonade of garden mint leaves

Directions
To make ice cream, place milk in a saucepan and bring to a simmer. Set aside. Place egg yolks and sugar in a medium-size bowl and beat until creamy. Pour half of the hot milk over the eggs and whisk to combine. Pour back into the saucepan with the rest of the milk. Place on low heat and, stirring constantly, cook to the consistency of a custard. Cool the mix and fold in the lemon zest and cream. Place in an ice cream freezer and freeze according to the manufacturer's instructions.

For the lemon curd, place sugar, butter, lemon zest, and lemon juice in a double boiler and stir until sugar and butter are melted. Beat and strain the eggs and continue stirring until the mix thickens. To avoid curdling, don't let the mix boil. Remove from heat and allow it to cool.

For the plum soup, place the sliced plums and pits in a pan. Add water and sugar. Cook on low heat for 6 minutes. Cool the mix and pass through a fine-mesh sieve. (Discard peel and pits.) Place the soup back in the pan (the soup should be still hot); add thinly sliced black plums and Sauternes. Allow the soup to cool, then chill.

For the garnish, bring the water and sugar to a boil. Cook for 2 to 3 minutes and add the lemon zest julienne; cook until dry. Set aside.

Presentation
Spoon the chilled soup with the black plum slices into deep plates and distribute the green plum slices between the plates. Top each soup with 2 spoons of lemon ice cream and place a tangle of lemon peel julienne on the ice cream. Drop the lemon curd in a carefree pattern and strew mint chiffonade on the soups.

4 servings

Indian Homemade Cheese: Chenna and Paneer

Chenna is a fresh curd cheese with the consistency of soft cream cheese. **Paneer** is made similarly except that it is compressed to a firmer texture.

Both of these unripened cheeses are easy and quick to make. You may use them in desserts as well as with vegetables, grains, and legumes.

It is crucial to use a large saucepan for the milk to prevent it from boiling over. Be sure to stir often to prevent it from sticking to the pan.

4 pints whole milk
3 tablespoons strained lemon juice

Directions

Place milk in a 3-quart, heavy-bottomed saucepan on high heat and bring to a boil. Reduce heat to low and simmer for 25 minutes, stirring often. Gradually add lemon juice and, using a metal spoon, very slowly stir clockwise. When strands of curd form and separate from whey (about 20 to 30 seconds), remove from heat and set aside for 4 to 5 minutes.

Line a colander with a double layer of damp cheesecloth and place over a container. Slowly pour curd and whey into the colander. Gather edges of cheesecloth and twist into a topknot to loosely enclose curd. Hold under running cold water and allow water to run through the curd. Twist the cheesecloth topknot and press out as much liquid as possible. (For paneer, place cheesecloth-wrapped curd on a plate, place another plate on the curd, and weight it down with a 10- to 12-ounce unopened food can for 2 hours. Remove weight and open cheesecloth.)

Unwrap; the curd will be gathered into a ball of soft curd cheese. Place on a work surface, and with the palm of your hand, knead the cheese about 5 to 6 minutes. (Use a scraper to scrape the cheese off the work surface while kneading.)

Use as called for in recipes. To refrigerate, form into a flat round shape and wrap in cheesecloth. Keeps well for 2 to 3 days in the refrigerator.

Yields 8 ounces

Crème Fraîche

It's luscious and tangy, lovely on fruit and on chocolate desserts.

For an easy dessert, layer fruit juice–soaked cakes with sliced fruits and crème fraîche, and dust with powdered sugar.

2 cups heavy cream
½ cup plain yogurt
½ cup buttermilk

Directions
Place cream, yogurt, and buttermilk in a saucepan and heat to 98°F. Pour into a sterilized glass container.

Cover with a kitchen towel and leave in a warm place (by the stove) for 15 hours. Thereafter, refrigerate for 24 hours.

Remove the thickened top part, which is the crème fraîche, place in a sterilized container, and refrigerate. Discard the liquid left at the bottom.

Crème fraîche keeps well for 4 to 5 days.

Yields 2 cups

Crème Anglaise

A sauce that enlivens many desserts, it is easy to make and can be stored in the refrigerator for 2 to 3 days.

Serve stewed or fresh fruits and chocolate cakes with crème anglaise.

1 cup whole milk
1 cup full cream
¼ vanilla bean
1 cup sugar
6 large egg yolks

Directions
Place milk and cream in a saucepan; cut open vanilla bean, scrape out the pulp, and put into the milk. On low heat, bring to a simmer for about 5 minutes and then set aside.

Place sugar and yolks in a medium-size bowl and beat together until light and creamy. Pour half of the hot milk on the eggs and whisk to combine. Pour the egg mix into the rest of the milk and strain into a clean saucepan.

Place on low heat and, stirring constantly, cook until thick. Strain, cool on ice for about 15 minutes, and refrigerate.

Yields 1 pint

Desserts

Conversion Tables

Oven Temperatures

Fahrenheit	Gas Mark	Celsius	Temperature Terms
225	¼	107	Very Slow
250	½	121	
275	1	135	
300	2	148	Slow/Low
325	3	163	
350	4	177	Moderate/Medium
375	5	190	
400	6	204	
425	7	218	Hot/High
450	8	232	
475	9	246	Very Hot

Solid Measures

U.S. and Imperial Measures		Metric Measures	
Ounces	Pounds	Grams	Kilos
½		14	
1		28	
2		56	
3 ½		100	
4	¼	112	
5		140	
6		168	
8	½	225	
9		250	¼
12	¾	340	
16	1	450	
18		500	½
20	1¼	560	
24	1½	675	
27		750	¾
28	1¾	780	
32	2	900	
36	2¼	1,000	1

Liquid Measures

Fluid Ounces	U.S. Measures	Imperial Measures	Metric Measures Milliliters
	1 TSP	1 TSP	5
¼	2 TSP	1 DSP (dessert spoon)	7
½	1 TBSP	1 TBSP	15
1	2 TBSP	2 TBSP	28
2	¼ cup	4 TBSP	56
4	½ cup or ¼ pint		110
5		¼ pint or 1 gill	140
6	¾ cup		170
8	1 cup or ½ pint		225
10	1¼ cups	½ pint	280
12	1½ cups or ¾ pint		240
15		¾ pint	420
16	2 cups or 1 pint		450
18	2¼ cups		500, ½ liter
20	2½ cups	1 pint	560
24	3 cups or 1½ pints		675
25		1¼ pints	700
30	3¾ cups	1½ pints	840
32	4 cups or 2 pints or 1 quart		900
36	4½ cups		1,000, 1 liter

Conversion Tables

Glossary

African coriander *(Eryngiceum foetidum)*
This herb, known by its common name eryngo, is used extensively in Thailand and Vietnam to flavor cooked dishes. As a garnish, the flavor and texture of this raw herb add spark to the famous Vietnamese pho.

Ajowan *(Trachyspermum ammi)*
The tiny, extremely fragrant seed resembles thyme, with overtones of oregano and pepper. It is a spice seed closely related to caraway and cumin. Use sparingly; it can be overpowering. A good substitute is thyme.

Amaranth *(Amaranthus gangeticus)*
There are many members of the amaranth family. The two main types grown as leafy vegetables are the green amaranth and red amaranth. The red amaranth plant has pink roots and dark green, oval leaves with patches of red along the center vein. Seeds of several *Amaranthus* species are used as grains. They are available whole, pearled, and as flour or flakes.

Arugula *(Eruca vesicaario, subsp. sativa)*
Arugula, also know as rocket, is a leaf vegetable with dark green spiky leaves and a very strong, spicy peppery taste. It is best used when the leaves are young; use in mixed greens.

Asafoetida *(Ferula assafoetida)*
Asafoetida is a dried resin obtained from several species of *Ferula* (fennel-related plants). It has the flavor of shallots or garlic and is used extensively in the regional cuisine of India.

Bain marie
A hot water bath used to cook foods gently or to keep cooked foods hot, a bain marie is also known as a water bath.

Balsamic vinegar
A dark Italian vinegar with a sweet and slightly sour flavor, it is made from concentrated grape juice, fermented and aged for twenty years or more in wooden casks.

Basil seeds *(Ocimum* spp.*)*
The seeds of the lemon basil plant are black, oval shaped, and half the size of a sesame seed. When soaked in cold water, they develop a whitish gelatinous coating. They are said to have a very cooling effect on the system and to relieve stomach ailments. Seeds of several *Ocimum* species are used in cooking. In India they are referred to as tulsi.

Basmati
Basmati is a generic name for a variety of long-grain rice grown along the foothills of the Himalayas in north India. It is considered the best rice in the world.

Batonnet
Batonnet describes food cut into matchstick shapes of approximately $\frac{1}{4} \times \frac{1}{4} \times 3$ inches.

Beluga lentils
Beluga lentils resemble beluga caviar in size and looks. These lentils cook fast and need no presoaking.

Black barley
The whole barley grains with only the outer husk removed. It requires overnight soaking and slow cooking.

Black cumin *(Nigella sativa)*
The seed of this annual plant is blackish in color and slightly thinner than the cumin seed. Botanically this plant is not related to the common cumin.

Black-eyed peas

Also called cow-pea, the black-eyed pea is the kidney-shaped seed with a black splotch, from the pod of the plant *Vigna unguiculata*. It is available whole or split and husked.

Black truffle

A fungus that grows underground, generally near the roots of oaks, it is spherical in shape and of various small sizes, with a thick, rough, wrinkled, black skin. The two principle varieties are black and white.

Blanch

To blanch food, cook it very briefly and partially in boiling water or hot oil. Blanching is generally used to assist preparations, as part of a combination cooking method to remove undesirable flavors.

Bok choy *(Brassica chinensis var. chinensis)*

A member of the cabbage family native to southern China, bok choy has long, wide, crunchy white stalks and delicate dark-green leaves.

Braise

To braise food, cook it slowly in a small amount of seasoned liquid with or without preliminary browning of the food.

Brown lentils

These lentils are also known as German lentils. They are unhulled and need to be soaked before cooking.

Brunoise

Brunoise describes foods cut into approximately ⅛-inch cubes and foods garnished with vegetables cut in this manner.

Buckwheat flour

Ground buckwheat has a dark color with darker speckles and a strong flavor. Buckwheat is neither a wheat nor a grain; it is the triangular fruit of a plant of the *Polyganaceae* family. The hulled seeds are also referred to as groats.

Bulgur wheat

Bulgur is a wheatberry that has had the bran removed, and then is steamed, dried, and ground into various degrees of coarseness. It is brown in color and has a nutlike flavor and texture. I used it in salads and stews or cooked like rice.

Burnet *(Poterium officinalis)*

The small grayish-green leaves of this plant are a wonderful addition to a green salad. Make sure the leaves that go in the salad are tender.

Butterfly

To butterfly, split fish, shrimp, or meat neatly in half lengthwise, leaving the two halves hinged on one side. This cut enables stuffing fish, shrimp, or meat and speeds up the cooking process.

Candied ginger

Candied ginger is used to add flavor contrast to savory dishes; it is a form of preserved ginger. It is cooked in a heavy sugar syrup to preserve it.

Capers *(Capparis spinosa)*

The unopened bud of this shrub is cured in a vinegary brine and develops a salty-sour flavor.

Cardamom *(Elettaria cardamomum)*

A member of the ginger family, its light green or brown oval pods have black seeds with a pungent, sweet lemony fragrance.

Cayenne pepper

This orange-red mix is blended from different varieties of dried chilies. It is extremely hot and has a fine texture.

Ceylon tea

Ceylon (Sri Lanka) black tea; it is world famous. When brewed, it has a golden color and delicate fragrance.

Chenna

Chenna is an unripened Indian cheese made from cow's milk and treated with an acid culture.

Chervil (*Anthricus cerefolium*)

One of the classic fine herbs, chervil has a delicate aniseed flavor. It is good in salads and soups and fresh as a garnish.

Chickpeas

Also known as garbanzo beans, these dried beans are ⅓ inch in diameter, with a pale brown, wrinkled skin. Chickpeas are also available canned.

Chiffonade

Chiffonade describes finely sliced or shredded leafy vegetables or herbs. A chiffonade of herbs or vegetables is often used as a garnish or bedding.

Chili paste

Many varieties of chili paste are available in Asian grocery stores. The most popular is siracha chili paste made in California. A condiment from Malaysia or Indonesia, this spicy, ground, red chili paste is known as *sambal olek.*

Chili pepper

Chili peppers are tiny bird's-eye peppers, 1 inch long or smaller and red or yellow in color; they are extremely hot. Generally the smaller the chili, the hotter it is.

Chili pepper water

Crushed fresh ripe chili, green or orange-red in color, with a thick crunchy texture and very hot flavor. The crushed chilies are soaked in water for a week or more. The chili pepper water is used to flavor food.

Choy sum (*Brassica chinensis var. parachinensis*)

This member of the cabbage family has slightly bitter tender stems and lemon-green leaves; all parts of the plant including its tiny yellow flowers are edible.

Chrysanthemum greens (*Chrysanthemum coronarium*)

The heavily dissected leaves of this herbaceous plant is a favorite among Japanese and Chinese chefs. The tender succulent leaves are generally plucked before the plant blooms. The very tender leaves are eaten raw as in salads. The mature leaves need to be blanched before use to rid them of the slightly bitter taste.

Cinnamon (*Cinnamomum zeylanicum*)

Native to Sri Lanka, the spice is the inner bark of the evergreen tree. It is rolled up and dried. Orange-brown cinnamon sticks or quills have a sweet, distinctive flavor and fragrance. The bark of several *Cassia* species is also sold as cinnamon.

Cloves (*Syzigium aromaticum*)

The unopened dried flower buds of the tropical evergreen tree have a deep red-brown color and a pungent and sharp astringent flavor. On drying they turn chocolate brown in color.

Concassée

Peel, seed, and dice tomatoes to make a concassée.

Coriander (*Coriandrum sativum*)

The tan-colored seeds of the coriander plant are also known as cilantro. They are available whole or ground. This lemony-flavored spice seed is the major component of many Asian spice blends.

Cornmeal

Dried ground corn kernels, cornmeal has a white or yellow color and a gritty texture. It is available in three grinds: fine, medium, and coarse.

Couscous

Couscous is a kind of hard wheat semolina that has been moistened and then rolled in flour. It is also available precooked in packets. The name *couscous* also applies to the whole garnished dish, the national dish of Morocco, Algeria, and Tunisia.

Glossary

Cumin *(Cuminum cyminum)*

This spice seed is the dried fruit of the cumin plant. It is a crescent-shaped small seed with an earthy flavor and aroma. Cumin is used raw or roasted in many Asian spice blends.

Curry leaf *(Murraya koenigii)*

Curry leaf is an important ingredient used in Sri Lankan, South Indian, Malaysian, and Fijian cooking. The fragrant small leaflets grow closely along a central axis and are referred to as a sprig of curry leaves. It is customary to throw a whole sprig into curries and other preparations.

Dandelion *(Taraxacum officinalae)*

The familiar weed is also cultivated for use in the kitchen. Young, tender leaves make an excellent salad tossed with a vinaigrette. Older leaves can be coarse and bitter, though cultivated varieties are milder than wild dandelion. The older leaves are best fast-wilted or cooked the same as a vegetable.

Endive *(Cichorium endivia)*

A member of the chicory family, endive has a long cigar-shaped head of compact creamy-colored pointed leaves with a bitter flavor. It is also known as Belgium endive.

Fennel *(Foeniculum vulgare)*

The spice fennel seed is the oval, pale, green-brown seed of the perennial plant fennel. It has a sweetish anise flavor and aroma. It is used in fragrant spice mixes of Asia and is also used as a mouth freshener.

Fenugreek *(Trigonella foenum-graecum)*

A small herbaceous legume, this brownish-yellow seed is flat and oblong in shape. It is used as a spice in curries and has a bitter-sweet flavor. It should be used with discretion. Young fenugreek plants are harvested when not more than 6 inches high and are used raw or cooked.

Field salad *(Valerianella olitoria)*

A plant with small dark-green leaves and a nutty flavor, it is used in salads or cooked as a vegetable. This plant is also known as corn salad, mâche, and Raub's lettuce.

Fish sauce

A strong-smelling, salty, amber-colored clear-liquid sauce is made from anchovies, shrimp, or other smaller fish fermented in brine. The Thai version, which is pale and milder, is *Nampla;* the stronger Vietnamese version is *Nouc Nam.*

Five-spice powder

This spice blend is commonly used in Chinese cooking; it consists of star anise, cinnamon, Szechuan pepper, cloves, and fennel.

Frenched

A roast, rack, or chop of meat, especially lamb, from which the excess fat has been removed, leaving the eye muscle intact, with all meat and connective tissue removed from the rib bone.

Frisée

Frisée is the same plant as curly endive or chicory, except that it is tender and less bitter. The outer layer of leaves are dark green; the inside leaves are pale yellow and feathery.

Garam masala

Garam masala is a highly aromatic spice mix. To make it, place 1 tablespoon black peppercorn, 3-inch piece of cinnamon stick, 1 tablespoon black cumin seed, 1 teaspoon whole cloves, 2 teaspoons cardamom seeds, and 1 teaspoon crushed mace in a spice grinder. Grind to a fine powder. Add ⅛ teaspoon freshly ground nutmeg, mix, and store in an airtight container.

Gooseberry

A large berry, gooseberry has a smooth or furry green, yellow, red, or white skin. It has a tart flavor and is used in preserves, chutneys, and baked goods.

Goraka *(Garcinia cambogia)*

Goraka is also known as fish tamarind, a yellow acidic fruit native to Sri Lanka. It has a fluted skin, dividing the fruit into six to eight lobes. When dried, the lobes turn black in color. It has a tart flavor and is a preferred souring agent in Sri Lankan cuisine.

Gotukola *(Centella asiatica)*

The green, quarter-coin-size leaf of a long wiry hollow stem, gotukola has a slight bitter tang. The Common English name for this leaf is Asian pennywort. Its medical uses are well known, and it is sold in nurseries as "the arthritis herb."

Green chili *(Capsicum annuum)*

A green chili is the young green pod of the *Capsicum* plant; when ripe, it is deep red. There are several varieties of capsicum; the fieriness can vary from one chili to another.

Green peppercorn *(Piper nigrum)*

An unripened berry of the pepper vine, it is either freeze-dried or pickled in a brine. Black peppercorn is the berry that is picked when fully ripened and sun-dried till it is black. White peppercorn is the ripe berry that is soaked and scarified, after which the coating becomes creamy white in color. Both black and white peppercorns are available whole or ground.

Haricots verts

One type of the French bean, the high-priced haricots verts, are slim and delicate and should be eaten young, when no larger than the prong of a fork. Outside of France they are rarely available that small.

Jaggery

Jaggery is the unprocessed sugar derived from various palms or sugarcane. It comes in cylindrical shapes and it has a delicious rich flavor somewhere between caramel and molasses.

Jalapeño pepper

Named after the Mexican city Jalapa, this dark green, thick-fleshed, crunchy pepper is mildly hot; it is also available canned.

Jerusalem artichoke

A member of the sunflower family (not a member of the artichoke family), this tuber is multipronged and brown with a crunchy texture and sweet nutty flavor. It can be eaten raw, cooked, or pickled. (It is also known as a sunchoke.)

Jicama *(Pachyrhizus erosus)*

A bulbous root vegetable, this legume grows underground. The tuber has a pale brown skin and a crunchy texture and sweet flavor. It is eaten raw or lightly cooked. (It is also known as mountain yam and Mexican potato.)

Julienne

Foods cut into a matchstick shape of approximately $1/8 \times 1/8 \times 2$ inches are julienned; julienne also describes a garnish of foods cut in such a shape.

Kaffir lime *(Citrus hystrix)*

The fragrant dark-green kaffir lime leaves are indispensable in Thai cooking; they have a piercing citrus aroma. Use whole leaves in curries and discard leaves before serving curry. For salads use the tender leaves finely shredded.

Kasha

The hulled roasted buckwheat groat, Kasha is reddish brown in color with a nutty flavor and chewy texture.

Kumu

A Hawaiian reef fish, Kumu is a member of the goatfish family. It is highly prized for its delicate white meat.

Lemon balm *(Melissa officinalis)*

The fresh lemon-scented leaves of this plant are ideal in a green salad.

Lemongrass (Cymbopogon citratus)

A tropical grass with long light-greenish stalks and grasslike leaves, the inner stalks have a strong lemony flavor and aroma.

Lima beans

A flat kidney-shaped bean native to Peru, it has a pale green to creamy yellow color. It has a waxy texture and is available fresh, frozen, or canned.

Limestone lettuce

Also known as bib lettuce, it is a variety of butterhead lettuce, with soft buttery-flavored and textured leaves.

Mace

The lacy outer covering (aril) of the seed of the nutmeg fruit, mace turns a brownish orange once dried.

Mahimahi

Also called dolphinfish (not related to the dolphin), mahimahi is an open-ocean fish, ranging in size from 8 to 25 pounds. Good substitutes are swordfish, pompano, and flounder.

Maldive fish

A staple of Sri Lankan cooking, bonito fish is processed in the Maldive Islands. The fish is cured by a process of boiling, smoking, and sun-drying until it turns hard as wood. This process enables the fish to be kept without refrigeration.

Methi

Methi are the mildly bitter sprouts germinated from fenugreek seeds. Wash sprouts and pat dry before use.

Millet (Pennisetum typhoideum)

The millet grain, widely used in India, is harvested from several cultivated grasses. Millet cooked by itself makes a delicious addition to salads. In combination with rice and spice it makes delicious pilaf and hearty stuffing.

Mirepoix

Mirepoix is a mix of coarsely chopped onions, carrots, and celery to flavor stocks, stews, and other foods.

Mirin

Japanese rice wine, Mirin is sweet and syrupy; it is used in sauces and marinades.

Mizuna (Brassica rapa ssp. nipposinica var. laciniata)

Mizuna, the Japanese name, means "water vegetable." The dark green, feathery leaves are often used in mixed-green salads; mature ones with the white succulent stems are excellent fast-wilted for a vegetable dish by itself or cooked with chicken.

Morels

Delicate spongy mushrooms ranging in color from beige to brownish black, morels have a meaty flavor. Dried morels are best soaked for 10 minutes before cooking. Morels should be washed thoroughly before use.

Mung beans

Also known as green gram beans, mung beans are seeds of the plant Phaseolus ouveus. They are available whole or hulled and split. The hulled split mung beans are a bright yellow. Mung bean sprouts, the germinated seeds, are available in markets or may be home-sprouted. They are commonly used in stir-fries and salads.

Mushroom soy

Mushroom soy is a dark soy sauce flavored with straw mushrooms.

Mustard seeds (Brassica spp.)

The tiny seeds of this annual herb of the cabbage family, with an erect stem and yellow flowers, come in 2 varieties: black mustard (B. nigra) seeds are hot, while yellow mustard seeds (B. alba) are mild.

Glossary

Navy beans

A variety of kidney beans, navy beans are small and oval in shape. These white-skinned beans are bland in flavor. Its generic name is white beans.

Neem *(Azadirachtra indica)*

One of India's most loved trees, the dark-green saw-edged leaves grow closely on a central stem. The leaves and flowers are used in cooking as bitter seasonings. Neem has astringent and antiseptic qualities.

Niçoise olive

A tiny black olive, it is native to the Mediterranean region.

Nonreactive

Nonreactive describes cooking utensils made of materials that do not react to acids, salts, and the like. Glass, enamel, and stainless steel are nonreactive materials.

Nutmeg *(Myristica fragrans)*

The nutmeg is the seed of the tree *Myristica fragrans*. It is encased in a dark brown, shiny, brittle shell. Around the shell is the scarlet lacy aril (mace). To use nutmeg, the brittle shell must be cracked and discarded. The kernel is grated or ground for use as a spice.

Ogo

Ogo is a seaweed that is highly nutritious; it has a crunchy texture and a sweet sea flavor. It ranges in color from deep yellow to brown to deep rose.

Olive oil, extra virgin

Extra virgin olive oil is produced from the first cold-pressing; the finest and fruitiest pressing, it has a bright green color and not more than 1% acid.

Olive oil, virgin

Virgin olive oil has 2% acid, a less fruity flavor than extra virgin olive oil, and a pale, yellowish straw color.

Onaga

The Hawaiian long tail red snapper, Onaga is caught in deep waters. It has moist, delicate pink flesh that turns white when cooked. You may substitute any other snapper.

Ong choy *(Ipomea aquatica)*

This plant grows in standing water and is commonly called water spinach. The leaves are arrow head-shaped and have hollow stems. The leaves and stems make a delicious stir-fry that is a favorite in China and Southeast Asia.

Ono

Also called kingfish, ono is in the mackerel family. It has flaky, firm meat that turns white when cooked. Good substitutes are mackevel, halibut, and swordfish.

Opakapaka

Hawaiian pink snapper, opakapaka has a delicate, moist flesh that turns white when cooked. Good substitutes are other snappers and sea bass.

Palm honey

Also known as treacle, palm honey is a form of palm sugar derived from boiling down the sap of the "kitul" palm (*Caryota urens*) or coconut palm (*Cocos nucifera*). In Sri Lanka, the thick palm honey is smoked, giving it a heady fragrance and a gorgeously rich texture and delicious flavor.

Paneer

A type of fresh Indian cheese, this unripe, sweet-smelling cheese is white in color and has the consistency of a soft tofu. With a flavor like farmer's cheese, paneer may be seasoned with herbs and spices.

Panko

Crispy Japanese-style bread crumbs, panko are more coarse than regular crumbs. You may substitute regular bread crumbs.

Glossary

Pea shoots

Pea shoots are the top few tender leaves of the snow pea plant. The raw, tender tips are excellent in salads. The more mature leaves and stems are equally good in stir-fries.

Pea sprouts

These are the sprouts of the germinated snow pea plant.

Pink lentils

Also known as *Masoor dal,* pink lentils are the seeds of the plant *Lens culinaris.* These salmon-pink lentils cook fast and need no presoaking; when cooked they turn a pale yellow.

Pomegranate *(Punica granatum)*

A large fruit with yellowish pink or reddish pink leathery skin, the pomegranate has a mass of ruby red, glistening seeds. The juicy pulp surrounding the seeds are sweet and tangy. Both seeds and juice are used in cooking. The dried seeds of pomegranate are used as a spice in India.

Poppadom

Poppadom are dried lentil wafers, mildly or highly spiced, available in packets. They should be grilled or deep-fried before serving.

Poppy seeds

These blue-gray, tiny seeds of the poppy plant are used in baked goods.

Portabella mushrooms

The portabella is the largest cultivated mushroom. It is actually an overgrown crimini mushroom and can even grow up to 6 inches in diameter.

Quenelle

Quenelle describes mounding food in an oval shape. It is also a dumpling made of seasoned ground fish, chicken, or meat, poached in stock and served with a rich sauce.

Quinoa

A bead-shaped, ivory-colored, delicate grain, quinoa is the staple of ancient Incas. It has a high-protein content. It is now prepared like rice, used in stuffing, or cooked with other grains.

Red kidney beans

Kidney-shaped beans with a dark red skin. Available fresh, dried, and canned.

Red oak leaf lettuce

This lettuce has red-tinged green leaves or red leaves similar in shape to leaves of an oak tree.

Rice paddy herb *(Limnophila chinensis var. aromatica)*

The small leaf, delicate, pale green herb is used in Vietnamese cooking to flavor soups and curries. It is also eaten raw with hot chili sauce.

Rice wine vinegar

Rice wine vinegar, clear and straw colored, is made from rice wine. Japanese rice wine vinegar is sweet and mild, while Chinese ones are sour and sharp.

Rock candy

Also known as rock sugar, rock candy has a richer, more subtle flavor than the refined granulated sugar. To use, crush the rock candy into smaller pieces with a rolling pin or mallet. It imparts an elegant luster to foods.

Rose geranium *(Pelargonium graveolens)*

An aromatic rose-scented herb with triangular gray-green leaves with toothed edges, the fresh leaves are infused for tea.

Sachet

A sachet is a cheesecloth bag filled with a blend of aromatic ingredients used to flavor stocks, sauces, soups, and stews. The sachet is removed and discarded, as indicated in each recipe.

Glossary

Saffron (*Crocus sativus*)

Saffron is the dried yellow-orange stigma of the saffron crocus. This expensive spice is used as a flavoring and coloring agent.

Sashimi

A Japanese dish of extremely fresh raw fish cut into thin slices, sashimi is traditionally artistically presented and served with condiments that include Japanese horseradish and dipping sauces.

Sauternes

A sweet, complex, and honeyed wine from Bordeaux region in France, Sauternes is made from overly ripe grapes, usually Sauvignon Blanc or Sémillon.

Semolina

A grainy, pale yellow, coarsely ground flour, usually durum or other hard wheat, semolina has a high protein content.

Serrano chili

A short plump chili, green or orange-red in color, the Serrano has a thick crunchy texture and very hot flavor.

Sesbania (*Sesbania grandiflora*)

This tree, also called West Indian pea tree, has dark green and feathery compound leaves. The leaves, stripped off their stalks, are cooked as a vegetable. The ivory-white flowers grow 3 to 4 inches long and can be stuffed or batter-fried.

Shiso (*Perilla frutescens, P. crispa*)

Shiso, also known as perilla, grows in green or red hues. This aromatic leaf is close to mint and basil and is served as a garnish, especially with raw fish preparations.

Siracha

A sweet and spicy chili sauce, siracha is offered in Vietnamese and Thai restaurants.

Soba

Japanese noodles made from buckwheat and wheat flour, soba are thin and grayish brown in color.

Somen

These fine Japanese noodles are made from wheat flour. They are available mainly dry and sometimes fresh. Somen is also available flavored with egg, green tea, or citrus.

Star anise (*Illicium verum*)

A dried star-shaped pod from a tree that belongs to the magnolia family, star anise has a strong licorice flavor. It is available whole or ground.

Sweet cicely (*Myrrhis odarata*)

This plant, with licorice-tasting leaves and seeds, is also known as anise chervil and is excellent in green salads. It adds fragrance and a slight sugary taste to foods.

Tamarind (*Tamarindus indica*)

The tamarind tree, with cinnamon-brown pods with brittle shells, is native to India. The pulp from the ripe pod has a sweet-and-sour-flavor and is chocolate brown in color. When ripe, the pulp separates easily from its shell.

Tarragon (*Artemisia dracunculus* var. *sativa*)

Native to Siberia, tarragon has narrow, pointed, dark green leaves about 2 to 2½ inches long and tiny gray flowers. Tarragon has an aniselike flavor. Strong and aromatic, it is available fresh and dried.

Thai curry paste

A paste of aromatic spices and herbs, it is used in Thai cuisine as a flavoring; the temperature range from mild to extremely hot.

Tobiko

Reddish-orange flying fish roe, tobiko is very tiny, with a mildly sweet fishy taste. Tobiko is available tinted black or flavored with wasabi (Japanese horseradish).

Toor dal

Toor dal is the seed of the plant *Cadjanus cajan*. They are hulled and split to yield golden-colored lentils.

Glossary

Totsoi *(Brassica chinensis* var. *rosularis)*

Totsoi is a variety of bok choy also known as rosette bok choy. Its round, thick, dark green leaves with white leaf ribs grow in tight, concentric circles flat to the ground. The leaves, with a slight bitter tang, are excellent in mixed-green salads.

Triticale

Triticale is a hybrid between wheat and rye grain, developed by humans. It has kernels larger than wheat and retains the crunch even after soaking and cooking. Triticale is available as flour or flakes.

Truss

To truss is to secure poultry or other food with string or skewers so that it cooks evenly and maintains its shape during cooking.

Turmeric *(Curcuma longa, C. domestica)*

A tropical plant, turmeric is related to ginger and has orange-yellow rhizomes. The rhizomes are dried and ground to a fine powder. The spice has a strong flavor and is used as a yellow coloring agent in food.

Urad dal

Urad dal are the hulled and split seeds of the plant *Phaseolus mungo.* Urad dal is ivory white; the unhulled, whole seed is black in color.

Wood sorrel *(Oxalis corniculata)*

A small herbaceous runner with trifoliate cloverlike leaves and tiny yellow flowers, in some countries small amounts are used as an acid flavoring. Larger amounts may cause discomfort.

Yellow split peas

Yellow split peas can be either yellow or green, and are dried, skinned, and split. Characteristic of split peas, they turn into a purée easily and do not need any pre-soaking.

Index

Index

Index

Index

Index

Index

Index

About the Author

Kusuma Cooray, a native of Sri Lanka, is an associate professor and chef-instructor at the University of Hawai'i, Culinary Institute of the Pacific. She trained at Le Cordon Bleu in London, the National Baking School, London, and Ecole de Cuisine La Varenne, Paris. Chef Cooray served as Executive Chef of the renowned Honolulu restaurant, The Willows, during the period the restaurant was awarded three consecutive Travel/Holiday Awards. She also was the personal chef for the late heiress Doris Duke.

Chef Cooray and her students prepare and serve international dishes during the school year to the public at the Ka'Ilena La'uae Restaurant, located at scenic Kapi'olani Community College, in the shadow of Hawai'i's Diamond Head.